WRITING FOR REAL

Each second we live is a new and unique moment of the universe,
a moment that will never be again . . .
And what do we teach our children?
We teach them that two and two make four,
and that Paris is the capital of France.
When will we also teach them what they are?
We should say to each of them:
Do you know what you are?
You are a marvel.
You are unique . . .
In the millions of years that have passed,
there has never been another child like you . . .
Your legs, your arms, your cunning fingers,
the way you move.
You may become a Shakespeare,
a Michelangelo, a Beethoven.

You have the capacity for anything.
Yes, you are a marvel.

  —Pablo Casals, 1876–1973

WRITING FOR REAL

Strategies for Engaging Adolescent Writers

Ross M. Burkhardt

Foreword by John H. Lounsbury

Stenhouse Publishers
Portland, Maine

National Middle School Association
Westerville, Ohio

Stenhouse Publishers
477 Congress Street
Portland, ME 04101
www.stenhouse.com

National Middle School Association
4151 Executive Parkway, Suite 300
Westerville, OH 43081
www.nmsa.org

Credits
Page ii: "You Are a Marvel" by Pablo Casals. Reprinted with permission of Simon & Schuster Adult Publishing Group from *Joys and Sorrows: Reflections by Pablo Casals, as Told to Albert E. Kahn*. Copyright © 1970 by Albert E. Kahn. Copyright renewed © 1998 by Harriet W. Kahn.
Page 28: *Rommel Drives on Deep into Egypt,* Copyright © 1970 by Richard Brautigan. Used with permission of Sarah Lazin Books.
Page 121: Excerpt from "Stopping by Woods on a Snowy Evening" from *The Poetry of Robert Frost* edited by Edward Connery Lathem. Copyright © 1951 by Robert Frost, copyright © 1923, 1969 by Henry Holt & Co. Reprinted by permission of Henry Holt & Co.

Library of Congress Cataloging-in-Publication Data
Burkhardt, Ross M.
    Writing for real : strategies for engaging adolescent writers / Ross M. Burkhardt.
    p. cm.
    ISBN 1-57110-358-9 (alk. paper)
    1. English language—Composition and exercises—Study and teaching (Middle school) 2. English language—Composition and exercise—Study and teaching (Middle school)—Activity programs I. Title.
LB1631.B775 2002
808'.042'0712—dc21   2002026824

Cover and interior photographs by the author

Manufactured in the United States of America on acid-free paper
14 13 12 11   9 8 7 6 5

For my students
and our simultaneously shared journey
at Shoreham–Wading River Middle School
1972–1997.

And, of course, for Jeanne.

Contents

Foreword

This unique book takes you on a vicarious visit to the classroom of Ross Burkhardt, where he first struggled to become more than a "comma corrector," to those years during which he became the creator of some of the most intriguing, engaging, and fulfilling writing assignments found anywhere in the world, and which led to his induction into the National Teachers Hall of Fame in 1998. Here, in a composite school year, you will meet and share in the thoughts of Heidi, Matt, Jessica, Bobby, and a host of other young adolescents who grew in lasting ways as they learned about themselves and life itself as well as how to communicate effectively.

For the last twenty-five years of his distinguished career, Ross and his math/science teaching partner guided the learning of some forty-five students per year in one of America's premier middle schools. To be in Ross's English/social studies classroom at Shoreham–Wading River Middle School was to be a participant in an educational adventure. In this environment, students were often teachers; and Ross, by his own admission, was regularly a learner. He saw his task as one of "nurturing a community of learners," where students' voices were solicited, heard, and acted on. He used his own prose and poetry as a teaching tool, and soon students found meaning and real satisfaction in expressing personal feelings through writing.

This rich resource is extremely well written. Having shared writing tasks with Ross, I know how carefully he crafts the written word, how he considers several possibilities until just the right word is identified—a procedure his students came to emulate. But the quality of writing is not what marks this work as well beyond excellent; it is the melding of imaginative activities with sound pedagogy, amply illustrated with samples of students' writing, that puts this work at the top of the list. This is not a "how to" book—but it is that. This is not an essay on progressive educational philosophy—but it is that, too.

Writing for Real is an expression of the author's passionate belief about kids, how they learn best, and how they can become active participants in their own education, learning the communication skills in what educators call "a functional context." The creative strategies that he honed over the years grew out of and rest on a progressive, constructivist theory of education. Ross Burkhardt is not one to simply provide clever, fun activities that keep students happy but may have little relationship to stated, long-term objectives. Rather, his teaching techniques encourage students to think, to reflect, to explore—in short, to learn fully in ways that change behavior, the ultimate aim of education. These ways, of course, reflect what common sense and research affirm: young adolescents learn best in an interactive, collaborative classroom. And while numerous powerful, individual strategies are presented here, Ross is sensitive to the reality that the most lasting lessons are cumulative in nature and more often than not center on the modeling of the teacher.

All too typically, the teaching of writing in school conjures up negative images of the rules of grammar, 250-word compositions, and obligatory topic sentences. After participating in a 1980 National Writing Project Summer Institute, Ross's teaching followed the more creative path of "How do I know what I believe until I see what I say?" Writing became not just something to be done correctly but a way to learn, to verify, to clarify, and to communicate to others one's findings or beliefs.

Teachers by the hundreds and, through them, students by the thousands will benefit because this gifted classroom teacher, this extrovert with imagination and erudition, has taken the time to distill his career and record in this volume "Ross Burkhardt in action." *Writing for Real* is a professional resource that is for real, a teaching handbook you will come back to time after time following a surprisingly engaging and thoroughly enjoyable first read.

As I became immersed in this manuscript, I kept thinking of what a marvelous illustration Ross's teaching was of the most meaningful mission statement I have ever seen. In an offbeat but effective message emblazoned on faculty T-shirts, the Freedom Middle School in Franklin, Tennessee, seeks to follow this maxim: "Where teaching consists of causing or allowing students to get into situations from which they cannot escape except by learning." Ross Burkhardt created such situations magnificently. And with this resource, you can too!

John H. Lounsbury
Milledgeville, Georgia
July 1, 2002

Preface

I believe in real writing for real reasons, and that is what I taught my students.

What is "real writing?"

When a student . . .

revises her interior monologue through seven drafts.

writes an article for the school newspaper knowing that everyone will read it.

composes a memoir celebrating a race in which he and his father competed, then gives the memoir to his father.

divulges a pressing personal problem in her journal entry.

volunteers to read his poem first.

writes a letter to a substitute teacher apologizing for misbehavior.

meets with his mother for half an hour to discuss writing.

writes twice as much for a personal time capsule assignment as required.

reads aloud to the class her personal essay about a family tradition.

When such things happen, writing becomes real.

And what are "real reasons?"

When a student . . .

defines for classmates on the second day of school such terms as *cooperation, respect,* and *responsibility.*

selects one of his three poems to appear in the class anthology.

enters an essay contest and wins $100 in prize money.

writes a "secret letter" to a classmate whom she admires from a distance, knowing that the recipient won't receive the letter until four years have passed.

publicly declares himself a learner by sharing with peers three important lessons he has learned since school began in the fall.

composes and delivers a farewell message to classmates at the end of the year.

When such reasons exist, writing becomes real.

For the twenty-five years I taught middle school, I tried many different strategies to engage students in writing. Some I invented; others I borrowed from colleagues and then tweaked; a few came from the students themselves.

Most of the ideas went through several iterations before evolving into their present form. Student response to a particular strategy introduced one year helped me clarify instructions, select appropriate models, adjust timelines, and invent ancillary activities the following year.

Eventually I learned how to formulate a ten-month curriculum, teaching with the whole year in mind, seeing it as a continuum from September to June. I knew before school started what I was going to do that year, although I made time for unanticipated events. I completed the writing assignments along with my students, which helped me to better understand the demands and challenges of each task and taught my students that I struggled, as they did, with the written word. I shared my writing on many occasions, composing model assignments over a period of years. My repertoire grew steadily.

I saw my task as nurturing a community of writers who practiced cooperation and mutual support. This required a shift in my thinking from a teacher-centered classroom to a more collaborative one in which students took ownership for their learning. Lecture and listening gave way to hands-on projects and inquiry.

All this did not occur overnight, nor without pain. I had to learn to trust students to be responsible. When I began, I had no prior experience in organizing groups effectively; allowing young adolescents go off on their own, unsupervised, was anxiety-producing. Would they learn? What if they frittered away their time?

Some students are drawn to attractively packaged activities; a community ethos will invite others in. Therefore, I designed enticing group work, weaving together a tapestry of projects and events, hoping for the best. Year after year I assigned the same tasks, tailoring them slightly to fit new students with new strengths, weaknesses, needs, and interests.

Over time I learned to teach writing by . . . teaching writing. I reflected on what worked, learned from my mistakes, and capitalized on my successes. In the process students moved from perfunctory prose to real writing.

And, year after year, kids loved writing letters to themselves, producing poetry booklets, making gifts of writing, and compiling individual magazines, because these activities accommodated a wide range of interests, abilities, and backgrounds, but mostly because, through these activities, students discovered that they were writing for real.

Ross M. Burkhardt
Las Cruces, New Mexico
June 2002

About This Book

Writing for Real: Strategies for Engaging Adolescent Writers tells many tales: personal reflections on my thirty-five-year career, anecdotes about my growth as a teacher of writing, and stories of my students' real writing experiences over the years. But before those accounts could come into existence, I had to change the way I taught and place students at the center of learning. Nancie Atwell (1987) put it this way: "[W]e have to organize our . . . teaching in ways that will help our kids begin to understand and participate in adult reality. This means more independent activity, more say in what happens in the classroom, and more responsibility for their own learning" (p. 26).

Writing for Real is about transforming belief into action. It advances the proposition that it is possible to teach writing effectively to most of the kids, most of the time, which is about as good as it gets; nothing in teaching is 100 percent guaranteed.

Part One introduces ten assertions about writing, then focuses on the first month of school and how to begin a writing program. Here I explain the first writing assignment of the year, students' initial public speaking experiences and sharing of writing aloud, the formation of early writing groups, and the creation of inaugural journal entries.

Part Two describes innovative teaching strategies based on the ten assertions presented in Part One. These strategies I used successfully in my middle school language arts classroom for almost two decades. Included here are such activities as the Gift of Writing, the Letter to Self, the Holiday Memory Piece, and Lessons Learned. Throughout, I present examples of student response along with reflections written by the same students several years later. Many chapters begin with "In a Nutshell," a short overview.

Part Three explains a series of culminating activities: the poetry magazine, the Parent Writing Conference, the individual magazine, and writing for closure. In the final chapter I offer reflections on the year-long writing program and its lasting impact on students.

Writing for Real celebrates developmentally responsive middle level teaching: motivating young adolescents, addressing their needs, and providing relevant writing experiences. National Middle School Association's position paper This We Believe (1995) describes early adolescence as

> a period of tremendous variability among youngsters of the same gender and chronological age. Dissimilar rates of growth are common in all areas of development—intellectual, physical, social, emotional, and moral . . . Individual differences proliferate, making dubious such assumptions as "All 7th graders

are . . ." It also is important to recognize that these areas of development are inexorably intertwined. With young adolescents, the achievement of academic success, for example, is highly dependent upon their other developmental needs being met . . . [B]ecause cognitive growth occurs gradually, most middle level students require ongoing concrete, experiential learning in order to develop intellectually. (p. 6)

How does one teach students in transition? I struggled with that question during my entire career. An activity that succeeded wonderfully one year flopped the next. As I attempted to link learners to their lives, I worked from the known to the unknown, from the simple to the complex, and from the concrete to the abstract. Teaching adolescents was an incredible learning experience, and eventually it all came together. Yet even in my last year of teaching I was discovering new truths about young adolescents.

How to Use This Book

Davy Crockett said, "Be sure you're right, then go ahead." A colleague put it more succinctly: "Trust your judgment." But how do you know you're right? The trial and error method takes time; asking students for feedback about an assignment provides helpful information, but after the fact. How do you know what will work in the classroom?

The activities described here are time-tested practices that work with kids, yet no one assignment gets the job done. Rather, it is the slow accumulation of skills, the exposure to different forms of expression, the time spent in writing groups, the sharing of models (from peers and from the canon), the reflecting in journals, the teacher's sharing his or her own drafts with students, the celebrating of writing by reading it aloud, and the regular publishing of selected pieces—all part of a sustained program of frequent writing based on an articulated philosophy—that make the difference. Some chapters include classroom dialogue. I invite you to use these dialogues as departure points for your own conversations about writing with students.

The activities I present flow from one to the next. However, each can stand on its own. I often varied the sequence; there is nothing sacred about the order, although some assignments are best done at specific times of the year. But when taught one after another, in whatever order, these activities create a reservoir of writing skills and experiences from which students and teachers can draw as the year continues.

Although the writing activities I presented in my classrooms grew in complexity over time, the school year I describe here never actually happened. It is, rather, an amalgam of typical events. The students and their writing, however, are real, though from many years; students from 1988–89, for example, are depicted alongside students from 1994–95.

Success Factors

The writing strategies presented are more likely to succeed in your classroom when you

Agree with most, if not all, of the ten assertions about writing presented in Chapter 2.

Modify these ideas to your own teaching style, students, and setting.

Allow for choice: of topic, form, audience, purpose.

Use cooperative learning techniques such as pair/share and writing groups.

Do the assignments along with your students, and share your drafts.

Create your own responses to specific assignments; within three years you'll have a set of personal examples to serve as models for your students.

Reflect on your pedagogy after using these ideas.

Ask students for feedback; listen to what they say as well as what they don't say.

Build trust with your students; have your classroom become a safe place for all writers, not just the able ones.

Honor and celebrate the writing that you and your students create.

Three Cautions

Keep in mind the following words of caution.

First, there is no handy formula to follow when teaching writing. The ideas presented here demand time, energy, planning, and reflection; they cannot be implemented casually or overnight. The idiosyncrasies of teaching make it an abstract art, not an exact science; consequently, replication is not the goal. But stay the course! If you are inspired by the voices of the students in the following pages, and if you adapt the strategies to your own style, you may do yourself and your students a great service.

Second, if colleagues at different grade levels in your school intend to use these activities, you might find it helpful to coordinate with them so that students aren't assigned a Gift of Writing or a Letter to Self, for example, every year. While it is true that student abilities and interests change over time, the activities could become diluted and less engaging if overused.

Third, you will encounter many examples of student voice in these pages: letters, journal entries, poems, reflections, essays, and more. The student writing in this book was composed over a span of fifteen years; much of it (particularly the journal entries) is presented just as students wrote it, in unpolished form.

A Word About Assessment

Every piece of writing is both an assessment and a documentation of learning. My goal was not rigorous assessment; rather, it was to turn kids on to writing. They were "assessed" in the process. In addition, I was working on higher-order thinking skills: reflecting, understanding, interpreting. As Lois Easton (2002), Director of Professional Development at Eagle Rock School in Colorado, put it, "The methodologies most likely to help us [measure higher-order thinking skills] are presentations, documentations, teaching experiences, portfolios, dramatizations, original art, technological media, and writing in various genres" (p. 76).

No student ever asked me what his or her grade was on the Letter of Appreciation, or the Holiday Memory Piece, or Lessons Learned, or several other writing assignments. Apparently, doing these assignments and sharing them with peers and family was sufficient reward.

A Final Thought

I saw my students as writers and, *mirabile dictu,* they were. If you regard your students as writers, you create a self-fulfilling prophecy: they write.

Acknowledgments

I am grateful to countless friends, among them a generation of former students, for their support of this book. While the words here are mine, the ideas, adventures, and activities they describe emanate from innumerable interactions with students and colleagues, all of which helped to shape my teaching over a thirty-five year career.

Many of the ideas about writing advanced in this book were initially suggested by teachers at Shoreham–Wading River Middle School where I taught for a quarter of a century. Thanks to Diane Burkhardt, George Dorsty, Esther Fusco, Jackie Grennon, Howie Katzoff, Maureen Powers, Bill Reffelt, and Liala Strotman for their contributions to my development as an English/social studies teacher over the years. Team members Bonne Sue Adams, Chris Cummo, Cliff Lennon, Nancy Lukoski, Nick Naccarato, Jerry Silverstein, Don Strotman, and Jim Traina enabled and encouraged me to grow in my understanding and practice as a middle level teacher. Principals Dennis Littky, Jane Wittlock, and Cary Bell were enlightened administrators who supported my initiatives in the classroom, and I thank them. In addition, Bob Kaplan, then the library-media specialist at Shoreham–Wading River Middle School, provided useful information regarding the school newspaper project.

None of the writing strategies described in this book would have merit if my students had not responded to them. I thank all my students, because by being themselves and doing what they did they contributed to the ideas that constitute this book. I appreciate their willingness to share their eighth-grade writing, and I acknowledge each contributing author whose work appears here, as well as the others for whom there was not enough space in these pages. Life indeed is unfair! A special thank you to those former students who in 2002 contributed reflections on writing composed when they were in eighth grade.

Thanks also to my writing teachers, Sondra Perl and Richard Sterling, who led a 1980 National Writing Project Summer Institute. My attendance at that event transformed my classroom teaching; Sondra and Richard's efforts led ultimately to my writing this book.

Here in New Mexico I thank my fellow Las Cruces retiree, Eileen Taulbee, whose years as a language arts teacher resulted in several excellent suggestions that improved the text, including her idea for the "In a Nutshell" summaries. I enjoyed afternoons reading to my octogenarian mother-in-law, Martha Gooden; sharing early drafts of several chapters with her enabled me to find my voice. My cousin Diana Bartnick Schmidt also read several chapters early on and guided them to clarity. My Albuquerque literary friends Linnea Hendrickson and Jeanne Whitehouse Peterson were enthusiastic in their response to the ideas in this book; their practical suggestions and comments about structure proved most helpful. I also thank the Institute of Historical Survey Foundation in Las Cruces, in particular Evan Davies and Anne Morgan, for their support. Their invitation to house my archives at IHSF helped make this project feasible.

The philosophy of National Middle School Association and its network of middle level educators, with whom I have worked for two decades, helped me understand the importance of developmentally responsive education for young adolescents; I hope that this book proves worthy of their regard. In particular, I thank John Lounsbury for writing the foreword, and for his kind words and friendship.

A recent book by Lois Easton, about Eagle Rock School, an exceptional educational enterprise in Estes Park, Colorado, helped me see possibilities for this book, especially how to use student voices effectively.

I am grateful to my editor at Stenhouse, Bill Varner, for his periodic praise and professional prodding. I appreciate the risk he took after attending my presentation on writing strategies at the 2001 National Middle School Association conference. His suggestion that I write a book describing the "powerful and authentic experiences with writing" that my students enjoyed was the genesis for this book.

To Jeanne, my wife, my friend, my librarian, and my muse, infinite thanks. She supported me through every stage of this book's development and made watershed contributions to it: helping with the index, editing every chapter, researching arcane facts, preparing the bibliography, checking release forms, creating breakthroughs when I was stuck, offering inspiration and consolation, and cheering me on. I could not have completed this book without her loving support and steadfast devotion. Jeanne, I am appreciative beyond words.

I thank my family—siblings, children, stepchildren, and grandchildren. Their love sustains me as I hunch over my iMac (and allow family newsletters and other projects to languish). Finally, the memory of my mother, who taught me to appreciate poetry, and my father, who taught me the meaning of service, lives in these pages.

Part One

The First Five Weeks

How do you get a snowball rolling down a hill to the point where it picks up momentum of its own?

When contemplating a year's writing curriculum, how do you address the many steps that need to be taken simultaneously on several fronts, teaching students how to:

draft
revise
edit
proofread
prepare text for publication
listen
share writing aloud
respond to writing
work cooperatively in writing groups
master specific forms of expression
trust other students
reflect in journals
participate in a community of writers
address the conventions of English, including grammar and mechanics
see writing as a joyous, fulfilling endeavor

Where do you start? What do you do after that? What specific classroom activities done early in the year lead to the development of a community of writers? What opening exercises can you conduct that will focus your students' attention on writing for real?

Chapters 1 through 8 explore these questions. I follow my class from the first day to the end of the first month of school, presenting a philosophy of writing and several assignments based on this philosophy. Here you will read about the first class, the first writing assignment, the first public speaking exercise, the first journal entry, the first poetry memorization, the first writing shared by the teacher, the first form of writing taught, the first time students read their writing to the rest of the class, the first writing groups, and the first class anthology.

Intention and design mark these activities. All support the development of a supportive community of writers, including the teacher. They share drafts and polished pieces, listen to and learn from one another, develop mutual respect as they practice collegiality and response, and grow into a community of writers embarked on a "simultaneously shared journey."

The activities described in this section of the book can be done at other times during the year; however, their placement at the beginning of the year is not accidental. Anticipating the more rigorous writing projects that come later in the year and mindful of the importance of taking day-to-day, incremental steps that nurture trust and cooperation among young adolescents, in Part One I offer a rationale for beginning the year so that students and teacher "hit the ground running." You will enter a writing class and see how a teacher begins, and how a set of ten assertions about writing provides a departure point for a year-long writing program with assignments accessible to all.

1

Writing for Real

In March, seven months into the school year, I asked my students to reflect on their writing experiences. They had just conducted a writing conference with their parents. Here are excerpts from their journals:

Since September I have become better at expressing myself. I am not afraid to write how I feel, and often if I am feeling down I write something on the depressing side, and when I am feeling happy I write a happy little something about the world or environment. I am better at descriptive writing than I used to be . . . I think about the picture I see in my mind [and] put every little detail from where the light is coming from to how loud the cricket is chirping.

I think my current writing strengths are report writing, personal narrative and interior monologues . . . The monologue I wrote about Jimmie from *Miracle Worker* went on in my head while I was reading the book . . . I may be one of the few people that like report writing. I feel I am pretty good at writing book reports etc. This is my basis for wanting to be a journalist.

My poetry needs improvement . . . I really don't like many of the poems I write, and it takes me a while to write them. Although the topics come easily [I] have to find the right word or words. It is almost a struggle. My story writing also needs improvement. I used to love writing story, but I find it hard to sit and type a fictional story. I'd much rather write a personal essay, one that I, along with the rest of my family, can cherish.

I love the way we write all of the time. My writing skills have stayed fresh all year long. Once the year ends I'm not going to want to stop writing, and I will be writing something each day. I want to write a long story, which would take me all summer . . . Thanks again for making this the best year of my life. Part of the reason it has been such a pleasure is my writing so often.

　　　—Jessica Cepelak, age 13

I learned that it is good to share your writing with your parents once in a while. My mom enjoyed reading the piece I wrote about my sister. She made me read it to her. I think she liked doing the conference with me. She asked me what my favorite piece of writing was. She made me read it aloud and it turned out that I changed my mind after I heard it.

I don't think [my writing] has improved that much. There hasn't been any big drastic changes in it, really. My current writing strengths are, I think, punctuation and spelling. I think I need improvement on keeping the reader's interest. Sometimes I go off on other subjects and it totally messes me up. I also need help on knowing where to put the paragraphs.

I've had a lot more fun writing this year. Last year we had to write about things that mostly didn't interest me. This year we're writing about stuff I like, for instance poetry. I love writing poetry. It's really hard for me sometimes, but I do it anyway. It's a nice challenge.

　　　—Heidi Lipinsky, age 13

My parents had a lot of questions, such as where I got my ideas, how I wrote my poems and things, and how I knew to edit and revise my pieces of work. I answered most of them easily but when asked where I got my actually concepts for poems, all I could say was the things that intrigue me. They also wanted to know what I like to write about, which was another easy one, fantasy.

My writing has definitely improved since September. I have learned how to [write] in a ton of different styles . . . I have also learned how to revise and edit my works and how to listen objectively to other people's work and how to bring up my criticisms about the piece in a constructive manner.

I really have no weak points that are very big at the moment though I am a little self conscious about reading my poems aloud. Oh yeah, I couldn't write a play script for my life.
—Mike Clair, age 14

These entries resonate with confidence, candor, and conviction. Jessica, Heidi, and Mike represent hundreds of eighth graders with whom I worked during twenty-five years as an English/social studies teacher at Shoreham–Wading River Middle School on Long Island, New York. In my classroom, we wrote almost every day. Because the writing activities addressed the developmental needs and characteristics of early adolescent learners, students were eager and enthusiastic when it came time to write.

Adolescents are "driven to communicate," and wise teachers take advantage of that reality. Jerome Belair and Paul Freeman (2001) note:

Try to quiet a middle school classroom, and you generally end up with the writing of notes and the passing of intricately folded pieces of paper. Their desire to communicate is insatiable . . . By channeling their natural desire to talk to each other, by focusing our efforts on relevant content choices, and by building on their innate abilities with the communication skills, we can engage them in instruction, feed their needs as social beings, and lead them to a deeper understanding. (pp. 5–6)

Parents and educators agree that by the end of middle school, students should be able to communicate effectively and fluently in writing. But what is the best way to achieve that end? Or, rather, what are the best *ways*, since an approach that works with one student does not necessarily succeed with the student in the next seat. How can we motivate adolescents to write with engagement? How do we develop positive attitudes about the writing process? What practices foster good writing skills? How do we get kids to write for real?

My approach to teaching writing stems from what I learned in a National Writing Project Summer Institute in 1980. Prior to that experience, my exposure to language arts consisted of two college courses: a forgettable freshman composition class and a memorable last-term senior year poetry seminar for English majors.

My Career as a Comma Corrector

Following two years in the Peace Corps as a physical education instructor in Tunisia; a year at the University of Pennsylvania, where I earned a master's degree in education and concurrently taught seventh-grade social studies half-time at Strawberry Mansion JHS in central Philadelphia; and seven years teaching high school social studies in my home town in New York's Hudson Valley, I moved to Long Island in 1972 to teach English and social studies in a brand-new middle school. Although by then I had been teaching for ten years, I was totally untrained in language arts and lacked any formal background in writing theory or literature. So I borrowed ideas from colleagues, cobbled together assignments as best I could based on vague memories of junior high, and experimented with any and all approaches to writing, including poetry and the five-paragraph essay. Gradually I began to feel comfortable teaching English composition to young adolescents.

Frustrated by sloppy papers, illegible handwriting, and other homework horrors, my language arts colleagues and I drafted and unanimously adopted a set of standards and introduced them to our pupils on the first day of school, September 1973:

Standards for Written Assignments for Grades 7 and 8

The following are rules to be observed for all written assignments in English and Social Studies, unless otherwise specified by the teachers. The purpose of these rules is to ensure that your written assignments will be both neatly written and clearly expressed.

1. Use 8 1/2" x 11" lined notebook paper with standard margins.
2. All papers must be written in ink, preferably black or blue.
3. Drawings and diagrams which relate to the theme of the paper are acceptable.
4. You may print, type, or use script, but all papers must be legibly written.
5. PROOFREAD all assignments for content, spelling, and grammatical errors. Make sure that you have written your paper in complete sentences.
6. A heading should be placed at the top of each assignment. This should include your name, subject, advisor, and the date. This is to avoid loss of paper.
7. All papers should be titled, except for short, in-class assignments.
8. Try to structure your papers to present your ideas clearly. In most cases this should include a topic sentence, followed by the body of your paper, and a conclusion. When your ideas are put in order, they are most easily understood.
9. All general statements should be supported with examples from your reading or from personal experience.

N.B. Papers will be accepted for final grading only when they comply with the above standards. Papers which do not meet these standards will be returned with a note informing you of the changes to be made. You are expected to make these changes and resubmit your paper within two days.

On the second day of school I anxiously gave a writing assignment as homework. The bottom line on the handout said, "In this assignment, as in all other written assignments, the *Standards for Written Assignments* are to be followed." My teaching log of September 9, 1973, records what happened:

I have just corrected the morning set of papers on the assignment we gave last Thursday. We instituted the *Standards for Written Assignments* in an attempt to create minimum standards for kids and make our jobs easier in terms of not having to read a paper written in yellow Bic Banana on white paper. The kids were to choose one of seven quotations and write an essay using the Standards to guide them. Sixteen out of the seventeen morning papers are being returned.

I cannot recall ever having taken so much time with any assignment in terms of reading and correcting it, and I find that my enjoyment is laced with a feeling that if I am as conscientious in correcting every assignment, I may actually help these kids improve their writing skills. I considered what they said, I pointed out to them as best I could how they could improve their work. Now I must await their reaction and see how my efforts are interpreted by them.

Clearly I was a conscientious teacher, struggling to do what was right for my students. Clearly the Standards were a step toward something positive; they provided students with support and guidance in their writing. Clearly parents were enamored with them; in a teaching log entry two weeks later, I noted: "Thursday night was Parents' Night . . . The Standards for Written Assignments got rave reviews . . . ('It should have been done a long time ago,' said one dad.)" And clearly my colleagues and I missed the boat.

Yes, we were proud of these rules. Our hearts were in the right place, but something was off. The Standards focused on mechanics at the expense of expression; and they allowed almost no time for revision. There was no mention of drafting and revising, barely a nod toward content, and an emphasis on appearance and neatness, as if those were the essence of written communication. I sensed vaguely that our Standards were flawed, but I did not know how to improve something I did not really understand: how to teach writing effectively.

An assignment given in 1976, during our two-week interdisciplinary study of the Civil War, stated:

You will complete three writing assignments. Please complete these assignments according to the *Standards for Written Assignments*. Use a proper heading, a title, and organize your thoughts so that you have an introduction, several paragraphs which develop the main idea, and a conclusion. PROOFREAD!!!

I offered no advance training in how to "develop the main idea," no inviting language, just terse terminology intended to set a high "standard." I must have assumed that students would learn to write well through some form of divine osmosis. They didn't. Their prose was passionless, perfunctory, painful.

In mid-1978 I gave this in-class writing assignment:

Seminars are over, high school schedules are being planned, *Inherit the Wind* has ended, winter sports are happening, and we play Jeopardy in a few minutes. How are things going? What kind of ideas, feelings, attitudes do you have about the year so far? What things bug you? What have been the good things? What should we do before the year is out? Evaluate what has happened by writing about it.

I felt good about this assignment; I was the interested teacher reaching out, asking the right kinds of questions, taking the pulse of the kids. One student's response set me straight:

I hate these things and these sheets bug me . . . I didn't like *Gone with the Wind*. I had a good vacation but at the end my great grandfather died, in the middle of the service my sister yells out, "Hey mom, who dressed the dead guy?" And every body turned around and gave us this "look."

I learned once again that students often respond in brutally honest ways when asked to write something in class.

But I persevered. In January 1979, I designed the following task:

You are to write six (6) paragraphs, each one developed in a different way (see list below) and each one on a different topic. Each paragraph must have at least five (5) complete sentences:

Paragraph Development
1. By giving examples
2. By giving details
3. By arranging details in chronological order
4. By arranging details in spatial order
5. By giving reasons
6. By comparison or contrast

I do not recall explaining this assignment to my students, and to this day I'm not sure what I meant by "spatial order." I was not seeking paragraphs that connected to one another coherently. At that time I saw paragraph development as a technical task, an exercise that posed a challenge to my students. I soon discovered that this assignment, like many others that preceded it, did not result in writing worth reading.

Every generation has a distinct youth culture, and sensitive teachers incorporate aspects of it into their lessons. Those of us from an earlier era may appreciate, as I did, watching my twin brother teach commas and quotation marks in 1965. The ordinary, yet extraordinary, sentence he asked his ninth-grade students to punctuate has stayed with me:

Paul said George will not be here today John said Ringo

I paid homage to that text in January 1980 on a comma worksheet, offering these gems to my students, mixing in their names in an attempt to brighten up what I saw as a dreary task:

Please put commas in the following sentences where they belong:

> Whose woods these are I think I know but his house is in the town.
> In November 1976 Carter beat Ford in the election.
> No Laura hasn't been in school for three days but she phones every day.
> John Robert and Jim went to the store but it was closed.
> If there is a natural pause in the sentence you should put in a comma.
> Carla has no problem putting commas in the right place however.
> Glenn however thinks that he can put commas wherever he wants.
> Mr. Burkhardt should I put a comma in this sentence?
> There should be two commas in this sentence Kathy so punctuate it
>   correctly.
> Do you really expect me to believe that Cindy?
> Mr. Burkhardt typed this without making any misteaks I think.

In retrospect, I'm pleased that at the very least I attempted to invent engaging curriculum and connect with my students. But after so many years I was still concentrating on commas, not writing, because I didn't know any better.

In December 1979 the school district administrators issued a set of "Administrative Regulations on Teaching Grammar":

> Grammar instruction is best presented in the context of writing, rather than in isolation from writing as a lesson for its own sake . . . Frequent writing with consistent presentation of grammatical and other information connected to that writing, and the use of common terms are expected in grades 3–12.

Picking up on this enlightened directive, the middle school principal sent all English teachers a memo in January 1980 in which she said that "the immediate direction for middle school English teachers at this point in time is to improve the quality of our students' writing by having them write often and regularly." She continued: "The teaching of grammar topics should be linked directly to the weaknesses found in your students' writing."

I remember reading the words and asking myself, *How do you do that?*

In July 1980, I depicted my teaching thus:

A comma corrector. That's how I can describe my role as a writing teacher last year. Typical assignment? Write a paper on a specific topic and submit a final copy in two days. I then took home the sets of fifty papers, read and red-penciled them and insisted on clean, corrected rewrites within two days. On a number of papers I would pen such illuminating tributes as "Good work, Cindy," "Great job, Glenn," or "Well done, Laura." I had very little interaction with the words, the content, the heart of the paper. And though my dutiful students were prompt in preparing assignments, they were, I felt, passionless writers. This was largely because I lacked a philosophy of writing.

National Writing Project Summer Institute

Richard Sterling and Sondra Perl, at that time codirectors of the New York City Writing Project, offered a summer writing institute for teachers in the Shoreham–Wading River school district in 1980. Colleagues of mine who had participated in a previous institute praised it highly. Even though I had been teaching language arts for eight years, I knew I was shortchanging my students. I saw the institute as a genuine opportunity that addressed a need, so I signed up. That summer I was introduced to the metaphorical "writing as bicycling" question: "Which is more likely to inspire youngsters to ride a bike—feeling the free wind in their faces as they glide downhill, or reading an instruction manual on bicycle spoke repair?" Those three weeks in June 1980 changed my life and revolutionized my language arts teaching.

For the participants, the summer institute was "learning by doing" at its best. We wrote every day. We rehearsed, drafted, and revised. We reflected in journals on our writing process. We shared drafts in writing groups, raising questions about titles, endings, names of characters, turning points, settings, and tone. We wrote about past practices and new insights. That July I wrote:

> Time was when I feared that, on a given assignment, my students might collaborate before writing, and thus one student would use the ideas of another. I actively thwarted then what I now know to be an important part of the writing process—rehearsal. Writers need time in the preparatory stage to let their ideas stew. Interaction with classmates in listening activities is just one of several good techniques through which students can rehearse.

We published. We listened intently to outside speakers. We read scholarly articles by Donald Graves and Lucy Calkins. We discussed writing theory. We anguished and apologized when we had to read aloud ("It's not done yet. I'm still revising it."). We experienced firsthand the range of emotions and behaviors that writers go through. Along with this we planned writing activities for our classrooms.

With Sondra and Richard as coleaders and colearners in the institute, we explored ideas about the teaching of writing then being promulgated by the National Writing Project (NWP). Sondra and Richard flooded us with writing ideas. I was a dry sponge soaking up every drop.

During the institute I was particularly impressed by an unusual set of guest lecturers—four eighth-grade students whose language arts teacher had taken the institute the previous summer. With only one year of experience implementing NWP theory in her classroom, she invited her students to talk about their writing. These eighth graders exuded confidence and passion as they shared their thoughts about writing, read excerpts from journals, discussed the power of reading aloud to peers, and answered our many questions. I knew immediately that I wanted my own students to be able to speak as knowledgeably and authoritatively as those four "experts" could. These four teenagers profoundly affected my teaching and consequently the writing experiences of all of my students for the remainder of my career.

Forging Ahead

Initially it was not clear sailing. That first year, armed with exciting ideas and good intentions, not to mention nagging concerns and complex questions, I forged ahead. Some writing activities worked, others didn't, and I continued to dwell in the question "What's the best way to teach writing to young adolescents?"

My second year using National Writing Project ideas is described in *Through Teachers' Eyes: Portraits of Writing Teachers at Work* by Sondra Perl and Nancy Wilson (1986). Sondra, a writing researcher and my instructor in the summer institute, spent three or four days a week in my English class recording every detail of how I went about teaching writing. In her book, Sondra began the chapter on me accurately: "This is the story of a successful teacher who had a bad year" (Perl and Wilson 1986, p. 119).

An entry in my teaching journal in late March of that year recorded my frustration:

> I'm disappointed in my failure to succeed—I'm scared the kids don't like me anymore—or that I've lost their respect—I do not know what to say or do or how to go on without first dealing with my breakdown on Wed. afternoon—confronting it—getting a sense from the kids of where they are at & what they are feeling—and then seeing or sensing what should be done next. It surprised me this morning when [a student] said he felt sorry for me—that he cared enough to say that. I didn't expect that. If he does, then maybe others do.
>
> I've thought about what I should do—read "The First Day," or this entry, or something special—but I am undecided. I am very nervous—I know what I want—to get back to teaching & doing joyful things with kids—but how? How can I go on when I feel so terrible?

I hasten to add that my distress had little or nothing to do with the theories of the National Writing Project. The year was a disaster primarily because I was unable to develop strong positive relationships with the majority of my students. Somehow I made it through the year, although the memories are painful to this day.

The Weekly Poem

The 1983 opening of school went well, and my muse was moved to compose a poem, "Day Three," and share it with my students. Mark Moritz, who had watched me recite "The First Day" two days earlier, asked, "Mr. B., do you write a new poem every week?"

"I sure do," I fired back, committing myself on the spot to writing thirty-eight more poems between then and June. Thus the tradition, and the challenge, began.

Every Friday I said to my students, "I was leafing through my copy of *Poems for All Occasions* last night and found this poem that seems just right for today." Then I read a poem composed the evening before, one that mentioned students by name and reviewed the activities of the week. *Poems for All Occasions,* an apocryphal tome, became a useful device that enabled this teacher as writer to appear regularly in class.

Why a weekly poem? First, I enjoyed writing verse and knew that words need an audience. Second, the poems documented events of the school year. These "occasional" poems provided an outlet for my creativity and sharpened my skills as a communicator. Ultimately I shared my writing—poems and prose, drafts and polished pieces alike—with students because it worked: it motivated them to write better. It also made the task of writing, seen by some students as a chore, more tolerable. As one student succinctly put it, "You're doing it with us, so it's not like you're torturing us."

In the weekly poems I constantly recycled student experiences, teaching the lesson that everyday life provides great material. The kids, narcissistic as only young adolescents can be, loved hearing references to themselves or allusions to something they had done, and thus they were attentive and receptive.

Nancie Atwell (1987) spoke to this, noting that teachers serve students "when we accept and build on the realities of . . . kids. We can't wish away, discipline away, or program away a time of life. Nor can we afford to devote our days to reviewing past lessons or introducing 'skills' to be tapped in some nebulous and assumed future. We're there to help our . . . kids open a window on adulthood, on what really matters in life; we help by opening our curricula to [their] preoccupations, perspectives, and growing pains" (p. 49).

One of my weekly poems described the practice some of the more socially advanced students had of meeting at the school exits at the end of the day to bid each other adieu:

The Phenomenon of the Eighth Grade Farewell
(dedicated to the Goodbye Guys and Gals)

Mirror, mirror on the wall,
What is happening in the hall?
When the school clock strikes two-twenty,
From within the library
If I stand on tiptoes, I
Can be an eighth grade romance spy.

Almost every single day,
J. and M. and N. and K.
And other "letters" linger late
For a most important date:
To say goodbye to someone sweet
And share the warmth of body heat.

If I wander through the exit,
Just like that my presence wrecks it
For the cuddling, clutching pair.
She turns red; he fluffs his hair.
Hurriedly they break apart,
Leaving matters of the heart . . .

. . . Till I am gone, and then resume
Their fond farewell—so I assume,
For I do not look back at them,
Nor walk right up and say, "Ahem!"
Nor tug upon their sleeves or coats,
Nor send their teachers quickie notes.

Rather, I recall my days
Of radiating in a haze,
Of wearing blissful grin on face,
Of glowing from a brief embrace.
And so, I ask, what's wrong with this—
A tender, eighth grade "goodbye" kiss.

Success

By the fourth year I was zooming along, feeling the wind in my face and no longer focused on bicycle spoke repair, thoroughly enjoying the teaching of writing and working diligently at translating my beliefs into action. Students kept journals, my writing assignments improved in quality and clarity, and the introduction of computers facilitated the drafting and revising process.

For the rest of my career I loved teaching writing because the National Writing Project ideas I had learned promoted schooling based on the nature of the learner rather than the convenience of the instructor. I shifted my teaching from primarily lecture method to a more hands-on approach; it was demanding, time-consuming, and wholly worthwhile. I was an enthusiastic writer doing assignments along with my students, reading and commenting in their journals, crafting poems for them, and publishing their compositions. Some activities became eighth-grade traditions, others were left by the wayside, and new ones were constantly invented. Poetry—reading it, writing it, reciting it—played a significant part in the overall transformation of my curriculum.

The students whose voices opened this chapter had many extraordinary writing experiences during the year. And they were not alone. If you want your students to be able to talk about their writing the way Jessica, Heidi, and Mike did, read on.

2

Assertions About Writing

After several years of translating National Writing Project ideas into practice, I began presenting a workshop entitled "Real Writing for Real Reasons" at conferences, often inviting students to assist me. We explained four activities: the Letter of Appreciation and Acknowledgment, the Holiday Memory Piece, the Letter to Self, and the Gift of Writing. Our enthusiasm inspired participants. One of our 1989 workshop handouts stated:

> Students write best when they are invested in their writing. The four writing activities described below have been used successfully with eighth-grade students for the past several years. Each activity calls for investment on the part of the student. In all activities, drafting and revising are part of the composing process. Each represents a form of publication.

Investment, publication, topic choice, drafting, and revising—the pieces were falling into place. And yet . . .

At a middle school conference in 1991, a teacher came up to me and said, "I was at your workshop last year. When I tried your ideas with my students, they didn't work. What happened?"

I thought about her question for several months and eventually realized what was missing in my presentation: the philosophical foundation on which the writing strategies were based. That incident led me to formulate ten assertions encapsulating the theory behind the practice.

These assertions were not new to me; they had permeated my teaching and informed my practice for eleven years. But I had not given voice to them until that moment. Here are the ten:

1. Every student is a writer and has ideas she or he wants to communicate.
2. Every student writes at his or her ability level.
3. Writers are more invested in writing when they select their own topics.
4. Writers are inspired by models, especially those created by peers.
5. Teachers who share their writing with students provide powerful coaching.
6. Writers discover their voice when they read their writing aloud to peers.
7. Student writers should publish frequently for audiences beyond the teacher.
8. Writing is a recursive process: invent, rehearse, draft, revise, edit, publish.
9. Writers consider audience, purpose, and topic when they compose.
10. Volume + Variety = Fluency.

The first nine come directly from the National Writing Project; the tenth is my own creation. It seems logical; the more one writes, and the more different forms of writing one explores, the more fluent a writer one becomes. (The tenth assertion assumes that our schools are committed to producing fluent writers.) Whenever I do writing workshops now, I begin by introducing these ten assertions.

I formulated these assertions after years of designing practical, engaging, and interrelated writing strategies, testing them over time, and refining them in the crucible of the classroom. If you find yourself questioning some of them, thinking, *That's just not how to teach writing,* then the ideas in this book may not work for you. If that is the case, why not compile your own set of assertions? What do you actually believe about the teaching of writing? What specific activities should you do with your students in support of your beliefs?

Belief into Action

If you can assert what you believe, you can then ask yourself two questions: How do my beliefs show up in action? What strategies can I devise that are consistent with my beliefs? Every writing activity described in this book can be linked to one or more of my assertions. In my classroom, all ten were present by the end of the first week of school, and they were constantly reinforced from September to June.

Every student is a writer and has ideas she or he wants to communicate. Some students are proficient writers the day they walk through our classroom doors. A few are far better writers than we will ever be, and we need to stand back and let them compose. Others are struggling writers who have difficulty organizing their thoughts. All of them are writers with ideas to share.

Every student writes at his or her ability level. This assertion demands a shift in attitude—from focusing on the piece of writing to focusing on the student who composed it.

If you want to know the ability levels of your students, collect several writing samples and read them—it's instant assessment. In the first eighteen days of school, I assigned three journal entries, two free-verse poems, three explanatory paragraphs, two in-class writing exercises, two interior monologues, and a letter of introduction. Reading through all those assignments, I came to know each of my students as writers.

When you read a journal entry, then a letter, then an editorial, then a personal essay, then a third-person narrative, all composed by the same student, you can see how this student responds to different challenges and expresses ideas using a variety of forms. Such information is very useful as the year progresses.

Writers are more invested in the writing when they select their own topics. The traditional "What did you do on your summer vacation?" essay may not appeal to a student who just lost a grandparent or whose parents just divorced. The Halloween topic "Write how it feels to be a pumpkin" might thwart the imaginative student who prefers contemplating the kumquat.

Providing choice became par for the course for me; options abounded in almost every assignment. Nicole Frovik (2001) underscored the importance of choice when she said of students:

> [B]y letting them choose their own topics and work at their own pace in this community environment, I have helped them take ownership of their writing . . . [Students] claimed that the most important factor in improving their motivation was their choice of topics. (p. 39)

As much as possible, let your students choose their topics. I dictated very few topics; instead, I provided suggestions for forms or modes of expression, and questions: To whom is your letter addressed? What is your poem about? Is your editorial pro or con? The decisions were left to the students.

Writers are inspired by models, especially those created by peers. Each year I used the best student writing from the previous year as models for a given assignment, intentionally passing off really good writing as average. I suspect that when some students saw the names of the authors, they thought, "I sat next to him on the bus—I can write as well as he can." Not surprisingly, the quality of my students' writing improved steadily over the years.

Teachers who share their writing with students provide powerful coaching. I began the first day of each school year with a poem I wrote especially for the occasion, and ended the year the same way. I also presented many occasional poems celebrating both special and quotidian events, which I published and distributed to students at the end of the year.

From September to June, when students had a writing assignment, I did it along with them, sharing my struggles in class discussions the following day. I distributed my own drafts covered with red revision marks to show them how I nudged ideas toward clarity. I believe that being an active member of the community of writers in my classroom had a positive impact on my students.

Writers discover their voice when they read their writing aloud to peers. The quickest way I know to encourage students to revise their writing is to ask them to read it aloud. In most instances they do not even get through the first sentence before changing something, because when they hear it, they know that it does not say what they are trying to communicate. In my experience, when students share their drafts with peers in writing groups, revision occurs.

Student writers should publish frequently for audiences beyond the teacher. In a March 1991 keynote address at a Long Island reading and writing conference, Nancie Atwell remarked that when students publish, something formal and permanent occurs. Publication raises the stakes; students invest more of themselves in their writing when they know that their ideas are going public.

One of the reasons students in my classes drafted, revised, and edited so diligently is that we published regularly and took the writing beyond the walls of the classroom. We sent epistles to the superintendent, produced class anthologies, composed for school and district newspapers, mailed real letters to real people, posted students' reflective passages in the hallway for the entire school to see, and read our pieces aloud to one another at celebrations of writing.

Someone once told me, "Every published piece of writing goes through a process, but not every piece of writing gets published." Part of a teacher's job is to provide opportunities for students to publish some, but not all, of their writing. When students are allowed to decide which pieces get published, they are empowered as writers.

Writing is a recursive process: invent, rehearse, draft, revise, edit, publish. How does an idea come into being? A familiar aroma triggers long-forgotten memories. A photograph evokes past experiences. Someone makes a suggestion, and the mind leaps to visions of what might be.

When we write, we begin with ideas, sometimes inventing them at random, sometimes purposefully, often unexpectedly. Once we have an idea— "I'm going to write a poem for my sweetheart"—we imagine words, consider messages, experience feelings, and begin inventing.

Before we begin to draft, we arrange our writing implements, settle in with a glass of water or a cup of tea, and make lists; in short, we perform rituals in support of our writing. We may talk over an idea with someone. We may draw a map, check a fact in the encyclopedia, look up a synonym, or study a picture. We may examine an artifact, read a passage, or jot down some thoughts. These, too, are prewriting activities, part of the rehearsal one does before actually beginning to write.

Next, we create a first draft, complete with false starts, erasures, crossed-out lines, arrows, key words, margin notes, possible titles, and questions. The draft is revised, and a new draft is created, then revised again. Seeking feedback, we ask others, "What's missing? What works?" Response to a piece in process can lead to more recrafting, more invention; response can send the writer back to rethink, reexamine, and in some cases recreate the idea. The drafts pile up; this recursive process continues until the author is satisfied that the piece is done.

Editing should occur near the end of the writing process, once the words have been selected and sequenced. Why spend time editing prematurely if major revisions lie ahead? I expected student drafts to conform to the norms of standard English, yet I didn't stress grammatical exactitude or correct spelling too early in the process, because of the editing and proofreading that I knew would occur in writing groups prior to publication.

Yes, spelling is important, but the third grader who has been told that correct spelling is absolutely crucial may, in attempting to write a story about a hippopotamus, experience frustration when heeding the admonishment of his teacher. The child writes: "The hip- . . . The hipper- . . . The hypo- . . . The hippoppo- . . . ," then abandons the piece for fear of making a mistake. Why not simply use a capital *H* to represent the creature until the piece is done, then look up the correct spelling in the dictionary? After all, in revising the story, the child may decide to write about kangaroos instead.

Writers consider audience, purpose, and topic when they compose. Students often ask, "Why are we doing this?" and "Why do we have to learn this?" Such questions, usually voiced by the more assertive students, are in fact responsible reactions to any task a teacher assigns and probably are also in the minds of those who sit silently. Teachers need to respond appropriately; real writing demands real answers.

The teacher may reply, "To whom are you writing? Why? What are you writing about?" The accomplished writer determines the answers to these questions before beginning a composition.

I always told my students, "If I cannot explain to you in advance the audience, purpose, and topic of any writing assignment this year, you don't have to do it." Somehow I always could, so they always had to be able to explain their writing as well.

Volume + Variety = Fluency. As I stated earlier, the more you write, and the more different forms of expression in which you write, the more fluent a writer you become. This is why I asked students to compose editorials, first-person narratives, third-person narratives, poems, descriptive passages, persuasive essays, interior monologues, personal letters, journal entries, analyses, forewords, brief autobiographies (About the Author), directions, plays, dialogues, dedications, business letters, reports, and more.

Nancie Atwell, speaking at another conference on Long Island in 1996, put it this way: "Quality in writing is supported by quantity and experimentation."

Environments and Expectations

Along with writing theory we need to consider the actual setting where it happens: the classroom. How well do you say "Hello" to your students each year? Is your room inviting? What assumptions do you have about your students before they walk through the door? Is your classroom arranged in ways that support writing? Are your expectations about writing clear? Are you excited about teaching writing? Does your enthusiasm manifest itself to your students? Is there a place for spontaneity in your classroom? Do you write with your students? Do you share early drafts as well as finished pieces? Is writing celebrated and honored throughout the year?

The teacher establishes both the expectations and the environment. An inviting classroom can reap dividends all year. You only have one chance to make a first impression; do it well. Think about how to begin; set the tone for the year with care and deliberation.

Let the kids know what you expect. I posted the ten assertions about writing and distributed copies to all students. I reminded them on day one to "Save all drafts!" They heard me repeat this throughout the year. Sometimes I would say, "Writing is like mathematics—show your work. I want to see all the steps you took to reach your final draft."

I rarely specified how long a piece of writing had to be. To the inevitable question about length I responded, "Do your best work." If a student fell woefully short of my expectations, I declared the assignment incomplete and raised questions to elicit further detail. An abundance of examples in my own writing served as a model for the kind of descriptive writing I wanted my students to create.

I was attempting to help my students become enthusiastic writers who enjoyed drafting and revising. Above all, I worked constantly at creating a safe community for writing, a place where students would feel secure, confident, and free from ridicule. How did I do this? By reading my own writing aloud, including early and polished drafts. By insisting that students listen to their peers respectfully. I never forced students to read aloud; rather, I invited them, and I respected their decision when they declined. I continued to invite them to share. Eventually, when they felt safe, they did. As a class we acknowledged with polite applause everyone who contributed to the lesson.

Many skills are addressed in a comprehensive writing program: taking notes, researching and organizing information, sequencing ideas, using specific detail and description, meeting deadlines, working cooperatively in groups, writing persuasively, actively listening to peers, drafting and revising, editing and proofreading, preparing writing for publication, using proper sentence structure, employing appropriate vocabulary, and maintaining consistent verb tense—to name just a few. I addressed these skills in the context of the students' own writing, not by focusing on them directly, but by saying, "We're going to publish your composition." I have yet to meet the student who wants to appear incompetent by having an error-filled essay in a class anthology. You raise the stakes for the student by asking, "What piece do you want to publish?" Students want to look good, and their writing will be better, when they know a particular piece is destined for the school library collection. They realize that their writing should be free of error, and they understand that they must revise, edit, proofread, and check to be sure the spelling and grammar are satisfactory.

Student effort needs to be acknowledged. If one student did seven drafts of her poem and another did only two, many would agree that the first student put forth greater effort than the second. It is also true that the second student may be a brilliant writer, capable of crafting a superb poem by draft two, and the first writer's verse may still require significant revision even in draft seven. Most teachers can distinguish between effort and quality; we should encourage both.

During the year one writing activity in my classroom would lead to another, which would lead to a third activity. I used Strategy B because it was supported by Strategy A, and I then used Strategy C because it built on the previous two. Some of the assignments became famous. Younger brothers and sisters of former students would enter class on day one and ask excitedly, "When are we going to do the Letter to Self?" Rituals and rites of passage are important to young adolescents.

Real Writing

What is real writing? First graders know that Santa Claus is real when they write letters to him. The eighth grader who jots a quick note to a friend about a certain someone engages in real writing. When a teacher reads his or her poem aloud to the class, the moment becomes very real.

I wanted kids to have rewarding experiences with real writing and simultaneously to develop communication skills that would serve them a lifetime. I was interested in having students put pen to paper, or fingers to keyboard, and enjoy the process of giving voice and structure to inchoate thought. When one writes, one necessarily has to think.

The strategies presented in this book, based on my ten assertions about writing, moved students toward that end. I learned that when students immersed themselves in these assignments, grammar, sentence structure, and usage issues usually took care of themselves.

Does every student master everything? Of course not. But over the long run, and without mind-numbing comma lessons and their ilk, most of the students, most of the time, demonstrated significant improvement in their writing skills. Can a teacher ask for more?

3

Day One:
Getting Started

Day One: Getting Started

Basic ideas: Make the first day of school a welcoming celebration featuring music, poetry, introductions, and the Distinctions.

Assertions addressed: 1, 2, 3, 4, 5, 9, and 10 (*see p. 17*).

Skills addressed: Letter writing, oral presentation, expository writing, listening.

Class time needed: One period.

Advance preparation: Select passages to be read on day one; prepare letter of introduction assignment sheet; prepare list of Distinctions; cut up Distinction lists so that you have one Distinction for each student in a paper sack; obtain 3-x-5-inch index cards.

Time of year: Day one.

Neat feature: All students stand and speak to the class.

Assessment: Two writing assignments provide the teacher with a preliminary indication of student writing skills.

Follow-up: Respond to each student letter. Hold class meeting on day two to share Distinction definitions.

Journal entry: None.

Caution: Return your responses to student letters all at once, not piecemeal. Keep track of which student selects which Distinction; this provides accountability.

Forms: Letter of introduction homework sheet; list of the Distinctions.

Questions to consider: What passages will you read aloud to students? What music will you play? What are your goals for day one? How well do you say "Hello"?

Why do this? To establish an inviting, positive tone at the beginning of the year; to get to know more about your students and their writing skills; to begin building a sense of community.

The year began with music and poetry. One minute before class, my partner Cliff Lennon, who taught math and science, pushed the "play" but-
ton on the CD; a rock classic blared through the speakers. In twos and
threes, the forty-seven eighth graders on Team 8-1, at last the "big kids" at
Shoreham–Wading River Middle School, entered the room and leisurely
took their seats, some on couches, some on the counter along the windows,
others in the chair-desks. They looked around at the posters, chatted ani-
matedly with friends, and waited for something to happen. A few kids
looked at Cliff and me curiously; we smiled back, enjoying the moment. As
the last notes of music faded away, I began reciting my poem.

The First Day

It's the first day.
In they come—
Some pausing hesitantly
At the door,
Wondering and waiting;
Others boldly asserting
Their presence
As they stride to seats.

Heads swivel,
Eyes contact the classroom:
Posters and pictures,
Multicolored images
Meet curious glances.
Saving seats for friends,
Adjusting clean-cover notebooks
Filled with clean ruled sheets,
They sit, expectantly,
In crisp clothing.

For some, the boredom of August
Gone at last.
For some, the restraints of structure
Unwillingly accepted.
For most, an unexplored world awaiting.
New seats permit new perspectives,
New possibilities, new patterns.

The student asks:
"What does he expect of me?
What is this room all about?
Who is this teacher?"
The teacher asks:
"Who are these people?
What are they all about?
What do they expect of me?"

A simultaneously shared journey
Through days and months ahead
Beckons. But for now,
All is new and trembling
Because
It's the first day.

"Welcome, everybody," I greeted them. "I'm Mr. Burkhardt, and I'm going to be your English and social studies teacher for the coming year. We've been expecting you, actually looking forward to your arrival, and we're delighted to have you as students. We know some of you already, and the rest of you we'll get to know soon. We're going to have some great experiences this year." Cliff then offered his words of welcome and spoke briefly about math and science. Four minutes into class, poetry had been introduced and the school year was under way.

Creating an Inviting Atmosphere

It took me eighteen years of teaching before I could envision "The First Day." I wrote it in 1980 during the National Writing Project Summer Institute after thinking through what actually happened in those first, fresh moments of day one. I wanted to capture September's promise of opportunity; the poem became part of the opening celebration for the rest of my teaching career.

What tone do you want to establish on the first day? Do you really need a seating chart? Must you seat kids alphabetically? What messages do such classroom management techniques communicate to students? Why start with the formality of an introduction, particularly if they already know who you are, when you can start the year with music and poetry?

Robert Rubinstein (1994) notes, "Students can pretty well tell what you're like, what learning will be like with you, and how you teach before you ever begin actually teaching. All they have to do is enter your classroom and look around" (p. 17).

The first day of eighth grade is an important occasion for young adolescents. They are intently focused on themselves and their appearance; above all, they do not want to do anything embarrassing and call attention to themselves.

Cliff and I wanted to create an inviting atmosphere, so we used rock music, something familiar and accessible. As students came down the hallway they could hear the music, timed to conclude two minutes into the period. This gave them an opportunity to look around at the numerous posters, check out their classmates all spruced up in first day of school clothes, and ponder Cliff and me, the unknown factors, all the while unconsciously adjusting to their new surroundings. The rock beat and posters of pop icons put them at ease.

It could have been otherwise. One of my favorite poems, "The Memoirs of Jesse James" by Richard Brautigan (1970, p. 4), speaks to that:

> I remember all those thousands of hours
> that I spent in grade school watching the clock,
> waiting for recess or lunch or to go home.
> > Waiting: for anything but school.
> My teachers could easily have ridden with Jesse James
> > for all the time they stole from me.

School should be fun, exciting, challenging, relevant, useful, and worthwhile, and it can be all of these if we work at it and are sensitive to our students. The first time I read Brautigan's poem, I resolved not to ride with Jesse.

If you want students to feel at ease on opening day, what piece of music would you select? The song I chose reveals my musical tastes: "Birthday," by the Beatles, from *The Beatles* (a.k.a. *The White Album*). The lyrics speak of new beginnings, having fun, taking risks, and dancing as a metaphor for participating in life. I don't think the students were deconstructing verses during those opening moments, although later on some may have thought about the words. I do know that I used that song year after year, not only to relax the kids, but also to remind myself of the special nature of opening day.

I believe that 99 percent of the students on day one are exactly where my poem "The First Day" suggests they are—"wondering and waiting," thinking, "What is this room all about?" But it is a qualitatively different kind of waiting than that described in "The Memoirs of Jesse James."

By reading an introductory poem written for the occasion, I made poetry come alive. I suspect that some students were thinking, "How does he know what is going on in my mind? I walked into the room wearing my new clothes and clutching my new notebook, sat down next to my friend, looked around to check out the classroom, and he read my mind—he knew exactly what I was doing. How did he do that?"

Well, I didn't read their minds. I just thought about what was likely to be occurring with most of my students in that situation, then put it into verse.

"The First Day" introduced the concepts of free-verse poetry and the teacher as writer. Such a poem makes a memorable first impression. If Rubinstein is right, you not only establish a great deal about the year in the first few minutes of class, you also need to do so intentionally.

On day one my students learned that poetry can speak to who they are at specific moments. I wanted them to see me as a writer, someone who understood their feelings, someone who thought about this defining moment—the opening day of school—and said, "I'm glad you're here. Let's get started."

Students learned soon enough that I was as nervous and excited as they were about the prospects before us, and that I saw them as partners on our "simultaneously shared journey." I then recited Robert Frost's "The Road

Not Taken," and Cliff read Max Ehrmann's "Desiderata." Our first class together was a ritual, a ceremony, an opportunity to create positive expectations for the year ahead. During the next ten months Cliff and I frequently referred to our "simultaneously shared journey" because we viewed the entire year as a shared experience, a voyage that we all traveled together.

I invite you, the reader, to compose your own version of the "first day" by describing yourself, your classroom, your students, the school, the community, and the world on your opening day. Save all your drafts; later, share with your students the jottings, scratched-out lines, and edited revisions you went through en route to the "final" piece. This would be better than using my poem, but if "The First Day" works for you, go ahead and use it.

If you feel nervous about sharing a poem on the first day, think of a line or two of welcome, write it down, and read it to your students as part of your opening celebration. Jot down several opening lines on a note card and use a different one to begin each of your classes that day. Add on to your "opening line" list the following year, and the year after that. Before long, you'll have an opening day address!

Among the many signs posted in my classroom, four had special significance: "Things change," "Life is unfair," "Follow the instructions," and "Do or do not. There is no try." On day one I asked students to read them aloud, and we discussed their meaning. Students often remarked that I was teaching them life lessons. Guilty as charged.

These four maxims addressed almost any class situation. Later in the year when a student protested because I switched the day of a test, or bemoaned a perceived injustice, or asked how long a writing assignment had to be, or confessed sheepishly that he "tried" to do his homework but didn't actually complete it, I would point to the appropriate saying, smile, then move on.

Introductions

Kids have strange notions about teachers. In a *Peanuts* cartoon, Sally is talking with her brother, Charlie Brown. She asks if it's proper to send a Christmas card to her teacher. Charlie says yes. Sally asks where she should send it. "To her home," Charlie replies. Last panel: a dumbfounded Sally asks, "Teachers have homes?"

Then there's the apocryphal anecdote about the third grader who, while shopping with her mother at the local supermarket one afternoon, rounded the corner of an aisle, saw her teacher reaching for the shelf, and said with amazement, "You eat Cheerios!"

Some students think their teachers do not have lives after the school bell rings at the end of the day. With that in mind, Cliff and I attempted to demystify ourselves by showing slides of us growing up. I used slides extensively in my teaching; three five-foot-square movie screens were mounted side by side where the wall met the ceiling. When all three were pulled down, the "screen" they created measured five feet by fifteen feet—an immense white space on which to project triple-screen images. We showed the students our baby photos, first day of school snapshots, and pictures of us in eighth grade with geeky haircuts. Predictably, the kids laughed. We reminded them that thirty years hence, their eighth-grade pictures would probably look just as geeky; we all laughed.

"Now we'd like to learn more about you," Cliff said. Since we had not assigned seats when they came in, where did students sit? Next to their buddies, of course. We counted on that.

"Pair up with a partner," Cliff continued. Immediately, elbows touched imperceptibly as kids connected; they handled it silently in less than five seconds.

"What we'd like you to do is take thirty seconds and interview your partner," Cliff instructed casually. "Then we want you to stand up and introduce him or her to us, because we don't know you yet." We gave each student a 3-by-5-inch index card for notes and sufficient time for each to "interview" the other.

Had we said, "Nick, take thirty seconds to stand up and tell the class about yourself," Nick most likely would get a hangdog look, barely whisper his name, turn red, hem and haw for twenty-five seconds, become embarrassed in the process, and ultimately waste his time and ours. However, when we asked Nick to introduce his best buddy, Max, you couldn't shut him up: "Max is on the soccer team, he scored the winning goal last year, he has a dog named Darth, he likes Big Macs and Britney and hates the Backstreet Boys, his favorite color is blue, and he has a sister in sixth grade . . ." Students who mumble incomprehensibly when describing themselves will speak fervently and at length about their friends. Note that we did not say, "Stand up and speak in front of forty-six of your peers." Our request was, "Please introduce your friend."

This exercise was not really about introductions. Cliff and I knew that the kids didn't need thirty seconds to prepare; they already knew what they wanted to say about their friends. By having each student introduce a peer, however, they learned about one another, and we learned something about them as well. But the really important thing that happened—the absolutely critical thing—is that on day one each student stood and spoke to the entire classroom, and everyone else listened. It was an activity they found they all could do, one that established several important precedents: in this class all students speak, all voices are important, we listen to everyone, and we learn from each other.

On the first day, kids are eager to cooperate. If we had an odd number of students, we asked for volunteers: "We need one group of three." Hands went up.

If there was a new student, I asked one of the positive kids, "Ben, this is Jason. He's new. Can you pair up with him?"

"Sure, Mr. B., and can Chris and Adam and Brian join me, too? We can all introduce him!" was the usual reply. Young adolescents love being asked to take on real responsibilities.

I don't exactly know how I can identify these "positive" kids—perhaps by their excited faces—but they usually surface in the first minute of the first class. You spot them very quickly, the ones who will throw themselves through the wall if you ask them to ("Want me to go through the top or the bottom? Feet first or head first?").

After introductions were complete, just thirty minutes into the school year, Cliff and I played the Name Game, an activity in which we competed with one another to see how many students we could recall by name. They loved it, particularly when on the second or third try we achieved 100 percent. It helped that we had studied the class lists and were familiar with all forty-seven names, and that we knew a few students from when they were in sixth and seventh grade. Also, earlier in the period, when each student introduced his or her partner, we were saying their names over and over, silently. Kids want to be known, and they want to know that they are known.

Introducing the Distinctions

Before teaching together in 1988, Cliff and I developed a set of thirteen behavioral guidelines we dubbed "The Distinctions"—words such as *cooperation, responsibility,* and *trust* (see Chapter 4). Those terms became the focus of the first writing assignment of the year.

Prior to class we put four of each of the Distinctions in a paper sack. I walked around the room with the sack, asking each student to draw out a slip of paper. Cliff followed me, recording which Distinction the student selected and distributing a master list of all thirteen to each student.

"Tomorrow we're going to have a team meeting," I announced. "Your homework is to define three of the Distinctions. You have to write about the term you just selected, and you may choose any other two terms on the master list. Your ticket of admission to tomorrow's class is three paragraphs, each one explaining a different Distinction. Any questions?" Usually there were none; this was a straightforward task.

But defining the Distinctions was more than an exercise in expository writing; we set a tone for the year ahead. Eight years later, Larissa Figari recalled:

> I clearly remember the first day of eighth grade, which was unlike any other first day of any other grade. I remember the Distinction that I chose: "Acknowledgment." It's such a distinct memory . . . just like the Distinctions were. The importance of acknowledgment has been incorporated into my life since that first day of eighth grade.

Letters of Introduction

With five minutes remaining in the first class of the year, I announced, "Your English homework for tonight is to write a letter of introduction to me. Yes, your partner just introduced you, but I don't really know who you are. What do you want me to know about you?"

"Since this is for English," I continued, "what do you have to say about writing? If we are going to be working together this year, what would be helpful for me to know about you?"

The assignment sheet went into more detail:

Write a letter of introduction telling me about yourself and how you feel about writing. Please include your view on the following points:

- Important information about you.
- How you feel about writing.
- Anything that's difficult for you about writing.
- Things about the writing you did last year that were successful for you or that you liked.
- Things about the writing you did last year that you didn't like or that weren't successful for you.
- Goals you have for yourself in writing this year.
- What you expect of me as your English teacher.
- Anything else you want to share with me.

I am the only person who will read this letter.
Your letter is due in class tomorrow. I will respond next week.

The letter of introduction was a developmentally appropriate assignment; students chose what they wanted to reveal. Incidentally, no student ever asked for a grade on the letter of introduction, probably because it was not a "made-up" assignment but a real letter to a real person for a real purpose.

Their responses, collected the following day, contained a treasure trove of insights into early adolescence. At Shoreham–Wading River Middle School, students were grouped heterogeneously; a range of skills, interests, backgrounds, and psyches were evident in the forty-seven letters. Fantasies, fears, and foibles were intermixed with specifics about siblings and summer travel. Hobbies and household pets were cited, along with concerns and character traits. Students revealed much, both by what they said and by what they didn't say; through this assignment, they began to emerge as distinct individuals.

Students want to be known for who they are, what they do, and how they feel; consequently, they freely mentioned problems and perspectives. One student informed me: "I like to write but I have trouble trying to phrase things. I'm also bad at grammar. I like to read but not every book interests me."

Another confided: "Because of problems at home, you can never expect what kind of mood I'll be in. But that won't matter because I always hide my feelings. I very often have the sudden urge to let people know how I feel, but I never do."

A third student declared: "I hate work that is way too simple, but if I get something that I don't understand and it is too hard for me, I get VERY mad. I hope that this class won't be too difficult, but still not too simple."

Most of the letters were positive; many students said they were looking forward to the year ahead. One student happily wrote:

Dear Mr. Burkhardt,

I'm Jessica Schechner and I'm thirteen years old. Over the summer I went to Florida. I went to Magic Kingdom, MGM Studios, and EPCOT. It was a lot of fun. Last year was a great year because seventh grade was so fun and easy and I had great teachers. My favorite things to do are to play sports. My favorite sport is soccer (I've been playing all of my life) and then basketball. I also love to dance. I've been dancing since I was two years old. I have a lot of friends I hang out with them in school and out of school . . . I had a great first day of 8th grade. I am really happy with my teachers and also my classmates. It seems like I'm going to have a good year and a lot of fun.

Sincerely,

Jess Schechner

Some expressed their anxieties. Jackie, for example, obviously concerned about her previous writing experiences and desirous of doing well, wrote:

I don't hate writing, but I don't love it. I find writing things that I totally have to make up out of my head difficult. I really like writing things like this [letter], it is structured, and it tells me exactly what to do. I enjoy writing letters, short stories—when I'm given a topic, journals, and essays. I don't like writing about fantasies, mysteries or science fiction. Almost everything we did last year was unsuccessful for me, as a matter of fact I can't remember anything that wasn't. My favorite thing we did last year was keeping journals. They were our own private journals, but they could be shared whenever we wanted . . .

The one goal I have in writing this year is to write one extremely terrific piece of work. Whatever it might be, a poem, story, essay, I really want it to stand out and sparkle.

The only thing I expect from you is a little help. A goal I set for myself this year was to [be the] best. I want to get the best grades I can and do the best work I can. If ever in your class, you don't think I'm doing my best, please tell me.

—Jackie Clinton, age 13

I answered every student's letter by the fourth day, having taken most of the weekend to compose my replies. Jackie's concerns merited a detailed response:

When you said, "I don't hate writing, but I don't love it," I was surprised, particularly because I was holding a three-page letter from you. I assumed that since you wrote so well and at such length, writing was something you enjoyed.

You spoke of finding it difficult to write about things when you have to totally make them up out of your head. Well, I find writing about my experience of something is the best source of inspiration for me. If I write about what I know or what I have done, I can call up emotions, sensations, memories, feelings, attitudes, and the like and make the writing more vivid. Like you, I also do not enjoy creating the whole thing right out of my head—I prefer to base my writing on an experience.

I was really surprised to hear you say you prefer being given a topic. I've made an assumption . . . that good writers (and I see you as being a good writer, certainly as a fluent writer) do not like being given topics but prefer to select their own. Your statement to the contrary was useful to me. Thanks, Jackie. You've opened up a new way of seeing things for me.

I was particularly impressed by the confidence and pizzazz of that line, "I want it to stand out and sparkle." Setting a goal such as that (to create a superior piece of writing) is valuable, Jackie. It lets me know clearly where you are headed, it allows me to see ways to help you, and it gives you a clear target to shoot for. It's also an example of clear writing!

Again, sincere thanks for your wonderful letter. I really appreciated the time you took to respond so carefully to my questions. It was a clear example of the kind of "best" work that you say you are striving for.

Sincerely,
Mr. Burkhardt

As I read through my students' letters of introduction, many implications for teaching occurred to me; I could envision opportunities for the coming school year. Yes, I had a specific curriculum to teach, but now I also had students with particular needs, clear (or vague) aspirations, marked individual differences, and varied skills. Their letters helped me get a handle on both how to teach them and what to teach them.

What do students gain from composing letters of introduction to their teachers? An opportunity to be known, a chance to share information about themselves with an important audience, the possibility of influencing a teacher's perception, an exercise in self-expression and awareness, a task that encourages them to celebrate who they are, and a real writing experience. Students feel welcomed and valued in classrooms where teachers make an effort to know who they are.

What do teachers get from sharing information about themselves and asking students to reciprocate? Each September, as I read letters of introduction, I was reminded of the nature of young adolescents in all their rough-edged glory. Their letters helped me formulate social and academic goals. As their English teacher, I gathered preliminary indications of their writing skills. Most of all, I gained a sense of the diverse yet distinct individuals participating in class each day. The task of building positive relationships for the year began with this exchange of letters.

This introductory activity worked because I was willing to share myself on day one, creating a model of response for my students. As I wrote personal replies to each student, I thought about who they were, what they told me about themselves, and what I wanted to say back to them. Reassurances, replies to their questions, comments regarding similar interests, and specific details about myself went into my letters. I was careful to hand back the replies all at once rather than piecemeal, so that every student received a response from me on the same day. This took extra energy on my part, but would you want to be the one student who didn't get a response when everyone else did?

Reflecting on Day One

The first day of class, as Cliff and I had planned it, was a highly structured, intentional, yet engaging lesson for the students. I introduced the idea of the teacher as writer, Cliff and I shared some favorite music and poetry, we told the students about ourselves, we briefly explained the curriculum, every pupil stood and spoke, the Distinctions were introduced, we played the Name Game, and by the end of the first class each student had two writing assignments: a letter of introduction to me and three paragraphs about the Distinctions. That first class, then, was a lesson about introductions and beginnings. We hit the ground running.

One of our tasks as teachers is to make students feel comfortable so that they can learn more effectively. A question I asked myself every year was, "How can I make this new group of students feel invited into my classroom so that they will be better learners?"

The importance of relationships cannot be overstated. In *Turning Points 2000: Educating Adolescents in the 21st Century* Anthony Jackson and Gayle Davis recognized "an essential truth about children's learning: relationships matter. For young adolescents, relationships with adults form the critical pathways for their learning; education 'happens' through relationships" (p. 121).

Eight years after leaving eighth grade, Jen Hodess reflected on her memories of day one and the anxieties she felt:

> I remember coming into 8th grade feeling sad and excited at the same time. I was sad because I knew this was my last year in the Middle School and the last year I'd be on the same team with that same group of people. And I remember being terrified of the thought of going to HS. I was excited because I had heard how much fun being in your class was from older students who had already moved on to HS.

The first class specifically left me with a feeling of intrigue. The music you played . . . resonated with me then and to this day has a meaning I'm not sure I can exactly put into words.

I also remember feeling like an equal to the other students in the class and to you from minute one. I think by seeing slides of you as a youngster and you introducing us to yourself through music, I felt comfortable. I didn't feel as though I was in a room with kids who constantly teased me, or didn't like me, and I didn't feel like I was in a classroom with an authority figure. I felt like everyone was starting on the same page and we were all equal. We could and were expected to feel comfortable and be ourselves.

The fact that everyone was treated as an equal helped me feel better about myself and helped me feel like the differences we all brought to the table were positive and I wouldn't be looked down upon for things I had been looked down upon in the past. The memory of those feelings still linger, especially when I hear "Birthday" by the Beatles.

Assertions Addressed

On the first day of school, the following assertions about writing were addressed:

- *Every student a writer:* Students had to write letters of introduction and define three Distinctions.
- *Ability level:* When I read the students' letters, I discovered the level at which they wrote.
- *Topic selection:* Students had a choice of two Distinctions; in their letters of introduction they could tell me whatever they wanted to.
- *Teacher as writer:* The first thing students heard in class was me reading a poem written for the occasion.
- *Publication:* Students went home on day one knowing that on day two they were going to share ideas publicly with other kids on the team.
- *Audience, purpose, topic:* In assigning a letter and three definitions, I forced students to consider two audiences (peers and teachers) and two purposes (advancing community; sharing information with Mr. Burkhardt).
- *Volume + Variety = Fluency:* Kids began their long journey toward June with two writing assignments on the very first day.

Closing Thoughts

As you plan for next year's opening day of school, here are some questions to consider:

- What do you know about this age level student?
- What can you do on day one that is consistent with that knowledge?
- What moods are the kids in as they return to school from summer vacation, as they see who else is in the class, as they take in the classroom, and as they meet the teacher?
- How do you build on those feelings and emotions?
- What is the first sound you want them to hear?
- What are the first words you will utter?
- What can you learn about your students from letters of introduction?
- How can that knowledge influence your teaching during the year ahead?
- How do the ten assertions about writing show up on day one?
- How do you introduce real writing?
- How do you move from theory to practice?
- What kinds of classrooms best serve students?
- How necessary is it to take attendance as the first order of business? Can it wait ten minutes, or twenty? Even then, does it have to be "attendance"? Can it be a game?
- Given that there is administrivia to be handled on the first day, does that have to be the first order of business in a forty-minute period?
- How fast can you learn the names of your students? Can you go around the room a couple of times and make an effort to get to know them?
- If you are attempting to establish a nurturing, caring classroom, should you place classroom rules as the top agenda item?
- If you were a kid, what would you want and expect? What would make you feel comfortable and welcome on the first day?
- How well do you say "Hello"?

Some of the answers to these questions can be ascertained by thinking through what you intend to accomplish during the months ahead. Some can be found by reflecting on past practice. Some will be dictated by who is in the class. And some may be answered instinctively on the spot. The answers you come up with will, in large measure, determine the direction of the year ahead.

4

Day Two:
The Distinctions

Day Two: The Distinctions

Basic idea:	Create a community of learners by having students define and discus the Distinctions, a set of community expectations.
Assertions addressed:	2, 3, 6, 7, 9, and 10 (*see p. 17*).
Skills addressed:	Expository writing, public speaking, listening, revising, editing, publishing.
Class time needed:	10 minutes on day one to explain the assignment; a double period on day two for the discussion.
Advance preparation:	Prepare a paper sack containing a number of each of the Distinctions sufficient for your class. If you have forty-eight students, for example, you should have four sets of the thirteen Distinctions, each one written on a slip of paper, in the sack.
Time of year:	Day two.
Neat feature:	Students begin the process of creating a cooperative community through their own definitions of words.
Assessment:	A student's three Distinction definitions can be assessed.
Follow-up:	Compile a class anthology containing student definitions of the terms discussed. Later in the year, conduct activities based on one or more Distinction, such as the Letter of Appreciation and Acknowledgment (LAA) in December or Reflections on Distinctions in April.
Journal entry:	None.
Caution:	When students draw their slips of paper, keep track of who selects which Distinction. During the double period, let your students speak first; trust them to say the right thing.
Forms:	A list of the Distinctions.
Questions to consider:	How is behavior affected when students think about, write about, speak about, and listen to their peers define terms such as "respect" and "cooperation" on the second day of school? How is a community strengthened by such an activity?
Why do this?	To start the year with a powerful, student-based conversation about the nature of community.

In the beginning of the year, I didn't really know that much about the Distinctions. I thought that it was a new thing that I had just learned on the first day of eighth grade, but then I realized that I had been using them practically my whole life. It's just now that I *notice* when I am using them. For instance, when we write letters to other people, whether it be pertaining to something they've written, or to just a nice, friendly letter, it usually has something to do with the Distinctions.

—Heidi Lipinsky, age 13

How can teachers foster a sense of community among a group of heterogeneously grouped students? What is the value of doing so for students, and for staff? What activities can teachers initiate that promote, support, and maintain a feeling of community? These were questions I considered when confronting the challenge before me at the beginning of every school year—how to create a community of writers out of a group of disparate students.

I was convinced that kids would be best served by having a sense of belonging, a place where they could feel secure, respected, and known. The team structure at Shoreham–Wading River Middle School supported this notion; we had forty-seven students on our team, a number large enough to include a diverse group of students yet small enough for everyone to know one another. I realized that if cooperative learning activities such as writing groups were to succeed, students would have to get along with each other.

In 1988, my teaching partner Cliff and I compiled a list of thirteen terms we called the Distinctions; they represented our philosophy of education. We each made a list of attributes of the ideal classroom; we then compared our lists using a Venn diagram of interlocking circles. The Distinctions emerged from the area that overlapped.

A team of teachers can create its own set of Distinctions. If teachers who philosophically are some distance apart identify shared values and attitudes about kids, they can build on common ground.

Toward the end of class on day one (as described in Chapter 3), we introduced the Distinctions. Each student drew a Distinction and was given the following homework assignment, which was due the next day:

In today's team lottery you selected one Distinction at random. For tomorrow, write a paragraph explaining that Distinction and why it is important. Also, select two other Distinctions and write separate paragraphs explaining their meaning and importance. These three paragraphs are your ticket of admission to tomorrow's Team 8-1 meeting. Be prepared to share.

The Distinctions
Acknowledgment
Appreciation
Commitment
Communication

Compassion
Contribution
Cooperation
Individuality
Respect
Responsibility
Risk
Support
Trust

What can we assume about our students on day one and their response to the first homework assignment of the year? I counted on the fact that most kids were glad to be back in school, eager to impress their teachers, and willing to do the first assignment because they hadn't done anything like it for two months.

This assignment was, by design, relatively easy: define three familiar terms, two of which you select from a list. Students had already drawn one Distinction from the paper sack (it's useful to employ the "fickle finger of fate" on some assignments during the year), ensuring that each Distinction would be defined at least once.

Acknowledgment

To me acknowledgment means to recognize a favor or service that a person did for me. A person could be my teacher or any teacher in the school, my friends, my coaches or my family. Acknowledgment is important because everyone likes to be recognized for the work that they do.
—Meghan Otten, age 13

What is the value to students, to teachers, and to the community of writers as a whole in having kids reflect on concepts such as compassion or trust and then verbalize their thoughts to peers on the second day of school? The tone in the room, not to mention the tone for the year, improves when students share such ideas. Students learn about public speaking when they watch each of their classmates stand and deliver. And they are reaffirmed when they hear those peers say what they themselves believe.

Appreciation

It is important to appreciate what people do for you and to acknowledge them. It is good to appreciate people if they take you to a restaurant, give you a ride

home, or do you a favor. I am thankful that I have a loving family and a house to live in. If you aren't appreciative, others know that all you think and care about is yourself. People don't only appreciate other people. For example, I appreciate good music.
—Ben Kalb, age 12

Because students had choice, they gravitated toward Distinctions that they knew. Some students who drew unfamiliar terms asked parents for assistance, others used a dictionary to come up with a definition, and still others consulted with friends. All of these behaviors were acceptable, because the purpose of the activity was to tease out the various shades of meaning of each Distinction.

If a student borrowed words from the dictionary (typically, few did), I was not averse to having Webster's definition read aloud in class along with several other student-based explanations of a given term. Because this was their first assignment, and because they had been advised "Be prepared to share," students came to class wanting to say the right thing. This worked to the advantage of all.

Commitment

Commitment means to pretty much stick to one thing. There's a commitment to many, many things in life. For me I kind of have a commitment to my friends, especially my music. I never try to do anything to hurt my friends, and I most definitely would never do anything to let anyone tell me anything that would make me dislike a band just because they did something wrong.
—Clayton Bowman, age 12

The most important aspect of the Distinctions activity for me was that each student stood up and addressed peers. This was the second time in two days they had been asked to do so.

Thus on day one, students began their public speaking training for the year by introducing a partner. This training continued on day two in a non-threatening forum: each student read from a prepared text.

Communication

I think communication is very important in a classroom. Student communication with other kids as well as a teacher is vital. I believe that without communication their can be no real learning at all. Without communication we cannot live.
—Dan Brickley, age 13

As students took their places in the circle of chairs, there was a palpable feeling of anticipation. They reviewed their "definitions," compared notes with friends, and prepared themselves for a serious discussion on the meaning and making of community. We did not assign seats at team meetings; we *trusted* students to behave, we took that *risk,* and we expected *cooperation.* In short, we practiced what we preached.

After a few introductory remarks reviewing the purpose of the gathering—defining the Distinctions—I asked, "Who wrote about 'Acknowledgment'?" Several hands went up. Cliff and I began calling on students, keeping track of who spoke so that everyone eventually had a turn.

Every voice was important, and the effect was cumulative. By the time five or six students shared with the team what they had written about a specific Distinction, there was little for Cliff or me to say except, "Amen!" The students said everything that we wanted to say about behavior, community, cooperation, and responsibility—and they said it directly to their peers.

Compassion

Compassion means to me that you should love one another and help anyone you can. If someone needs help or advice you should be compassionate and give it to them. Compassion is something you either have or you don't. Compassion means being loving and being a good friend!!
—Jen Hodess, age 13

The Distinctions assignment was one of the few writing tasks I did not do with my students. Cliff and I wanted the definitions to come from the kids, not us, so we refrained from voicing our interpretations. After five or six students had read their passages about a specific Distinction, we would reflect on what they had said, tying together ideas or highlighting a significant point. We let students know that we had heard what they said by saying it back to them. Defining the Distinctions created expectations of behavior for the year.

How do you teach caring or any other abstract concept? One way is to have students talk about it. As they discussed a Distinction, the students verbally committed themselves to the concept of community. They spoke publicly, in front of their peers, in a serious, sustained, and demanding discussion that lasted eighty minutes.

Peer influence can be very powerful. I often wondered what was happening in their heads and hearts when they heard classmate after classmate say the right thing (and kids do say the right thing on day two). I suspect that some students were saying to themselves, "Hey, I believe that, too. I agree with that definition."

Contribution

> To me contribution means when everyone participates in class, and when they contribute different ideas to the class. It is important because we can learn many things from one another. You also get different thoughts and views from people.
> —Carolyn Makar, age 13

Writing is central, integral, and real in this activity. The Distinctions discussion, powerful as it was, would not have occurred if the students had not first thought about their ideas regarding the meanings of these thirteen terms, and written them down before reading them aloud to the rest of the class.

Kids learn behaviors by observing those around them; the Distinctions exercise was based on that premise. As one student after another stood and spoke while the rest of the group listened, they were modeling thoughtful behavior. We established a significant expectation for the year: in this class, participants listen to and learn from one another.

Cooperation

> Cooperation means people working together, striving for a common goal. This goal can be as major as flying a shuttle to the moon or as simple as putting together a 1st grade science project. Yet, as long as those involved help each other and act as a team, they are cooperating. Cooperation is what makes society work.
> —John O'Brien, age 13

The assignment sheet made our expectation—a public sharing of ideas—clear to students. There were no surprises; that is very important early in the school year. If you want students to share writing publicly, let them know in advance.

In addition, the novelty of the Distinctions assignment was a success factor; most of the students had never done anything like this. Writing became real, kids had to think, and the unique demands of the assignment drew them in.

Devoting two class periods to such a discussion on the second day of school represents a significant investment of time as well as an important step toward creating community of learners who will be willing to cooperate, trust, risk, and commit for an entire school year. This is also a safe assignment: there are no "right" or "wrong" answers, simply kids' notions about meanings of words.

Individuality

In the dictionary, individuality means something that distinguishes one person from the other. To me, individuality is more than that. It's an art. Individuality is a way to express one's self. It gives you zest, or a gentleness. It helps you to stand out in a crowd. Individual people light up a room when they walk into it. They usually gain admiration from others, sometimes jealousy. So stand up, have confidence, use your imagination, and be an individual.
—Nicole Guippone, age 12

As a follow-up activity, we asked students to type their Distinctions and prepare them for publication. The edited passages were printed, then posted outside our classrooms for all the world to read. I noticed many a sixth or seventh grader reading what a "big" eighth grader had to say about commitment or compassion. We also used the typed passages to create the first class anthology of the year; each student contributed a page to the booklet, a copy of which was subsequently given to everyone.

Respect

I think respect is recognizing that there's something good in someone else and being happy that they have that special talent that you don't have. Respect is important because without it people would destroy what is important to other people.
—Kevin Brown, age 14

When, during the school year, one student hassled another, the Distinctions came into play. Following the altercation, I would ask the transgressor to reread what he or she wrote about respect, or compassion, or cooperation.

"Do you believe what you wrote back on day two?" I would ask.

If the student answered, "Yes," I then asked why he or she was going against personal beliefs by engaging in negative behavior.

If the student responded, "No, I don't believe what I wrote," I asked him or her to write down what he or she did believe about respect or cooperation so that we could continue working together.

If the alleged perpetrator had not defined one of these terms originally, I asked that student to read what a peer had written and whether he or she agreed with those viewpoints.

By consciously appealing to students to live into their words, Cliff and I handled many discipline situations expeditiously. However, our aim was not to trap a student in semantics, but rather to have kids confront the fact that words have meaning, people are accountable for both their words and their actions, and one ought to be consistent in word and deed.

Responsibility

Being responsible is when you borrow a pencil and it breaks or you lose it, you should be held fully responsible. Responsible is like being obligated. If you want to succeed in life you should be very responsible.
—Jen Feeney, age 13

As the year progressed, the kids took the Distinctions to heart. In one memorable incident, a group of students returning from a community service activity at a nursing home were accused by the minibus driver, a teacher's aide, of tossing a pencil at her while she was driving. The seriousness of this issue was not lost on Cliff and me, so we rounded up the students who had been in the minibus and began questioning them. They were good kids, not at all the usual suspects. They insisted they had done nothing wrong, that they would not endanger their lives in that manner, and that the pencil had dropped from the visor when the minibus hit a bump, temporarily distracting the driver. Jamie protested her innocence by observing, "One of the Distinctions is respect. Are you showing us respect now?" We realized that she had a point; the Distinctions went both ways.

Risk

When I think of risk taking, I think of a negative outcome. Although I have discovered that without risk taking life will never progress. I think back at when a baby takes his/her first risk when taking those first steps, eventually he/she will learn to walk. Sometimes a risk can affect your entire life. If that baby did not take that risk then he/she would never have learned to walk and later more importantly learn to run.

As a teenager, every day consists of taking risks and making choices. It is my choice whether to do my homework or not. If I do I will be rewarded, if not I might be risking my grade. There are even things like drugs or alcohol, when someone says "yes," then they are taking a major risk that could affect them in life. But by saying "no," you are also taking a major risk. Will they still like me, or be my friend? I know that in my life I will have to take many risks. I just hope that I take the right road, such as the traveler did in "The Road Not Taken" by Robert Frost.
—Meredith Montenare, age 13

In ten years of my conducting this activity, only one student refused to share his Distinction definitions. Brian Kisiel, a very bright young man, was fully prepared; I was the "ticket taker" at the classroom door and admitted him when he showed me his three typed paragraphs.

I still marvel at the courage Brian demonstrated to not go with the program on day two. Asked to share, he emulated Bartleby the Scrivener and said, "I prefer not to."

Brian's resistance finally abated in the spring when I invited him to assist me in presenting a workshop in New Jersey. There he heard me describe my philosophy of writing to a group of educators.

"Why didn't you explain this to me sooner?" he demanded; he was cooperative for the remainder of the year. I learned from Brian that it is best to be explicit with students and share with them your plans, philosophy, and approach to teaching.

Support

Support is another important Distinction. To me it is important, especially in school, to support people in their triumphs and in their flaws. Support is even more important in the home, not only for children, but also for adults. Lack of support could lead to someone going out and getting drunk, using the alcohol as their support.
—Bobby Unterstein, age 13

Is there a parent in America who would object to his or her child exemplifying these thirteen traits? If so, I haven't met that mother or father yet. Cliff and I didn't come in and say, "Kids, we're going to teach you values." We just asked questions: "What does 'responsibility' mean? What does 'cooperation' mean?" Our students did the rest.

Trust

Trust is a very important Distinction. Trust means when confidence is placed. Trust is important because you have to be able to depend on someone when you can't do everything. You can't survive without others help. Trust is also linked to Responsibility because you have to be responsible to be trusted.
—Larissa Figari, age 13

By posting, publishing, and referring to the Distinctions over and over again during the course of the year, we kept them present and part of the conversation. We sprinkled homework sheets with references to the Distinctions.

A typical tag line at the bottom of an assignment would read:

This assignment addresses the Distinctions of *respect, communication, responsibility,* and *trust.*

Reflections on the Distinctions

In April, we asked students to reflect on the Distinctions; we were curious to learn how they viewed them in action.

Our assignment read:

Reflections on the Distinctions

Last September you defined three of the thirteen Distinctions and shared those definitions with the rest of the team on the second day of school. We are now beginning the fourth quarter—less than ten weeks remain in your middle school career. It's time to look back and reflect.

Using your original three Distinctions definitions, cite specific examples of and instances when you or another member of the team "practiced" each of those three Distinctions. Be specific as to who did what and why you think that was important.

Also, write a paragraph or two explaining what the Distinctions mean to you now, three-quarters of the way through the school year, and how they have affected and/or influenced your team experience.

Be prepared to share your "Reflections on the Distinctions" in class on Thursday.

Jessica Cepelak, age 13, offered the following:

The Distinctions have meant a lot to me all year. Actually, they didn't mean that much to me on the first day of school when we received this list called "The Distinctions." I think that the only reason it appealed to me at first was that the title was so catchy. "The Distinctions." It sounds like something Darth Vader would say.

The Distinctions have meant a lot to me ever since the second day of school. Right from the beginning I saw that these thirteen words would be used countless times throughout the year. I was right, and they mean more to me, then I ever thought possible. I do not think a day goes by without my expressing at least three of the Distinctions. I usually do not realize when I am using the Distinctions. Still, these words are in the back of my head, and anytime someone says "Let's Acknowledge so-in-so" I can picture the black and white sheet of paper. With "The Distinctions" underlined in large black letters, and Acknowledgment the first word down.

Bobby Unterstein was similarly thoughtful:

If only the Distinction *communication* was used by everybody and more often, the world would be a lot better place. But, as far as [the team] is concerned, I think that this was the most important *communication* of the year so far. Actually, it was more like a major lack of *communication*. Everyone remembers the Team's little encounter with violence this year. If someone had used their ability to *communicate* (including myself) the whole mess wouldn't have happened.

One time the team has shown *responsibility* this year happened quite recently. With Ms. Lukoski's neck injury she has not been in school to look after the recycling program. But by using the Distinction of *responsibility,* the team has been able to keep on it's toes and get the job done.

There were quite a few times the Distinction *Support* was used so far this year. But this one in particular stands out in my mind. As we all know, Mr. Burkhardt and his family had to experience his mother passing away this year. During this time the whole team came together to *support* Mr. Burkhardt. Between our donation to the scholarship fund, or just the way we behaved for the substitute, without the *support* (as well as compassion) I think this time would have been even harder for Mr. Burkhardt and his family.

Now it's early April, and although the Distinctions do come up every now and then in class, they aren't ever presently on my mind anymore. But I've discovered that everyday I still use them at least twenty times. I've been able to permanently include the Distinctions into my life. By using them so much previously, they've been pounded into my head, improving me and all the people around me each and every time I use the Distinctions.

Who do we want emerging from our classrooms? Jessica and Bobby come pretty close to the definition.

As we had done in the fall, we created another anthology filled with student passages and distributed a copy to each student, this time containing their April reflections on the Distinctions.

Community Terms

One year, as an alternative to the Distinctions community-building conversation, I asked students to do the following:

Community Terms

As homework for tomorrow, select two (2) terms that relate to the idea of community (at least one term should come from the list below). Write a paragraph or more for each term, explaining how that term relates to the idea of community. Be prepared to share your two passages tomorrow in class.

trust
honesty
excellence
humor
participation
appreciation
cooperation
exploration
communication
memories
competence
reflection
struggle
opportunity
fun
acceptance
civility
responsibility
consequences
risk
originality
partnership
support
education
change
excitement
community
encouragement
courage
tolerance
respect
organization

In this activity, students selected terms that they felt were significant for a community, as opposed to a teacher's predetermined list. Guess what? They came up with all the right answers! As with the Distinctions, students wrote about, then shared with peers their ideas on the meanings of these words, all the while nurturing the development of a community of writers in the classroom.

Assertions Addressed

When they defined the Distinctions through a class discussion, the students addressed several of the assertions:

- *Every student a writer:* Each student contributed to the Distinctions anthology, and each had his or her words posted in the hall. Looking at their written definitions afterward, I discovered kids struggling towards articulate expression, students who wrote glibly, and serious thinkers whose thoughtfulness was evident and admirable.
- *Ability level:* Students wrote their definitions of the Distinctions at their differing ability levels.
- *Topic selection:* Each student had to write about one specific Distinction and had choice for the other two; this sweetened their task.
- *Publication:* The Distinctions passages were printed in an anthology of student writing.
- *Volume + Variety = Fluency:* Students wrote their definitions in the fall and reflected on them later in the year.

Closing Thoughts

The Distinctions represent values—trust, respect, cooperation, responsibility—that are important to me personally, not just in teaching but in real life. But my list is just that, *my* list.

Based on your teaching experience, what "distinctions" do you think are most critical when creating a community? Have you shared them with your students? What would happen if you did?

What is the benefit of having students contemplate the Distinctions on day two? To encourage them to commit themselves to a culture of caring early in the school year.

5

Free-Verse Poetry

Free-Verse Poetry

Basic idea:	Students examine selected models of free-verse poems written by previous students, then compose two or three of their own.
Assertions addressed:	All ten *(see p. 17)*.
Skills addressed:	Writing poetry, drafting and revising, listening, reading aloud, publishing.
Class time needed:	Two periods: (1) review models of free-verse poems; (2) have students share poems they created as homework.
Advance preparation:	Compose three free-verse poems yourself. Select several good models from student work of previous years to share with this year's students.
Time of year:	The first week of the school year.
Neat feature:	Free-verse poems are a very accessible form of writing: there are no rules, anything goes, they are short and nonthreatening.
Assessment:	You can assess a student's journal entry, drafting and revising process, and final draft of the poem selected for publication.
Follow-up:	Each student selects one free-verse poem for publication in a class anthology.
Journal entry:	"Writing My Poems": a. What did you like best about writing your poems? b. What was hardest for you when writing your poems? c. What did you learn while writing your poems? d. What else do you have to say?
Caution:	In class, ask for volunteers to share their poems, and be prepared to share yours first. Do not force kids to share; rather, create an inviting and safe atmosphere where writing is celebrated.
Forms:	None
Question to consider:	What form of expression should you teach first at the beginning of the year?
Why do this?	It is a great way to start your year in writing because the free-verse poem is accessible, easy to do, and fun. Kids achieve instant success in writing short poems.

Performance

My fingers silently close over the soft keys
My lungs slowly let out warm breath
My body expressively moves
while my
foot steadily taps
My fingers are now moving freely
though my eyes are watching carefully
As I hold out that last silvery tone
I hear the sudden commendment
from the astounded spectators
I lower my head in a bow
and give my flute a tight squeeze

     —Nicole Guippone, age 12

The Flower

Shovel, hoe, gardening gloves,
some seeds, and some dirt.
I dig and plant,
I water and wait.
The sun shines brightly.
Time passes and it blooms.
Radiant and beautiful she stands alone,
Sweet smelling and looking graceful.
Just waiting to be loved.

     —Tori Schappert, age 12

Right to Left and Down to Up

Your roller blades go right to left when you skate.
A roller coaster goes down to up.
a typewriter goes right to left.
A plane goes down to up,
while a pendulum goes right to left.
A football goes down to up.
Clock hands go right to left.
Your grades go down to up.

     —Kevin Morgenstern, age 13

Joanna, would you please distribute these poems, one to a customer?" I asked. It was the second week of school.

Joanna walked around the room, handing each student a single sheet. On it were four poems, two per side, each quite different from the other three. The poems, written by two boys and two girls from the previous year, had been selected because they were good models of free-verse poetry.

When presenting peer models to kids, I always picked the cream of the crop from previous years and passed them off as average.

"Who would like to read the first poem?" I asked. It was a safe request. Perri raised her hand.

"Thanks, Perri. Go ahead." She read the poem as her classmates listened intently.

"Thank you, Perri. We need to hear the same poem again. I find that I learn more the second time I hear it," I observed. "You may, too. Who'd like to read?"

Clayton signaled me. "Okay, Clayton." He gave a slightly different reading to the words.

"Let's acknowledge Perri and Clayton," I said. The class applauded politely.

"Okay, now that you are familiar with the poem, read it three times silently to yourself," I instructed. "As you do, circle any words that you don't understand. Put a star next to the line you like best. And if you have a question about anything, write it down. Go."

Heads bent to desks, eyes pored over words, and all was silent save for the occasional cough and the scratching of pens and pencils on paper. I avoided mentioning the term "free-verse poem" for the time being; this process was designed to lead students from the known to the unknown.

After a few minutes I asked, "What did you notice about this poem?"

"Well, it doesn't rhyme," Tori began.

"It has different numbers of words in each line," Jake noted.

"It expresses emotion," Joanna volunteered.

"I could see it happen in my mind—it has lots of details," added Érica.

"I think it's kinda short," Clayton said.

"I liked it," said Heidi. "It was funny."

"Did Kevin really write that?" Ben inquired. "I sat next to him on the bus last year."

We discussed the text for a while longer, then moved to the second poem. After two students read it aloud, their peers jotted notations and then shared observations similar to those made about the first. Poems three and four evoked almost identical reactions.

"Kids," I finally said, "each of these is a free-verse poem. Now look at all four of them. What do they all have in common? What makes each one a free-verse poem?"

Students noted the absence of meter and rhyme, the free-form structure, the focus on one event or object. We discussed meaning, and students explained why they preferred this poem or that one. Eventually I was satisfied that they understood the poems and had a basic grasp of free-verse poetry.

"Your homework this evening, my friends," I announced, "is to create at least two free-verse poems. They can be about anything at all—you get to pick the topic. Also, write a journal entry about one of your poems, explaining what happened when you drafted it. What problems did you have, what successes? What worked for you, and what didn't? Most important," I said, my voice rising in volume to get their attention, "if you do a second or third draft, be sure to save it. I want you to save every, and I mean every, draft that you do this year. Jake, what did I just say?"

"You said, 'Write two poems and save all drafts,' Mr. B.," he replied.

"Good job, Jake," I responded. "Now, let's get started. You have the rest of the class period." And so they began composing poems.

Why Free Verse?

Why did I begin with free-verse poetry each year? Robert Frost once observed that writing free verse is like playing tennis with the net down. He had a point. But young adolescents who are learning to write need support and success. If you can remove some obstacles and open some doors early on, you do your students a service. You can always intensify the rigor later in the school year. Also, I discovered that kids really enjoyed crafting poetry.

Several factors affecting learning came into play when my students explored free verse:

- *Challenge:* Young adolescents like to be challenged. Creating a free-verse poem challenges them ("Can I actually write a poem?"). Writing a poem is a complex task that calls for many decisions ("What's my topic?" "Where do I end the line?" "What should my title be?" "What's a good word that I can use here?").
- *Novelty:* Summer vacation was over; the students were starting a new grade and were ready for something different. Many had not heard of free-verse poetry before, so there was a novelty to the task; young adolescents are attracted to novelty.
- *Peer models:* Sharing good writing composed by other students is important. If I had said, "Here are some poems by Robert Frost and Edna St. Vincent Millay—go home and write like them," that might not invite success. Later in the year we paid deference to the canon, delving into Frost, Poe, Dickinson, and others. At the beginning, however, the poets I wanted my students to emulate were their peers.
- *Accessibility:* The free-verse models we analyzed were easy to understand and emulate, selected specifically for these reasons.
- *Length:* The models I shared were short, quick reads of eight to twelve lines. Not surprisingly, students composed short, quick reads of eight to twelve lines as homework. And because they were short, we were able to discuss four models in one class period; the next day we had time for each student to read at least one poem to the class. Later in the year, when we did lengthier pieces such as first- and third-person narratives, fewer students were able to share.

- *Topic choice:* Students could write about anything; they were free to pursue their interests.
- *Ease:* Drafting two short poems in one night is not an overwhelming task; also, I assumed that in most cases students preferred one poem to the other, thus committing themselves to a piece of writing early in the year.
- *Revision:* I was teaching the skill of revision; a short piece is generally easier to revise than a longer piece. The brevity of the poems preempted any "It's too long, I'll be revising forever" resistance.
- *Exposure:* The students had already experienced the power of free-verse poetry when I recited "The First Day"; this mode of expression was not unfamiliar to them.
- *Teacher interest:* I enjoy writing free-verse poems, and my passion conveyed itself to students; some were carried along by my energy and enthusiasm.

The Process

The following day, students arrived for class bearing journals and first drafts. A few students had done second and even third drafts. We began by discussing the process of writing their poems. Several students read from their journals. Heidi's was a typical entry:

Writing My Poem

A. I was laying in bed at night, thinking of what to write. So I thought of two poems "Night time" & "Bedtime." After that I went downstairs to get a cup of tea, and I saw my dog Murphy. That is what made me think of the poem "Dogs."

B. I think the poem I wrote about "Bedtime" was the best one of the three. "Nightime" is a very short one and Dogs is pretty stupid.

C. It took about three hours to think about what to write. I was talking on the phone while writing "Bedtime," so the person on the phone helped me a little. She gave me other ideas, but I didn't use them.
—Heidi Lipinsky, age 13

Tori shared her journal entry as well:

Free-Verse Poems

I just sat down at the kitchen table and started writing. Yesterday in class I started to think of one so I just finished it at home. That one is called "Grandma." The other poem was pretty easy because there was flowers on the table and I looked at them and starting writing down some thoughts. That poem is called "The Flower." I really enjoyed writing my poems, I didn't think it was that hard. I like my poems a lot. I haven't written a lot of poems in the past couple of years so I was surprised that they came so easy to me. I had a little trouble ending my poems because I thought it was hard to just end it with some kind of thought. I never really thought much about poetry, but now I really like it.

—Tori Schappert, age 12

After acknowledging Heidi and Tori with brief applause, other students shared, providing more models of what a journal entry could include. We then turned to the homework: the free-verse poems written the night before.

"I'll read my poem first," I offered. My job was to make the classroom a safe place for writing, so I modeled good habits. I always did this assignment with my students, composing a new free-verse poem each year.

When sharing early drafts, we read them aloud twice before inviting comment; the first read-through was for familiarity, the second for understanding. After reading my poem twice, I circulated all three drafts, each awash with red ink, evidence of my revision. I asked the students about the title, the ending, the main idea, what they liked, and anything that didn't seem right; they told me what they understood and raised a few questions.

And then, as nonchalantly as possible, I asked a crucial question. This was day five of the school year, and I knew that the success of the community of writers would be affected by the response to this one question: "Who else would like to share?"

Before I took the National Writing Project Summer Institute, when I assigned writing students would show their pieces to me or to close friends, but not to everyone. The challenge is getting a critical mass of young adolescents to the point where they trust one another and are willing to share their writing aloud.

Wait time can seem interminable, especially if you are the teacher waiting for a student to volunteer early in the year. Once the ice is broken, everyone wants a turn. But at the beginning, who will bell the cat? Nobody wants to go first.

I was on edge until some brave volunteer raised his or her hand and said, "I'll read mine." And it never failed—someone always rose to the occasion.

Consider all that happened prior to this moment. Both the classroom environment and my expectations were intentional from day one; I had been working toward the goal of getting students to feel safe enough to read their writing aloud to peers. One reason we acknowledged kids so often during the first four days was to establish a pattern: if you contribute in class, you will be acknowledged.

On day one kids spoke to the team when they introduced their partners. On day two each student stood and read a Distinction definition from a prepared script. On day three they heard me read a poem created just for them and for that moment. On day four they discussed poems written by peers. Just moments earlier on day five they heard me struggle with word choice ("It's still a draft!") as I read draft three of my free-verse poem to the class.

In five days they learned that writing was valued and honored in this classroom. Asking them to read aloud their own free-verse poems was a natural step toward building a community of writers. I purposefully didn't ask students to stand when they read; they sat at their desks—it was safer.

After a moment that seemed eternal, Clayton, a self-assured young adolescent, volunteered to go first. We were off and running.

Lost Nights

On all of my sleepless nights,
I think of all of the people bedded
down in nice comfy beds,
with comforters sleeping the night away,
not even noticing how lucky they are.
    Then I think of myself,
I'm not up late to watch the moonlight
come through my window,
      nor' am I scared,
I'm just waiting to lose sight on reality,
and drift off into a lovely land of nice,
comfort and calmness,
I wish with all my heart to get away
    yet keep a grip on reality,
      until I notice,
I've already lost the night.

        —*Clayton Bowman, age 12*

We acknowledged Clayton's poem. Mike, encouraged by Clayton's example, asked to read next.

The Dragon

Your scales glisten in the noon sun
as you walk down the path through the woods.
You are the king of the wilderness, but
something is troubling you.
Your brow furrows,
you twiddle your claws,
but you can't pinpoint your trouble.
Then it hits you like a sharp pain in the chest.
You look down at your chest.
and see a glowing arrow stuck deep into it.
You look up and see a man and a woman,
one with a bow and the other with a shimmering cloak.
Your roar fills the noon air as you slowly
crumple down on the ground.

You see the man with the cloak chant words
and your world is suddenly filled with red.
Your last thoughts are,
"At least I know what was bothering me."

    —Mike Clair, age 13

After we acknowledged Mike, Jake, inspired by both Mike and Clayton, volunteered.

The Drag Day
RED,
YELLOW,
YELLOW,
YELLOW,
GREEN
The Pirellis spin
laying
heavy smoke.
I'm getting gription
starting to move.
I'm tacing her up,
shifting six grand,
losing in the
dust.
A few seconds more.
The race is won.

    —Jason Esper, age 13

Jake got a nice round of applause.

"Can I go next?" asked Érica. Other students also raised their hands. Clayton, Mike, and Jake had started something.

Near the end of the period, after most students had shared at least one of their poems, I said, "Let's acknowledge everyone who read a poem today." We did.

Then I raised the stakes.

"This evening, kids," I announced, "your homework is to revise one of your free-verse poems. Take it to draft two, or three, or four, based on what you heard in class today about language, word choice, and vocabulary. How good can you make it? And when you do revise, there's one very important thing you have to remember: *save all drafts!*"

"But Mr. Burkhardt, what if we don't need to revise?" Jake asked. "Didn't you say last week that when we write something, we get to say when it's done?"

"Indeed I did, Jake," I responded. "What I actually said was that when you compose a piece of writing, you are the judge of when it's done. We're going to do a lot of writing this year, and you are always the final arbiter of what you write. You get to declare it finished. That's because I don't know when it is done. I may have some suggestions, but all of you, Jake and everyone else, should exercise that responsibility. And I'm going to respect that. Some pieces of writing are done right away, and some—most?—take a while."

"But Jake," I continued, "I also know that revision—which is when you look at a piece of writing, see it anew, and then make it better by changing sentences, deleting or adding words, rearranging the line sequence—revision can make a real difference and turn an average piece of writing into something eminently worth reading."

"Great, Mr. B., but mine is done. I say so," Jake declared.

"Fine. Now kids, remember that tonight when you revise—"

"I'm not going to revise," Jake interrupted. "My poem is complete."

"I got it, Jake. Thanks. Now," I pressed ahead, "I need two volunteers. Nicole and Larissa, come on up here," I instructed.

The lesson had been building toward this moment.

The "First Day" Drafts

"Larissa, take hold of this and hang on. Don't drop it." I handed her one end of a laminated scroll, keeping most of the unscrolled portion for the moment. Students could see a single sheet of white paper with a list written in red ballpoint pen.

"Do you kids remember my poem from day one?" I inquired.

"Yes," Chad replied. "You recited Frost's 'The Road Not Taken.'"

"Good answer, wrong poem. No, I meant 'The First Day.' Can you see this list?" I asked. "Up on the top left it says, '7/14—Noon—Poem—First Day.' These are the original notes for that poem. I wrote it in the summer of 1980."

I then read the lines of notes to an attentive audience.

Theme—poem about school—1st day—kids coming in—excited faces—
new clothes—anticipation—who else is here—the teacher—new papers,
new patterns, newness
Seeds of the future planted to grow through the months
—Kids' upturned questioning faces
—New seat, new perspective
—September—the boredom of August, the sense of a fresh start—the unexplored possibilities ahead—
What does he (Teacher) want from me?

"Nicole, take this," I said, handing her the scroll. "Stand still right there. Larissa, walk slowly to the window, unrolling the scroll as you do."

Larissa edged away from Nicole, revealing draft one, two pages containing a forty-one-line poem titled "First Day." Students could see five arrows, seventeen crossouts, two questions in the margins, but no separate verses, just one continuous poem handwritten in red ink and splattered with black notations. The opening line read, "It's September and . . ."; the second and third words had been crossed out and replaced by "the first day." At the top left were the date and time: "7/14, 1 P.M."

Larissa continued to follow the instructions; she moved further away from Nicole, unscrolling draft two, composed on two sheets of paper at 6:30 P.M. that same day. The word "The" had been added to the title, and the poem, again written in red ink, was divided by four thick black lines into five chunks. "New seats allow new perspectives" had been changed for alliterative purposes to "New seats permit new perspectives."

"Draft three, please, Larissa?" She drew closer to the window. A handwritten, forty-two-line draft composed at 7:00 P.M. had only five cross-outs on two sheets of paper. Draft four, typed at 9:00 A.M. the following morning, was down to forty-one lines on one sheet of paper. Draft five, typed at 2:00 P.M., was back up to forty-two lines and a new title, "It's the First Day." Draft six, composed in red ink at 9:00 P.M. that evening, recycled the title from draft five.

Larissa reached the window. The final draft, typed on July 16, had thirty-nine lines and a three-word title. Larissa and Nicole held the nine-foot scroll for all to see.

"That's how I composed 'The First Day,' kids. I did seven drafts over three days. Now when you go home this evening and revise at least one of your free-verse poems, remember what I said: Save all drafts! I want to see them all. Staple your newest draft on top of the earlier ones, so that what I will see first is the latest version of your poem."

After we acknowledged Larissa and Nicole, I said, "Any questions?"

Jake raised his hand. "I'm not going to revise my poem, Mr. B.," he said. "'The Drag Day' is done! I like it the way it is!"

"Jake, it's a good poem. You say it's done, so it's done. *No problemo, mi amigo.* But would you mind if I took it home and read it? I may have a question or two about it."

"Well, okay, but I'm not going to change it. I like it the way it is," he reiterated.

"Fine, Jake. As for the rest of you, remember to save all drafts as you revise. See you tomorrow."

Jake handed me his poem as students filed out. I knew he was testing me. I contemplated my response.

The "Drag Day" Letter

After class I posted the laminated scroll of "The First Day" in a prominent place on the wall of the classroom; it was on display for the next three months, my composition process visible to all. The scroll became a useful point of reference when explaining drafting and revising.

That evening I carefully read Jake's poem and composed a five-page letter to him in which I posed a multitude of questions.

Dear Jake,

No question about it—"The Drag Day" has form, substance, excitement, and a sense of presence. It clearly communicates the quick excitement of a drag race—a roar, a cloud of smoke, and seconds later, it's all over. That aspect of drag racing is something you have conveyed very well, Jake. So in fact, the poem can stand as it is. For you to like it as it is, is fine. And, as an exercise in having you look and see what's missing, I raise the following questions, comments, suggestions, and observations. Read them, consider them, and then either leave the poem alone or revise it, whichever you feel so moved to do. The point I make is that only rarely does a poem achieve final form in its first draft.

Title: "The Drag Day"—is this poem about an entire day or about one race? Would "The Race" be a better title? What about "Eat My Dust!"—"In the Dust"—"Winner"—"Heavy Smoke"—"Victory"—"One on One"—something that changes the sense of the reader's expectation from a whole day with lots of races to a single race. When I read the title "The Drag Day," I expected to find a whole lot of races in the poem, a whole afternoon of cars blazing down the track. Instead I got one race and, as a reader, feel cheated. The title doesn't work for me. If you add more races to the poem, that would support the title. Your poem is about one race, I think, not about a whole day at the track.

"RED, YELLOW, YELLOW, YELLOW, GREEN"—are there actually five lights? Do they go down fast, or does the guy behind the wheel think about things as they are going down? Or do they go up? What is the driver of the car thinking about? What kind of car is it? What color? Is he on the left or the right side of his opponent? Does he glance over at his opponent? Can he see his opponent? Is he wearing a harness or safety belt? Does he feel strapped in? How does he feel in those brief moments before the light turns green? What is going on in his mind? Do you want the reader to think about what is going on in the driver's mind? What do you want the reader to think about? What if your poem went—

RED
(beads of sweat)
YELLOW
(trickled slowly)
YELLOW
(down. . .)
etc.

so that you gave the reader a sense of time passing slowly? Or do you want the time to pass fast?

I moved into the body of Jake's poem, tossing more questions at him about word choice, descriptive language, and imagery:

How many Pirellis are there? What if you used the total number on both cars rather than the word "The" in line 6?

Do the Pirellis do anything else besides "spin"? How fast do they spin? Do they scream? whine? make other noises? What noises?

"Laying/heavy smoke"—what's a synonym for "laying"—emitting? giving off? creating? dispensing?

"I'm getting gription"—there is no such word as "gription." Did you know that? Have you consciously created a word just for this poem? The meaning is clear, so you don't have to change it. I understand it perfectly and like it, in fact. Who gets the grip—the driver, or the tires? How long does that take? Seconds? Milliseconds? Should you say so? What if you gave the reader a sense of the clock running as this race was run? How long does a drag race take, anyway? Three minutes? Six seconds? What if you included a clock in the poem and stated the time with each event, so that you have a verse for each second that passed and told all that happened during that second? Again, I see the poem as being about one race, not a whole day, and about the sense of victory that the driver feels at blowing away another driver.

"starting to move"—What's a synonym for "starting"? Do you mean commencing? beginning? advancing? edging forward? something else? And what about sound? Where's the sound? Are there vibrations? What does the wheel feel like to the driver? What does the driver see? Is his view blurred? Is this race being run in sunshine or under the lights? Is the windshield blurring his vision? Is he cramped? How long has he been driving? Is this his first race? Is he a veteran? I want more about the driver. I sense he is a veteran because he seems to know how to drive the car. How old is he?

I asked Jake about the possible use of "top fuel" and suggested he make a list of technical terms related to drag racing.

"I'm tacing her up"—"Tacing" is spelled incorrectly. It's "taching" from the word "tachometer." Who is "her"? Does the car have a name? What color is the car? What color are the tires? Does the driver have a white flame suit on? Is there color at all in this experience? Poems depend on the senses—sight, smell, taste, touch, hear. You have used only two—sight and sound. What if you were to use aspects of touch—how is the driver holding the wheel? What does it feel like to him inside the cockpit of the car? How many horsepower is the car? What are the smells of the race? What are the tastes inside his mouth? . . .

Do they actually say "six grand" in drag racing? Don't they say "six thousand"? You are referring to RPMs, I think. Aren't they measured in thousands? "Grand" is a slang term for a thousand, and yet I have never heard it used in referring to drag racing. Do they use it in drag races? If so, what other slang terms are used with drag racing? Make a list of slang terms used in drag racing and see if you can use more of them in your poem. Again, it is the use of specific technical language that makes a poem rise from good to great!

I asked about the number of fans in attendance, the track surface, and other details. Then I moved to the ending:

"The race is won."—What are other ways of saying this? Here's a useful exercise, Jake. Write your last line five different ways and show the list to five people and keep track of which ending they like best. Then see if you want to keep the one you have. When you write a poem, you are working to communicate something inside of you and get it inside of someone else. Be aware of audience. Here are two possible last lines: "The race is history." "The victory is his." What are some others that you can write?

So, these are just some thoughts on your poem. Read over this letter carefully and consider all the questions and suggestions. Then reread your poem. Is it absolutely your best possible effort, so outstanding a piece of work that not one single change more can be made in it? Can you answer YES to that question with no hesitation? If so, leave the poem alone. If not, do what is appropriate—do your best. I can ask no more of you than that, in this as in all you do . . .

Thanks for allowing me to share these thoughts with you. I am committed to your doing well, and the poem you wrote has a lot of merit to it—it is not a beginner's poem—it has structure, short choppy phrases (appropriate for the event), cuts and jumps, short bursts—it's a good poem. You don't have to change a thing and it will stand by itself and be fine. My thoughts above are intended to help you see how you can go to another level with it.

Thanks for playing. I enjoy having you as a student.

Sincerely,

RMB

Students walked into class the next day proudly bearing second and third drafts of their poems. I spotted Jake and handed him his original poem and an envelope bearing his name. Jake went to a desk, opened the envelope, and began reading. He became absorbed in what I had written, oblivious to the students around him who were sharing new drafts with the rest of the class.

Tori volunteered to share her revision process. Amanda, smiling, protested that Tori had shared yesterday, it wasn't fair, and everyone should get a turn.

I pointed to the appropriate sign. "Amanda, you're right, it's not fair. You'll be next after Tori," I said, delighted that kids wanted in on the action. "Go ahead, Tori." She began to read from her journal:

Revising My Poem

When making my revisions a few people helped me. In "The Flower" I added a word at the end of the 5th line. In the poem "Grandma" I changed a lot of things, I explained the afghan the rocker and the cookies, but I still can't find something better for line 2. Maybe you can help me?

The first time I read my poem I thought it was fine, but after reading it over and over you always find something wrong.

—Tori Schappert, age 12

We acknowledged Tori. Amanda then read her journal entry, and before the end of the period, more than half the students shared either a journal entry or a revised draft. I collected most of the free-verse poems; a few students, while reading theirs aloud, discovered new possibilities for revision and wanted to draft and revise further. I did not object.

Class ended; Jake left without saying a word. I wondered what he was thinking.

The "Drag Day" Drafts

The next day Jake brought in his first draft of "The Drag Day." Stapled on top of it were drafts two and three.

"Good job, Jake," I said, thinking to myself: (a) sometimes kids do listen after all, and (b) my gamble had apparently paid off. Jake took the letter to heart, because it addressed something of interest to him—he really liked drag racing. He saw that I both understood and appreciated his poem.

Later that period I saw Jake showing my letter to some of his buddies; I had hoped he would do that. Word began to circulate that "Burk is totally serious about writing." I was. Still am.

Jake eventually declared his poem complete at draft five. It jumped from sixteen lines and thirty-six words in draft one to forty lines and ninety-five words in the final version. "The Drag Day" was now a carefully crafted, much more textured free-verse poem. Jake selected it from among six pieces he had composed as his entry in the class anthology. He was proud of his poem, and I was proud of him.

The Drag Day

As I
creep to the
line
in my double A Fuelie
and sit there patiently
ready to go
RED
(scared to look over at my opponent)
YELLOW
(my foot shakes on the clutch)
YELLOW
(I hit the gas)
GREEN
My tires
start to spin
and they're
screaming
for some
traction
I'm taching her
up

SIX grand
SEVEN grand
EIGHT grand
NINE
I lose my
opponent as
I shift through
the gears
soon
the finish
line
grows nearer
POP the chute
HIT the binders
and the world comes
slowly into
focus
And the race was
WON!!!

—Jason Esper, age 13

We do not have time to write five-page letters to every student. But one letter can go a long way.

The Dude Poet Society

If you had told me before I attended the National Writing Project Summer Institute that eighth-grade boys would get excited about writing poems, I would have been skeptical. Girls? No problem. Boys? Maybe. But they did.

Why? A combination of factors, I believe.

The cautious approach I used when introducing the task of writing poetry—slowly, gently, invitingly—did not scare off the students. Before drafting free verse, we discussed and analyzed models written by peers; this made the form accessible. Also, frequent poetry memorizations during the year exposed students to all kinds of poetry, which in turn provided them with ideas, models, and inspiration. Finally, I shared my own passion for poetry, regularly reading to my students selected verse from my tattered copy of *Poems for All Occasions*.

Significantly, the boys saw the girls getting into and enjoying both writing and reading poetry. When one boy finally shared a "sensitive" poem in class and the girls acknowledged him for it, other guys took the hint; writing poetry became cool. One year a group of boys went so far as to form the Dude Poet Society, vying with one another to go first when it came time to read poems aloud in class, competing for the attention of the girls through verse. They invited me to join the society; I did. We "dudes" nourished one another.

"Bookends"

All kinds of things happen when kids compose, and we often miss them in the everyday swirl of events that is middle school.

In September, Joanna, an amazingly able student who always did her best, dutifully created a free-verse poem as a homework assignment. Three months later, Joanna shared the story behind her poem. I was stunned; her revelation reminded me once again that even students who make writing look easy may be exerting tremendous effort behind the scenes.

Joanna wrote:

Writing has always been difficult for me. From the time I was in second grade 'till I was in fifth grade, I had trouble getting the courage to put a pen to paper and write a few sentences. As I had to write more and more for school, I learned to just write whatever I was thinking. I still hadn't really gotten the hang of poetry until this year, though. The first poem we had to write this year was a nightmare. When we got the assignment I freaked out! I must have started twenty different poems, then scrapped them because I thought they sounded dumb. Finally, my mom suggested that I look around and find something that inspired me, so I did, and saw this picture in the hallway. This gave me the idea for "Bookends." Once I got the idea, the words just sort of, well, happend.

Emulating Jake, Joanna selected her poem, whose words "just sort of, well, happend," for the class anthology:

Bookends
There's a photo on the wall.
An old woman, smiling,
a bouncing baby on her knee

Her face, though wrinkled
        with age,
is hopeful, eyes gazing upward,
        to the future
that her daughter's daughter's daughter
        represents.

The baby is me.

We are bookends,
holding our family together,
years of stories between.

— *Joanna Kalb, age 13*

Assertions Addressed

When students write free-verse poems, they simultaneously address several of the assertions about writing. The assertions could be paraphrased as follows:

- Every student is a poet and has poems she or he wants to create.
- Every student writes poems at his or her ability level.
- Student poets are more invested in their poems when they select their own topics.
- Student poets are inspired by models, especially those created by classmates.
- Teachers who share their poems with students provide powerful coaching.
- Student poets discover their voice when they read their poems aloud to peers.
- Student poets should publish frequently for audiences beyond the teacher.
- Poetry is a recursive process: invent, rehearse, draft, revise, edit, publish.
- Student poets consider audience, purpose, and topic when they compose poems.
- Volume + Verse = Poetic fluency—the more poems you write, and the more different forms of poetry in which you write, the more fluent a poet you become.

Closing Thoughts

When they wrote free-verse poems during week two, students celebrated their passions. In doing so, they revealed aspects of themselves that helped me get to know them as writers—their interests, ability levels, drafting and revising skills, vocabulary, and creativity.

I followed free-verse poetry with two other modes of expression: interior monologues and personal essays. We were building up to the first anthology of creative writing. Writing groups were about to be introduced. A community of writers was coalescing, one step at a time.

6

Interior Monologues and Personal Essays

Interior Monologues and Personal Essays

Basic idea: Students examine models of interior monologues and personal essays created by students from previous years, then draft and revise their own.

Assertions addressed: All ten *(see p. 17).*

Skills addressed: Sentence structure, paragraphing, sequencing ideas, listening, reading aloud, drafting, and revising.

Class time needed: Two periods for each form: (1) introduce the form and assign homework; (2) have students share their pieces.

Advance preparation: Prepare a set of examples of interior monologues and personal essays. Create your own models to share. (Save all drafts.)

Time of year: The second and third week of school.

Neat feature: Students work toward a class anthology.

Assessment: Journal entries can be graded; students can be assessed on their drafting and revising process; final drafts can be assessed. Also, the teacher can assess a student's ability as a writer by reading and comparing that student's interior monologue, personal essay, and the journal entries written about them.

Follow-up: Students create a class anthology.

Journal entry: Students describe the process of creating their interior monologues and personal essays:
a. What happened as you wrote it?
b. What successes did you have?
c. What difficulties did you encounter?
d. What else do you have to say?

Caution: In class, ask for volunteers to read their drafts aloud, and be prepared to share yours first.

Forms: Photocopied examples of interior monologues and personal essays.

Why do this?   To teach two new forms of expression to your students; to enable students to engage in real writing by using forms that encourage them to draw on real-life experiences.

When students base writing on personal experience, they should be able to call on a range of adventures, details, emotions, sensations, and memories. They discover that writing about their lives imbues the text with meaning. Putting words on a blank page becomes an easier task because they can draw from a well of experiential information; the writing becomes real as they celebrate themselves and the events of their lives.

These ideas lay behind my decision to introduce interior monologues and personal essays as the second and third forms of expression of the school year. Both forms placed more demands on the students than the free-verse poems created during week two. Those were, for the most part, short and sweet. The form precluded complete sentences, and brevity did not encourage delving too deeply into the human condition.

Interior monologues and personal essays, however, require sentence structure, paragraphing, appropriate vocabulary, and a substantial number of words; students have tales to tell. In short, I wanted my students to move from short poems to longer, more complex prose pieces and their concomitant increase in demand.

The class lesson in which I introduced the new forms was familiar. First, I distributed models of interior monologues and personal essays for stimulation, inspiration, and, I hoped, emulation. We read the models aloud, discussed them, did drafts of our own as homework, and celebrated our work by sharing in class. Finally, the kids wrote reflective journal entries about the process.

What I knew, and what my students would soon learn, was that all three forms of expression were part of a publication plan—we were working toward our first writing anthology. Within two weeks students would form writing groups and take pieces intended for publication through revision, editing, and proofreading.

I did not say to students, "You are writing for publication." I wanted their attention on the immediate piece of writing before them for the time being. Instead, after they had drafts of all three forms, I said, "Which two of the five or six pieces that you created do you want take to a writing group and prepare for our class anthology?" We moved toward publication in incremental steps.

The Interior Monologue

"I'm going to read you a piece of writing," I said at the beginning of class on day nine, the third week of school. "When I'm done, I'll have some questions for you." Free-verse poems, letters of introduction (and my responses to them), the first poetry memorization, two journal entries, and three celebratory "occasional" poems were the background of writing and learning against which the present lesson occurred.

I told the class that the piece I would read was my own and was called "Question Session."

Should I raise my hand? If I do, he'll probably think I know the answer, especially if I wave my arm. But then he just might call on me. He always does that; he always calls on kids who have their hands down. Rats, why didn't I read the chapter? If I get through this one, I promise I'll read all the assignments for the rest of the year. Just don't have him call on me today. I'll look like such a jerk if he asks me the question and I don't know the answer.

Oh, no! He's going right around the room in order—that's three in a row coming towards me, and now he's asking a kid only five seats away. Wait—now he's asking Billy. Thank goodness. Billy's on the other side of the room. Saved from my doom just a little bit longer.

Groan. Thirteen minutes left. I'll never make it.

Yippie! He called on Frank. Good old Frank takes ten minutes just to clear his throat and say his name. Attaboy, Frankie. Keep talking. Good old Frankie boy, just keep those old lips flapping. C'mon, Frank, you can do it. Give him words, any words, just—Frank? *Frank?* Don't quit on me, man.

Oh no, I don't believe it. Frank just gave the shortest answer in history. You bozo!

I feel sick. *Sick?* Hmmmm, maybe if I throw up and run out of the classroom with my hand over my mouth, he'll send me to the nurse.

Ooooooh, too close for comfort. He just called on Samantha. She sits next to me. He's sure to ask me next. Please don't let him ask me. Have him go in another direction, please . . .

Yes! He went the other way. Seven minutes left now. I can make it. *I can make it!* If I shut my eyes and concentrate real hard, I might be able to get him to call on someone else. Or maybe . . .

I know this is a strange thought, but what if there were an earthquake, or maybe a plane crash right outside the window? Yeah, a training flight, like a Piper Cub or a Cessna, so no one gets hurt—well, maybe just the pilot and copilot. A plane crash right now would just about do it, yes sir. I only need a few more minutes and I'm home free. A big burst of flames, sirens, ambulance, police, fire trucks, newspaper reports, TV cameras—hey, I might even get on the evening news. "Eighth grader George Johnson, eyewitness to the spectacular crash of Cessna XV14-J on its training flight over Long Island earlier today, filed this report: 'Well, I was sitting in social studies participating in a discussion about the American Revolution when I momentarily glanced out the window and saw this humungous plane coming right at me. I raised my hand to get the teacher's attention and alert him to the possibility of danger when—'"

"Yes, George?" The teacher's familiar voice intruded from the front of the classroom. "I'm happy to see you know the answer. Thanks for volunteering, unlike some of your classmates who don't seem to have read the assignments. Now, tell me, George, what were three results of the Townshend Acts and how did they set off a chain of events that led to the Revolution?"

"What happened in this piece of writing, kids?" I asked.

Alicia raised her hand. "Well, the boy didn't do his homework, so he was thinking about how to get past the teacher, and he accidentally raised his hand and . . ."

"That happened to me once," Jake interrupted.

"Why am I not surprised?" I said to Jake. We laughed.

"What else did you notice?" I continued with the class.

"I liked it, Mr. B.," said Larissa. "It seemed real, like I was there."

"Good observation, 'Rissa. What else did anyone notice?"

"It was like we saw inside your head," chirped Magda.

"Good point, Magda. What else, anyone?"

"It was funny," Beth Ann began. "He did himself in."

"I liked the part where he dreamed about the plane crash and the TV reporter and he thought he was being interviewed," said John. "My mind sometimes goes like that."

"Good, John. Okay, let's acknowledge everyone who contributed." Applause ensued.

Students understood the theme of my interior monologue—trying to get one over on the teacher—because it tapped into their experiential knowledge base and touched a familiar chord. My choice of topic was intentional: I wanted to attract kids to the power and possibility of the interior monologue.

"Okay, here's another one by a student from last year. Who would like to read?"

John was first to get his hand up. He began reading; the rest of the class listened intently.

I Tried

I tried my hardest to please you but it is not good enough. If I don't get an A then you say you're not perfect enough for me. If I miss a shot in a game you yell just because everything is not done your way. You always ask me why can't you be like your brother and get A's on everything. But just as many times I have tried to tell you that I am a different person. No matter how hard you try I will never be like Billy Bob in any way. So I hate to say it but just deal with me as my own person.

—Meghan Otten, age 13

"Thank you, John," I said. "Now, in this piece, who is speaking?"

"It's a girl who is listening to her dad yell at her," Érica noted. "Sometimes my folks yell at me like that."

"It was like she was thinking aloud," said Tori.

"Parents are always on your case," said Chad.

"I could just see her there," said Clayton, "clenching her fists and getting angry as she listened, but she didn't say anything."

After a few more comments, I asked for a volunteer to read a third interior monologue, "The Game," to the class.

"So, what about that piece?" I inquired when the reading was finished.

"It was like yours, Mr. B. It was all thinking, all thoughts," noted Shannon.

"That was cool," said Chad. "It was like you were right in the middle of the game."

"Well said, Chad and Shannon," I responded. "Now, kids, here's the real question: what do all three pieces have in common? You heard "Question Session" by yours truly, then "I Tried" about the girl being yelled at by a parent, and "The Game" just now. In what ways are they all alike?"

Silence for a moment. Thinking in progress. A hand.

"Well, in each one of them, someone was thinking," suggested Rebecca.

"Yeah, and there was just one thing going on, like a class, or a football game," noted Dan.

"Good points," I responded. "Let's try an experiment. Everybody, close your eyes and listen to yourself think. Just follow the instructions."

Students sat quietly with their eyes shut. An occasional giggle escaped.

After a moment I asked, "What happened? What did you hear?"

"I didn't hear anything," said Chad, "just a voice saying how dumb it was to sit there with our eyes shut."

"Great, Chad. But that's what you heard—a voice. That was your interior monologue, sometimes called your 'inner voice.' You have a conversation going on in your head all the time—it's called an interior monologue." I paused, then asked, "What does *monologue* mean?"

"When one person speaks," Beth Ann said.

"Was anyone speaking in these pieces?" I prodded.

"Well, no, not really, but it was like they were speaking," Beth Ann continued.

"But if you had been there, you wouldn't have heard anything," said Shannon.

"Bingo!" I replied. "Nothing was said, but we knew what was going on. Why?"

"Because it was their thoughts," Shannon answered.

"And that's exactly what these are—examples of thinking," I explained. "Only we call them 'interior monologues,' because it's just one person, and the conversation is taking place inside the person's head. They go on all the time; you can't shut them down."

We had a brief discussion about the difference between monologue and dialogue. The young adolescents mentioned both Jay Leno and mononucleosis.

"Okay, here's your homework for tonight," I announced cheerfully. "Create two interior monologues. Remember to save all drafts. We'll share them in class tomorrow. Now, what are some situations where an interior monologue might be happening?" I asked.

Kids suggested possibilities—being at bat, worrying before a test, choking up at the free throw line, having lunch with someone who eats strange food, performing a solo, nervously waiting after being told by your mom that she has something important to tell you after dinner. I could tell by their responses that they had grasped the essentials.

The next day, students shared their work. Eileen couldn't wait to go first.

Cross Country

Okay, here I go jogging slowly, pacing myself. My, Mr. Sullivan has a lot to say today. When is he going to start talking to me? Oh, well. Today I think I can run the whole thing without stopping. No, I know I can.

Here we go around the first turn, Hey, this isn't so bad. Breathe. Take deep breaths. Okay, let's think of something else. Disney World, Space Mountain, Dumbo ride. Whew it sure is hot out here.

Holy, here comes the second corner. O.k., o.k., pace yourself, you still have a long way to go. Hmmmm, how can I think of something else? I know! I'll sing a song. "Is that a booger in the sugar . . . ." Nah, let's not. Boy, I wish I had my Walkman.

Hey, almost halfway done and I'm not even tired yet. Uh-oh, I am starting to get a stitch. Oh, what did Mr. Sullivan say about a stitch? Oh yeah. Push your stomach out, breathe in. Pull your stomach way in, breathe out. Push it, pull it, push it out, pull it in. Ahh, now it feels better.

I'm so bored. What do we have for homework? Let's see. English, Science, Math, Home Ec, Social Studies, and French! They really loaded on the homework tonight, didn't they. When is this straight-away going to end? Ow! My ankles hurt. I really should get good running sneakers.

Ah, the turn. Which way do I turn? Oh yeah, left. Okay. Back on the straight-away. I am 3/4 of the way there. I am not going to stop now! I am soo hot. I need something to drink very badly.

It's getting hard to breathe. Deep breaths. Take deep breaths. That makes it feel a little better. Ow! My ankles really hurt now. These shoes aren't very good.

I'm almost there. I know I can make it. I want to stop, I want to stop. No, I am not going to stop. I want water. Please, give me water! Look! There's where we started. Almost there, almost there . . . . . .

I made it!
—Eileen Wind, age 13

Eileen based her interior monologue on her cross-country running experience. The day before, she had been out on the course, running and panting through the woods, carrying on an interior monologue in her head. Her ability to take the reader there, to drift off into nonsense and then pull the reader back with a reference to the heat, or a stitch, or the pain, made her piece work. A mature writer for her age, Eileen clearly understood the form; she demonstrated mastery on this assignment.

David loved playing deck hockey. His interior monologue celebrated that passion:

On the Ice

C'mon, drop the puck already. Good, I got it. I got to score. C'mon, Dave, skate faster.

What's that? Oh great, a fat defenseman. He's gonna run me over. Skate faster, Dave. UNHHH! That schmuck made me eat ice. Stupid ref, call a penalty. Good call!

A power play—now we're gonna kick butt. Damn! I lost the face off. C'mon, Jeff, steal the puck. Oh, what a beautiful steal. Jeff, don't go all the way. Don't try to be a hero, Jeff! Don't shoot! Jerk.

I got the rebound. Okay, Dave, don't choke. Here it comes . . . NOW, shoot!

I scored? Well, I guess I scored (I had my eyes closed). I did? We won the playoffs? Awesome!

Oh no, not a pile on. AHHHH. C'mon, guys, get off. This isn't cool. We won, we get the big trophy. I hope we have this on tape.
—David DeTurris, age 13

Thirteen years later I asked David what he recalled about composing his interior monologue. He responded:

I remember writing "On the Ice" simply because it was a piece of writing that reflected something that was a very big part of my life in eighth grade. I found the assignment easy because I just wrote what I knew. [The interior monologue] was the type of writing that was easy for me. No real format, no constricting guidelines, no topics already set for me. Just put down your stream of thought . . . It was real. I actually went home after a hockey game, thought about what had happened, and put it on paper.

This is a great way to get kids to write. They don't have to worry so much about form and punctuation. It's just a matter of putting what you know on paper. This process helped most when I was in college. Whenever I was stumped on an essay test I would take a sheet of paper and just start writing what I knew. Soon I would have the answers I needed and I would then put them into the form that the question required.

That is how I learned to write. I didn't read "On Writing Well" and then suddenly know how to write. I wrote what I knew. After I learned how to express myself, only then did I start worrying about the form it needed to take.

Students enjoyed writing interior monologues because:

- The form was novel; most had not written interior monologues before.
- The interior monologue drew upon a real-life experience.
- The students could place themselves at the center of the action.

The Personal Essay

As with free-verse poems and interior monologues, I introduced personal essays by distributing a photocopied set of models written by previous students. Given the increased length of this form, we did not read each piece twice. Otherwise, the procedure was the same:

- A student read a sample personal essay to the class.
- Kids spent a minute or two jotting down their reactions.
- I invited comments, questions, criticisms, and compliments.
- We repeated this process with two more personal essays.

The students had done this exercise—read, consider, discuss, then agree on the central elements of the form—twice in the past two weeks. By comparing several models selected specifically as good examples, most students were quickly able to understand the personal essay form.

After having read the three pieces, I asked the kids what they noticed as being the same about all of them. Students began constructing a list of the common elements of the personal essay. They noted the following:

- It is longer than the free-verse poem or interior monologue.
- It is written in the first person.
- It describes a significant event that happened to the author.
- It has a "you are there" quality.
- It concerns the author having learned or realized something.

The homework assignment was, of course, to create the first draft of a personal essay. I expected sustained writing for this task, and thus did not assign two as homework.

The next day, students brought in first drafts and, as before, we shared aloud. Again, I went first to model proper volume, voice, speed of delivery, and, of course, the assignment itself. After I had finished, Greg volunteered to read his essay to the class:

Stitches

When was about 9 years old I went to BOCES 2. I picked up a program called chess and games where you played games all the time. Toward the end of BOCES 2 some of my friends discovered a great bannister to slide down on.

Three days before the program ended, I had to bring some letters down to the office with someone else. On the way down we passed the bannister, so we decided to slide down. We did, and at the end a teacher saw us. We both jumped off, and as I did I felt a sharp pain in my hand.

At the time I thought nothing of it, but it steadily hurt more and more, so I looked at it. An ugly gash from my pinky down to the edge of my hand was there. I suddenly felt very stupid because the teacher was still there. I showed him the gash, and he asked how it happened. I looked at my shorts and on it was a broken key chain (it broke earlier that day). Suddenly I realized what happened. When I jumped off the bannister the key chain caught me in the pinky and slashed downward. I went to the nurse's office, and she bandaged the cut. She said I should stay there for a couple of hours to see if I needed stitches before she called my mom. In about two hours my mom came and took me to a doctor.

When I got there a lady looked at the cut to make sure I needed stitches. She said yes and showed me to a room. The doctor came in with a tray and set it on a table next to the bed. He had antiseptic and injected it into my hand. After about three minutes my hand had no feeling to it, and the doctor began to give me stitches, 13 in all.

After I got stitches I resolved to never, ever, get on a bannister and slide down. Whenever I pass a bannister now I remember and move away a little bit.
—Gregory Megara, age 12

Eighth-grade boys have a passion for blood and guts, and when they can legitimatize their predilection for plasma through personal essays, they are in heaven.
John continued the theme:

A Visit to the Doctor

My mom had insisted that we see the doctor about a bad infection I had on my wrist. It had been there for a while and gotten worse. So my mom made an appointment and drove me to the office.

When we arrived at Dr. Pohl's waiting room my mom told me to sit down in one of the chairs. She then went up to the desk and spoke to the lady behind it. I don't remember exactly what was said but it sure didn't sound good!

I was led into one of the small observation rooms and instructed to have a seat on the table. Dr. Pohl came in and looked at my arm. He told me that he would need to lance the wound. He took out a scalpel, which, to me, looked like a kitchen knife, and told me to look away. I asked what he was going to do with the knife and he told me that he was going to quickly nick the infection. I questioned as to why he had to do this and he said that the infection was very close to the bone underneath. He warned me again to look away. I said I was going to watch. This worried him.

He hesitantly took his blade and plunged it into my diseased wrist. A sharp pain shot through me and fresh blood spouted from the spot of the incision! I let out a high scream! He then removed the knife and cleaned up the cut with a clean pad. He put a bandage on it and announced that it was done. My mom comforted me and I felt better. We then got in our Toyota and went home.

I'm never sure why, but this memory has always stuck out in my mind. Although some of it has faded, I can recall the moment of the incision with

nearly photographic detail. Maybe it's because this was one of the scariest things that has happened to me. Oh yeah, and if any doctor tells you to look away, just listen to him!
—John O'Brien, age 13

John was clearly a mature writer, able to stand back from his topic and comment on it. When an eighth grader composes a sentence such as "He hesitantly took his blade and plunged it into my diseased wrist," I relax and enjoy the rest of the story, knowing that I am in the presence of a writer.

Alicia described herself as an average writer and a middle-of-the-road student. For her, school was at times a challenge. Yet in the piece below, one sees love, understanding, sorrow, compassion, and an ability to tell a story, sentence after sentence, using real writing.

My Grandfather

It was 1987. I was in fifth grade. It was about halfway through the year.

It was 7:30. I just woke up. I heard my father on the phone. Afterwards my father told me and my sister that my grandfather died. I was sad but I did not cry. I knew my grandmother was very sad. I did not have to go to school, but I decided that I wanted to go. I could not concentrate real well, but I survived.

That night I went to my grandma's house. When we walked in everyone could hear her crying. Everyone felt so bad. I can not recall what I ate but it does not matter. Back to my grandma, every time she went to say "Andrew", she started crying harder. I kept on floating in and out of my aunt's bedroom and the kitchen. It was not a pleasant night.

That night the funeral home held the wake. I did not go because I do not like to think of death, so I stayed at my grandmother's next door neighbor's house. I watched a movie over there. The movie was good.

The next day the funeral was held, I went to that. I really did not like the idea of going but I was okay. First they had the final look at him. I felt really bad. I did not go to the wake. But I would not have felt well. So I know I would not have felt well. Then they had the priest come up and say a last prayer. Then everyone else came up to the coffin and said their last wish or prayer. After that they had the mass. I really did not understand what the priest was saying but I stayed quiet. After the mass that was the end.

Everyone went to my grandma's house. We divided the flowers between everyone. Then we went home.

The End
—Alicia Naeder, age 13

John wrote a sequential story replete with detail, commentary, good grammar, proper paragraphing, strong vocabulary, a sense of when to shift the scene, and an ability to step back and draw out the moral of a personal event. Once I read his essay, my assessment of John as a writer was that he did not need a lot of help with the basics; I needed to provide him with higher-level challenges that would further develop his already advanced skills.

Alicia started at the beginning and went straight through chronologically to "The End" using primarily simple sentences. Through detail, she helped the reader see the setting. Her essay revealed ways that I could assist her development as a writer: beginning sentences with words other than "I" or "It," combining sentences to make them more complex, developing more interesting beginnings, and improving the endings so they offered readers a reflection on the experience.

Writing as Therapy

Jane's distress, unknown to me when she composed her personal essay, was palpable. Jane (not her real name; she requested anonymity, even many years later) used the assignment to explore an enduring question among young adolescents: who will be my friend? Although not an easy assignment for her to complete, she managed to capture the uncertainty of shifting social relationships among middle school girls along with her personal anguish.

Jane did not share her essay with the class, nor with me immediately, because she knew how personal, how real, it was:

Best Friend

I don't know what to do. I feel trapped, like a nut in a shell. She's so much better than me. How can I compete? She's so popular and so smart. But yet she tells me we're best friends. Well, maybe we are. I want to be hers, but I'm not totally sure she wants to be mine.

I remember two summers ago. She spent it with two other girls. I really didn't mind much then because we weren't as close. But as she recollects on it, I feel so bad. Now one of the girls isn't friends with us anymore, but the other is. She has been with her since elementary school and they are still very close. It's hard for me because I like them both and don't want to hurt any of our friendships. But when we are together I feel so left out. It seems I'm only there because they don't want my feelings hurt. Only every time I try, I just get pushed away. My belief of our friendship isn't very strong. My strengths keep fading away and soon I'll have none left.

We got into a fight about a week ago and I realized that it didn't affect her. I don't even think she thought about it. All I know is that I did, and knew that if it wasn't over soon, I would be drawn farther away from her, while she would be drawn closer to someone else.

We have made up and we talk a bit more, but I'm still not sure if she wants to be my best friend. I've been doubting this ever since that fight we had. I try

so hard to please her and know I can't afford to lose our friendship. But can she? Starting now I'm going to do my best in pleasing her. Because right now I'll do anything to get us to be real, true, best friends.
—Jane, age 13

Jane was writing for real in the most meaningful sense of that phrase when she composed her essay. She was not writing for her teacher, but rather for herself, grappling with a dilemma—a classic example of writing as therapy.

We need to respond sensitively to students when they use a writing assignment to share a personal crisis, and students do. Sometimes they do not want response; other times they just want reassurance that someone else knows; still other times they want to talk about the problem. If a particular assignment prompts a student to reveal closely held emotions, we cannot turn away or pretend that it didn't happen. Our responsibility as teachers is to be sensitive to young adolescents as they struggle to communicate the triumph, turmoil, and tranquility in their lives.

Assertions Addressed

As they explored the dimensions of interior monologues and personal essays, students also addressed many of the assertions about writing:

- They communicated ideas that celebrated events in their lives.
- Their essays helped me understand their varying ability levels.
- They became invested in self-selected topics.
- Student examples from previous years proved inspirational.
- My own interior monologue and personal essay helped them to understand these forms of writing.
- Interior monologues and personal essays added to the volume and variety of student writing.

Closing Thoughts

When introducing interior monologues and personal essays, you may wish to use the student examples in this book. Feel free to reproduce them and have your students discuss them in class. Ask them to design alternative endings, new lines, better titles. Invite them to write what came next. Use these models to prompt your students to write their own essays and monologues. After the first year, you will have your own models to use and inspire students in the future.

Students enjoyed composing their personal essays, in part, I believe, because they were given the freedom to select an event worthy of celebration or work through an unresolved issue or chronicle a family memory. They were encouraged to write about something memorable, a real topic that had meaning for them and that helped them make sense of their lives. Students honor their own lives through this form of real writing.

7

Anthologies and Writing Groups

Writing group: a subset of the community of writers who meet regularly to share drafts with, provide feedback to, and get response from one another when they read their pieces aloud.

In the National Writing Project Summer Institute, we discussed our unfinished pieces in writing groups. That experience taught me the value of response. Working with students over the next several years, I learned a great deal about the dynamics of writing groups. Here is the short version:

- Keep the size of the groups to three or four students (five is too many).
- Arrange groups in which the writers are at roughly the same level of competence.
- Model appropriate writing-group behavior before sending students off to meet and discuss writing.
- Provide a set of instructions and expectations to each member of the group.
- Allow groups sufficient time to coalesce and learn to function.
- Hold students accountable for their behavior.
- Vary group members during the year.
- Later in the year, ask students whom they would like to have in their writing groups, and use their input.

Writing groups are a developmentally appropriate activity for young adolescents in that they address both academic and social skills. Alyce Hunter and Peter Blat (1994) praise cooperative learning activities in which "students as group members actively pursue learning goals, display appropriate behavior, and participate in group dynamics . . . [C]ooperative learning not only facilitates subject matter retention, but also promotes social skills such as leadership and decision making" (p. 17).

Young adolescents are usually focused on their peers. When students work in groups, they develop collaborative skills in purposeful settings that address their social needs as well. Most of the time, heterogeneous groups work best for middle-level students. They learn to cooperate with others in circumstances that foster the development of self-esteem.

In my own classes, I found that if the students in a group had too wide a range of ability levels, they had difficulty providing useful response to one another. For the most part, once the year was under way and I had a sense of where my students were developmentally, I arranged writing groups in which the participants were at roughly the same ability level.

In an article in *Middle School Journal*, Alan Weber (1992) addressed the issue of response. He was speaking to teachers engaged in correcting written work, but his comments also relate to oral response. An authentic writing group member, Weber said,

> responds to a piece of writing emotionally, intellectually, and critically. A corrector responds to technique alone. A reader becomes engaged in a work while the corrector stands apart from it. For example, a corrector circles misspellings and underlines run-on sentences; the reader reacts to the writing personally with comments like, "The incident you describe reminds me of my childhood." By asking genuine questions and perceiving yourself as a helper rather than a cynic, responding as a reader becomes a much easier task. (p. 24)

Constructive response is the critical factor here; if the members of a writing group feel their needs are being met by useful feedback on their writing, they benefit from the experience. Response from peers sends the student back to his or her piece to resee it, recraft it, and revise it.

Follow the Instructions

Before students began to read and respond in groups, we did three things. First, I gave them a set of instructions, which we reviewed in class:

Writing Group Instructions

1. Sit facing one another. The fewer distractions, the better you can concentrate on the task at hand—responding powerfully to writing.
2. Be prepared—have your pieces of writing, a writing implement, and scrap paper for taking notes.
3. Determine an order for your group. Have each participant take turns "leading" the group. Be thorough in discussing the writing—don't rush.
4. Each author should prepare questions about his or her piece to bring to the writing group's attention.
5. Each listener should listen carefully and make contributions to the improvement of the writing that comes out of the group. Responses to writing should be nonjudgmental and should enable the author to see options and possibilities for revision.
6. At the end of the writing-group discussion, the author should have a clear sense of how he or she can revise the piece.
7. What works best are questions for the author: Did you consider this? Why did you say that? What time of day/year is it? What's missing? What do you need help with? Did you consider . . . ? What if . . . ?
8. Ultimately, each author is responsible for his or her work.

Second, we established and reviewed the basic procedures that each group would follow.

Procedure:

1. Author reads piece two times; listeners take notes.
2. Pause 30 seconds—listeners think and prepare initial response; author writes questions also.
3. Each listener responds briefly to major impact of piece.
4. Discussion/feedback—compliments; questions; what worked for you and why; what didn't work; suggestions.
5. Author's Time—author raises questions; shares concerns about piece; sees revision possibilities in next draft.
6. Start process again with another author.

Third, we did a demonstration in class. I selected three students whose performance in class since day one indicated that they would be good at providing response. Our group sat in the center of the room; the rest of the students sat around us, observing. While we discussed a piece of writing in our "fishbowl," the outer circle of students took notes in their journals on the manner in which our group interacted. Afterward we discussed how the writing group functioned, what worked and what didn't. We did a second demonstration just to be sure everyone understood what was involved. Then the kids broke into their groups to discuss their writing.

Students improved as the year went along; some were naturals, while others struggled with response. I visited groups to observe their interactions and provide coaching.

Sometimes when you put young adolescents in loosely supervised small groups and allow them to run their meetings, not everything goes smoothly. In his journal, Dan shared a problem:

> I liked the writing groups a lot. I feel that most people have great things to offer to a piece of writing. However their are a few who just don't take notes or anything. That's a sure fire downer!
> —Dan Brickley, age 14

I arranged to monitor Dan's group and rectify the situation.

The Imperative of Publishing

Anthology: a published collection of writings, often connected by a unifying theme.

There may be an eleventh assertion about writing: *If you know your writing is going to be published, you want it to look good so that you do not look bad.* This is one of the reasons we created class anthologies—to get students to care about their writing.

I have yet to meet the student who wants to look like a fool. Play the fool? Yes, I've met that student. But be perceived as the fool? No.

Consequently, publishing automatically raises the bar for kids. When I said, "We're going to publish your writing in a book," they understood the message, and they wanted to be represented by their best writing. Immediately, writing groups and proofreading skills took on new significance as kids prepared pieces for the class anthology. The desire to have the writing be "correct" shifted from the teacher to the student; we became partners as we raced to our deadlines, making our writing as error-free as possible.

One day during the fourth week of school I said to my students, "Okay, you've written two or three free-verse poems, two or three interior monologues, and one or two personal essays. Now select two of those pieces, revise them further in writing groups, and prepare them for publication in our class anthology. You need to select two different forms. You cannot use only poems or only interior monologues. Which two do you want to represent you forever and ever in the class anthology? Everyone will get a copy. We'll also put the anthology in the school library. So, which are your best pieces of writing?" The ball was now in their court.

I let kids decide which pieces to publish. If a student wanted to use her interior monologue but I preferred her poem instead, we went with the monologue; I respected the author's choice.

Celebrating Authors

For homework on the day the anthology appeared, I asked each student to write letters to two authors, commenting on their pieces. The first letter went to a classmate selected by lottery from a paper sack; the second went to "any other author in the anthology." Through letters, students celebrated their friends' writing. They had to leaf through the anthology and read all the writing from their peers; also, the lottery assured that every author was acknowledged for his or her writing.

During a typical year, my students and I published ten anthologies:

1. Poems, Interior Monologues, and Personal Essays
2. The Distinctions
3. The Pocono (PEEC) Field Trip

By March, students had composed over twenty-five original first drafts of writing and had taken at least fifteen of those through the revision process to publication. In April and May students created two major pieces of writing: an individual poetry booklet and an individual magazine. Together these two projects resulted in a minimum of twenty-five published pieces, all created in the fourth quarter of the school year.

Consider for a moment the impact of all this publication, along with multiple drafts and proofreading, on a student's written expression and skill development. When you also consider the weekly journal entries and the letters and in-class writing exercises, the assertion "Volume + Variety = Fluency" takes on new resonance.

Putting an Anthology Together

Creating an anthology took concerted effort by many individuals. Page makeup and proofreading alone demanded careful, attentive work. Recognizing that many hands make light work and that young adolescents enjoy real tasks, I asked for volunteers to stay after school one day to put the anthology together. Several students answered the call. Their efforts strengthened the bonds of the developing community of writers.

Our after-school publishing group began by loading student disks in the computers and calling up pieces intended for publication on the screen; each student had previously selected two pieces for the anthology, revised them in writing group, edited and proofread them, and selected a title. We did a final spell check, formatted the text and changed font sizes so that the piece would fill one or two pages, and printed out a hard copy. I invited a student to write the introduction; occasionally student artists drew illustrations to enhance the written work. Finally, we numbered all the pages, then sent the packet to the district office for photocopying.

Inside the front cover were the credits. One year they read:

Credits

Cover created by Mike Caracciolo
Table of Contents typed by Andy Hanulec
Printing by Karen White
           Andy Hanulec
           Robin Derwitsch
           Keith Colantropo
           Matt Short
           Mike Caracciolo

Assertions Addressed

Writing groups and class anthologies are powerful tools for teaching writing. They support the publishing process. In my class, every student became an author when the first anthology appeared. The heterogeneously grouped class composed a range of writing samples; and, as students read through the anthology looking for an author to honor with a letter, they learned about other writers. Each student could appreciate the work that went into every piece of writing, because each of them had been through the same process of drafting, revising, editing, and preparing the text for publication.

Kids kept their anthologies as treasured souvenirs. I received an e-mail from Shannon in 1999, just after Halloween during her senior year in high school. She wrote:

Last Saturday night Katie Joos, Beth Ann McEnany, Kim McCarrick and I planned on having a fun evening at the haunted house nearby, but when the fog turned out unbearable that was called off . . . We came back to my house . . . I went down in the basement and pulled out all of "our published works" and of course, *Poems for All Occasions*. We sat there for hours looking through the books, playing our [eighth-grade] tape in the background. Needless to say it was a quality night.

It was so refreshing to look back and remember what it was like in 8th grade, and realize how much we have grown. Katie, Beth Ann and I laughed for hours while we read our pieces of literature, and we all started crying realizing that this was four years ago and in six months we will be in college. Those were some good days . . . some of the best.
—Shannon McCarthy

Closing Thoughts

If your school district cannot afford to print multiple copies of student work, assemble one copy for the classroom and one for the school library. It's still publishing, since all of your students know that their writing can be found inside the covers of the book. It's there on the shelf, a laminated class booklet that nurtures student pride and ownership.

8

Journals

On the first day of class, a Wednesday, I informed students that they needed an English journal with ruled sheets and lots of pages, and that their homework was to bring it to class that Friday.

On Friday, I said, "Write your name inside the front cover of your 'EJ'— that's another name for your English journal." Then I asked two of the kids to collect all of the brand new, now-identifiable journals. I said I would return the journals on Monday.

We spent the rest of class discussing the first poetry memorization of the year, scheduled for the following Friday.

Over the weekend I put a big white label in the upper right-hand corner of the outside front cover of each journal. In that white space, using a permanent magic marker, I printed each student's name and class period:

EJ–2 Meghan Otten

Rules for English Journals

When the students came to class the following Monday, I pointed to the pile of journals stacked neatly on a small desk by the classroom door. "After you complete your first journal assignment, which is due tomorrow, stack your EJ neatly on the desk. Any questions about those instructions?" (Usually there were none, but it's always good to ask.)

"Okay, now get your journals," I instructed. "You'll need them for today's class."

Two students closest to the door began calling out names: "Brickley, Hodess, Schappert, Wind, Unterstein, Clair . . ." In moments, all the students had their journals, and we were ready to write.

"Okay, open up your English journal," I said. "Inside the front cover, copy the following." I pointed to the chalkboard:

Rules for English Journal

1. Bring English journal to class daily.
2. Use only for EJ entries.
3. Use only one side of the page.
4. Do not rip out pages.
5. Use proper heading.
6. Keep until June.
7. Entry due the next school day.

They set about the task.

A hand went up. "But my cover is dark green, Mr. B.," said Mike. "I can't read what I wrote."

"In your case, Mr. Clair, put the rules on the first page," I responded. "Anyone else who has the same problem, follow Mike's example. And let's acknowledge Mike for bringing this problem to our attention." They laughed and applauded Mike.

Soon each student had copied down the rules. We spent a few minutes discussing them.

I raised a question. "Chad, if I assign a journal entry on Friday, when is it due?"

"Monday," he replied confidently.

"How do you know?" I pressed.

"Because Rule 7 says 'Entry due the next school day.'"

"Good job, Chad. But what if Monday is a holiday?"

"Well, I guess it would be due on Tuesday, then," he answered.

"Let's acknowledge Chad for his clear understanding of Rule 7," I said. They laughed again as they applauded.

"Now, ladies and gentlemen," I continued, "a proper journal entry heading looks like this. And woe betide the miscreant who strays from the stipulated path. Or in other words, 'Follow the instructions'!" They chuckled. I turned to the chalkboard and wrote:

EJ # _____   Date due
                                   "Title"

"Copy that sample heading inside the front cover below the rules. That's how you label a journal entry," I said. "No exceptions."

Clear, direct language. Simple instructions. Useful practices. Journal protocols were now in place, and the system worked because:

- All journals were labeled for easy identification with the student's name and class period on the front cover.
- The rules were written inside the front cover, along with a model of a proper journal entry heading.
- Students knew where to hand in their journals when they completed an entry and where to retrieve them once I had read and graded them.

What can journals teach us about students and their writing? How can we use them effectively? What kind of grading system is best? How often should students do journal entries? What about spelling? How do students see the role of journals in their learning? These are useful questions to address if you plan to have students write in journals.

The First EJ Entry

For the initial English journal entry of the year, titled "Learning My Poem" and assigned intentionally four days before the first poetry memorization as a wake-up call ("Hey, you have a poetry recitation due this Friday!"), I asked students to respond to three questions:

a. What poem did you select to memorize, and why?
b. What strategies are you using to memorize it?
c. What else do you have to say about anything?

I wanted to learn how they were progressing with the first memorization of the year. Nicole, a dedicated flutist, began her entry by writing from memory all twenty lines of her poem as a self-test of what she had learned so far. I noted that she made nine minor errors. She continued:

> To memorize that poem, I had to be patient and take my time.
>
> First, I stood in front of my mirror and read the poem a few times until I got the hang of it. Then, I said as much of the poem as I could. Whichever lines gave me trouble, I said ten times in a row and soon knew each line perfectly. Now I can speak the poem very fluently.
>
> I didn't really have any help learning this poem from any people. Tara helped me out a bit, though. She held the poem while I said it and then told me which words I missed, etc.
>
> This poem, "A Road Not Taken" by Robert Frost, gave me a lot of different messages. I think the most defined message is that which is clearly stated in the last stanza. "Two roads diverged in a wood and I—I took the one less traveled by and that has made all the difference." This means that—who cares what everybody else is doing—do your own thing and you'll probably have a great time. When Robert Frost spoke of the two roads, he really could have been speaking of anything. You will come to many forks in this highway we call life and it's up to you which way you go . . . You could follow the herd and make a left or you could go your own way and make a right. Who knows what lays ahead of you when you make that left—smoking, drinking, drugs—eventually death. But you can avoid all this simply by following an old poet's advise . . . and making the right decision.
>
> This poem was easy for me to learn. I really liked the way it was written and the crucial words that were written. I've always liked this poem, and my opinion didn't change before or after I finished my assignment.
> —Nicole Guippone, age 12

Nicole's forty-seven-line journal entry (excluding her rendition of the poem itself) earned an A. I commented:

> Nicole—
>
> This entry is a model of what I expect in an EJ—complete, detailed—I have no questions. I appreciate the time you took with this—good job. Isn't it a great poem? It's one of my favorites—I like Frost, as you'll learn—he has a lot of wisdom.
>
> Sounds as if you handled this assignment well. Good job, Nicole, & thanks for being a great student.
> —RMB

Another student, Mike Clair, a tall, gangly soccer player, wrote about a different poem:

> I chose the poem Ozymandius. I chose this poem because I think it tells how the passage of time is not only the great healer but a two-edged sword that can destroy and kill as well as heal.
>
> One of my strategies for memorizing my poem is to read the poem once or twice through, just to get a feel for it. Then you read one line, close your eyes, and then recite that line. Do this to every line and helps greatly.
>
> I have joined soccer for school. It is hard work!
> —Mike Clair, age 13

Using red ink so that my comments would stand out against Mike's black ball-point pen, I responded to his nine-line entry in four places:

1. I circled the words "two-edged sword" and noted, "Well expressed!"
2. At the end of the last sentence in the second paragraph, I added the exhortation, "Good luck on Friday!" (the day students would recite their first memorization).
3. At the end of the third paragraph I added the words, "Go for it!"
4. As a final comment I wrote, "Mike—Thanks for sharing! RMB."

Mike's entry earned a C+. I usually graded the first journal assignment low, figuring that some students would write more if they thought it meant a higher grade; also, I was not yet clear about their abilities and did not know, in Mike's case, for example, whether his nine handwritten lines represented Herculean effort or perfunctory performance.

Looking at other first entries besides Nicole's, I noted that on the same assignment Meghan wrote seven lines, earning a C; Bobby, who penned twelve lines, took home a B-; Jessica, at twenty lines, received a B; and Adam, with twenty-four lines, got a B+. I was grading length, among other things (volume + variety). But as I read the students' entries, I also was evaluating them on the completeness and quality of their responses to the three questions.

The Second EJ Entry

Returning their journals the next day, I heard whispers of "Whadja get?" along with the rustling of pages being turned as they read my comments. These students, who had been together as a team in sixth and seventh grades, all knew one another; they were used to comparing notes.

Once they had their journals, I said, "Open your EJ to entry number two. The title is 'Writing My Poem.' The due date is tomorrow." I wanted to strike while the iron was hot; they had just read my coaching comments about their first entry.

For the second entry, I asked students to explain the process they went through when creating their free-verse poems:

a. What happened? Your thoughts, time needed, drafts completed, and decisions made about one of the two poems you wrote.
b. Share your reaction to one of your free-verse poems.
c. What else do you have to say?

The next day, the first thing I noticed about Mike Clair's second entry was the contrast with his handwritten first effort. Mike had drafted three different poems (only two were required), then typed a thirty-five-line entry, including sentences such as "The first draft was the important one, the one that looked for the way the poem was written and the way it had turned out" and "So I finally made a poem about a majestic dragon who had been trailed by two adventurers who then killed it with an arrow of dragon slaying."

Mike concluded his entry with this paragraph:

As looked back on that poem I thought that I had done a pretty good job. I liked the way I had described the dragon and how the adventurers had killed the dragon with a magical arrow. I then looked back and saw that something was missing. So I incorporated the part about the feeling of something troubling. Unfortunately for the dragon he was never going to be able to figure out what the troubling feeling was. My main reaction was good, mostly since I like to write about fantasy. I thought that after I looked over it and made it perfect that the poem was actually perfect.

Assessing Journal Entries

I was ready to put an A on Mike's journal entry, and I had read only the first page. On page two I discovered an additional ten lines of typed text:

Soccer practice is getting a little easier now that I am getting in a little better shape. I would also like to ask why you gave me a C+ on my first E.J. entry. I saw that it was a little short compared to some others, but I think a B- not a C+ would be a fairer grade. I would like to hear some of the reasons behind your grading system. This is not meant to criticize you, not do anything of that sort, it's just that if I get all A grades this year in all my classes then I can get a laptop of my choosing (remember that I told you about this already?) That is why I want to know about your grading system so I can figure how to write the way you would like me to. I would also like to thank you for being a good teacher and making us work hard in the first week of school, and to get us into the swing of things quickly.

Mike had been a student of mine for five days; I barely knew him, but he was surfacing fast. He jumped from nine handwritten lines and ninety-three words in his first entry to thirty-five typed lines and over seven hundred words in his second. I was impressed, and I knew that my response needed to communicate that:

> Mike—
>
> You're welcome.
>
> First, thanks for typing—it's easier to read. Also, thanks for a fine job of describing what happened as you wrote your poems—very clear!
>
> Compare EJ #1 to EJ #2. Which is better? Why? EJ #1 was barely better than satisfactory, Mike. Thanks for asking.
>
> If all future entries are this detailed and this complete, you'll have no problem earning an A, Mike. This is an excellent EJ entry.
>
> —RMB

Jessica, a gymnast whose grades on the first four English journal entries were B, B, A-, and B+, raised the assessment question in her fifth entry:

> One question is all I have . . . What method do you use to grade journal entries?

I responded with a combination of criteria and mathematics:

> Jessica—an outstanding entry—you clearly responded to all [five] parts of the question, and I am very clear about your thoughts on writing.
>
> As for how I grade, remember that I read some 25 English and 25 social studies journal entries a year times 45 kids—that's 25 + 25 x 45 times 14 years that I've been doing journals. So I've read lots of entries and know (as a gymnastics judge knows) if a student has responded fully, authentically & thoughtfully to the questions. I look for clarity, completeness & originality in entries. Your entry is an example of quality work, for example. Thanks for asking.
>
> —RMB

Jessica's three-and-a-half-page handwritten entry, one of over thirty thousand I had read since attending the 1980 National Writing Project Summer Institute, received an A.

Reviewing Writing

What could you learn about your students and their writing habits if you gave the following journal assignment early in the school year? Then what could you do to enhance their writing with the information they provided?

Your assignment is to write as much as you can on the topic

"What I Know About How I Write"

The following is a list of factors that may be part of how you write. Write about the ones that are true for you, as well as any other factors you can think of.

> Where you write.
> Your body position.
> Music or TV or neither.
> A certain kind of paper/notebook.
> Pen or pencil.
> Asking for help, ideas, suggestions from others.
> When you do writing in relation to other homework.
> Interruptions, eating breaks, etc.
> Time of day.
> Alone or not.
> Bothered by spelling or punctuation, etc.
> Concerned about neatness.
> Handwriting: print, script, etc.
> Do you have trouble beginning?
> Do you plan in advance?
> Does your mind wander from what you're writing?
> How frequently do you reread what you're writing?
> Do you evaluate as you are writing?

On October 6, I assigned the fifth English journal assignment of the year. I asked the kids to consider all the writing they had done since day one, then comment on it. My goal was to understand how my students perceived writing and learn from their comments. Bobby turned in the following entry:

A. PEEC pieces
B. FVP, IM, PE
C. Journals (11 so far)
D. Other thoughts of writing Burk system
E. Other

A. The PEEC [Pocono field trip] pieces were probably my favorite pieces. I put every part of every day in each of them. From breakfast, to orienteering, to the talent show, I tried to include every detail. Even before we were at PEEC, and were writing about our goals, I could still picture PEEC and how I would apply my goals, as well as the team goals.

I tried to write the entries with this in mind. That if I were to read the entries in a year or two that I would still be able to remember everything. I think I did a pretty good job, too.

B. The free verse poems, interior monologues and personal essay that I have done so far were very beneficial pieces of writing for me as a writer. They showed me a form of writing that I thought I could never be good at. When I first heard the assignment for the free verse poems, I frowned. I had never done anything like that before. But when I got home and started fooling around with two subjects I was familiar with, it became much easier. When I wrote about lacrosse, I just pictured myself on the field in a clutch situation. For the fishing poem, I just pictured myself on the beach as the sun was setting, hoping for a fish. After getting these two ideas everything just fell into place. The interior monologues and personal essays were all the same once I got an idea I just typed away.

C. The total of eleven journal entries so far have done more for me than just help me become a better writer. I'll never look at movies as just actors doing their work just to get paid. After writing the Forrest Gump entry, I now look deeper into movies and get much more involved in the story itself. I never really liked reading that much, but now reading is fun, and seems more than just more homework. With all we've been doing on poetry, I'll never look at a poem the same again. I've learned to visualize and look farther into poems, now. I can actually understand them a lot better.

D. There is really only one more thing I have to say about writing. I only experienced it two days ago when we were reading our personal essays out loud. When I finished other people, specifically Mr. Burkhardt, gave me ideas and suggestions to make my piece better. It turned my paper from a one page decent piece of writing, to a two and one half page essay full of details and examples. It made a 100% difference in my essay. I would love to do the same with all my pieces of writing whether it be a report, or poetry.

E. Writing was never so fun for me. With all the ideas and forms of writing I working with, it should get even better!
—Bobby Unterstein, age 13

I appreciated Bobby's entry; he helped me see that the writing program was working for him, five weeks into the school year.

By October 7, Bobby had completed the following assignments in English and social studies:

- a letter of introduction;
- three Distinctions definitions;
- two free-verse poems (multiple drafts);
- two interior monologues (multiple drafts);
- a personal essay (multiple drafts);
- two poetry memorizations;
- three pieces about the Pocono Environmental Education Center (PEEC) field trip;
- a United States timeline (1865–present) poster project, including a report;
- two in-class writing assignments;
- eleven journal entries (five in English, six in social studies);
- seven pieces of writing edited and proofread for publication in four separate class anthologies.

And Bobby was not alone. Each of his forty-six classmates did the same assignments. Their reflections on them in the fifth EJ assignment provided a wealth of feedback. Reading through all the journal entries in one sitting, I could see the degree to which the way I taught writing was working, or not working, both with the students as individuals and as a group. Collectively, their journal comments furnished me with ideas for strengthening the writing program, ways to approach certain students who were not fully engaged, and a sense that my efforts to create a community of writers were paying off.

Students used journals to explore ideas, record understandings, share reactions, communicate with me, learn through writing, and vent.

I used journals to gather information, assess understanding, promote writing and thinking, monitor student attitudes, diagnose writing skills, process unanticipated events, and engage in a continuing conversation with each of my students.

"What Else Do You Have to Say?"

"What else do you have to say?" or "Other" was the last question in every journal assignment. That invitation to digress encouraged a number of students to add to their entries as they wished (volume + variety). Kids would share their latest success, announce an upcoming birthday, air a concern, or offer a philosophical insight. Adam, no slouch when it came to thinking, took issue with one of the "life lesson" signs that I pointed to three or four times each day:

> "Do or do not; there is no try"—Yoda. WHAT! I have to say, Mr. B., I agree with all of your signs—except this one. If there is no try, great accomplishments would not be accomplished. I know the sign means "JUST DO IT," but knowing you may not succeed & that's OK is a great comfort to those who have great dreams about what they will accomplish. And after all, I am TRYING to explain this to you, and yet there is no guarantee you will agree with what I'm saying. That's OK, isn't it?
> —Adam Silver, age 14

If you invite response, you ought to reply. I circled the word "agree" in Adam's next-to-last sentence, drew an arrow from my comment to where he had written the word "TRYING," and put a red "X" through it:

> Adam—You weren't trying—you explained yourself. And so what if I don't "agree" with what you say—you are at perfect liberty to disagree with what I say. As for Yoda, my sense of this quote is that, in life, you should approach things from the point of view that "I can do this" and figure out how rather than the words "I wonder if I can do this—maybe if I try . . ." frame of mind. Too many people make one stab or two stabs at something difficult & then fold

up. That's no way to live your life. Me? I run the videotape in my mind ahead &
see the task accomplished & then work backwards from there, thinking about
how I got it done & what decisions I needed to make to get the job done. Mine,
Adam, is a life of results, not reasons. People who "try" have lots of reasons as
to why they didn't get the job done.

Thanks for stimulating these thoughts.

—RMB

Meghan used the "What else do you have to say?" question to report on
a time management talk she had with her father:

So far school is good. It seems like we've been in school longer than 2 months,
probably because we've done so much. At one point I was having trouble keeping up with school work because I was playing field hockey after school but me
and my dad had a talk and he told me how he had the same problem when he
was in high school. He told me he learned to manage his time management. So
I've been working on my time management and it's working. Field hockey is
over now so it should get easier to fit in school work.

—Meghan Carey, age 13

If you use journals with kids, I recommend that you include a "What
else?" question so that students feel encouraged to communicate whatever
is on their minds.

Thirty-Five Journal Entries

In one year, which was not at all atypical, I gave the following English
journal assignments between September and March. A few were assigned
as in-class writing; most were done as homework.

1. Learning My Poem
2. Writing My Poem
3. Movie: *Forrest Gump*
4. Reading
5. Writing
6. The Artifact Project
7. Decisions
8. Leadership
9. Lessons Learned
10. Current Events I
11. Current Events II
12. The Fall So Far
13. The School Paper
14. Three Newspaper Ideas

15. My Newspaper Article
16. Doing My Article
17. Reading This Fall
18. Being a Reporter
19. Evaluating the Paper
20. Movie: *The Long Walk Home*
21. Poem: "Stopping By Woods on a Snowy Evening"—observe, question, interpret
22. Poem: "Not in the Guidebooks"—observe, question, interpret
23. Poem: "My Papa's Waltz"—observe, question, interpret
24. Poem: "Mending Wall"—observe, question, interpret
25. Poem: "anyone lived in a pretty how town"—observe, question, interpret
26. Doing My Letter to Self
27. Doing My Gift of Writing
28. Communication
29. Movie: *Twelve Angry Men*
30. Blind or Deaf?—preparation for *The Miracle Worker*
31. *The Miracle Worker:* My Favorite Character
32. Parent Writing Conference
33. Poem: "The Red Wheelbarrow"—observe, question, interpret
34. Poem: "As the cat . . . "—observe, question, interpret
35. Poem: "The Great Figure"—observe, question, interpret

Students averaged five journal entries a month. Their final English journal entry of the year was due on March 23. But we were not finished with journals. In April, after completing their poetry magazines, students composed a series of journal entries documenting the development of their individual magazines.

Responding to Reading

One English class a week was devoted to reading; the students and I would engage in sustained silent reading for an entire forty-minute period. When they walked into the classroom, students found me already reading quietly, modeling appropriate behavior. They sat at desks, on couches, under tables, on the window ledge, on pillows, or lay prone on the floor; they made themselves comfortable and began reading. There were a few simple rules:

- Always have a book to read.
- Get a new book before you complete your current one.
- Read by yourself; do not disturb others.
- During the last five minutes of class, jot down notes on your reading: what you read, how many pages, what you enjoyed, and what ideas were prompted by your reading.

In late fall I assigned students a journal entry in order to learn about their reading habits and attitudes. By posing the question, I reminded them that reading was an important part of the English curriculum:

Look back over your weekly reading notes. Consider the reading you have done, the books you have begun and completed, and your experiences as a reader. Then respond to the following questions:

a. What books have you read this fall? List them.
b. Which was your favorite/best book this fall? Why? Explain fully what you got out of that book.
c. What has been the value of the weekly reading period for you?
d. What comments, observations, and/or suggestions do you have regarding the weekly reading period? How has it affected your reading ability?
e. What else do you have to say?

Heidi's response was informative:

A.   *The True Confessions of Charlotte Doyle*
     It Happened to Nancy
     part of: *A Summer to Die*
                  For All Their Lives
     I've started: *The Client*

B. I think *It Happened to Nancy* was the best book I read this fall because it was a true story and it was written by the person that got AIDS. It was very sad. I learned what I should do or shouldn't do to prevent getting HIV or AIDS. There was a question and answer section in the back of the book.

C. I think the reading period has been good for me. When I'm home, I usually only read over the weekend. Now I can read during the week.

D. I think we should have more time to read during school. It has affected my reading ability a bit. Now it seems to me that I am getting more into the books I am reading.

E. When are we going to Boston?
      —Heidi Lipinsky, age 13

Assertions Addressed

Having students write in journals all year long addressed a number of the assertions about writing:

- *Every student a writer:* All students were expected to do all entries.

- *Ability level:* By reading both in-class entries and those done as homework, I got a good sense of where students were in their development as writers.
- *Peer models:* I asked students to share excerpts from journals on a regular basis. When other students heard how classmates responded to a particular topic, they saw new possibilities for their own future entries.
- *Volume + Variety = Fluency:* The impact on a student's writing of thirty-five English and twenty-five social studies journal entries composed during the first seven months of the school year, in addition to all the other assigned writing, was substantial.

Closing Thoughts

Journals are an excellent tool for promoting writing and thinking, for documenting progress in written expression, and for developing relationships with each student. They are particularly appropriate for young adolescent learners. As Alyce Hunter and Peter Blat (1994) observed:

> Journal writing can be used as a way to help middle-level teachers and pupils monitor and assess learning process and product . . . They can be used as a basis for dialogue between instructor and student. The teacher can ask the learner to finish such statements as "From today's lesson, I am confused about . . ." Then the teacher can alter the next day's lesson to clarify the learner's confusion. Journal writing can also be utilized to evaluate how much a student does know about a subject. (p. 17)

They recommend Toby Fulwiller's *The Journal Book* and Les Parsons' *Response Journals* for their suggestions that teachers

> can help students use journal writing to explore themselves and their learning. Such exploration delights many middle-level students as they attempt to clarify and solidify their lives and values. (p. 17)

By the end of the fifth week of school, journals were an established part of the program, a place for students to explore ideas, reveal understandings, and ask questions. The journals provided me with regular opportunities to assess the written expression of each student. The quality and quantity of the kids' responses satisfied me that they, as did I, saw journals as an important part of the overall writing program.

Summary

What writing activities are best suited for the opening month of school? The ones I described in this section can be done at any point in the year; but the combination of their novelty, the intermingling of journals and letters and published pieces, and their incremental degrees of complexity and demand make them best suited for September.

There are many ways to teach writing, and many ways to interact with students. The possibilities presented in this part of the book have the clear goal of creating a community of supportive writers. During the first five weeks of school, the activities one employs can establish expectations that will endure until the end of the year and simultaneously nurture the development of community.

Do you need to create a set of Distinctions that serves as a framework of behavioral expectations for students? No, but every teacher has values, ideals, and expectations. Why not be explicit about what you really want to have happen in your classroom?

Do you need to do homework assignments along with your students? No, but it does help to share your prose and poetry, and not only the polished pieces; let them see early drafts as well.

Do you need to begin the year's writing program with free-verse poetry? No, but it is useful to consider using an accessible, engaging form of expression that becomes a building block for later activities.

Do you need to have students write entries in journals weekly? No, but it is beneficial to establish a vehicle for communication between your students and you, something that allows you to see their insights and struggles, and something that allows them to express opinions and share information.

Do you need to have students work in writing groups? No, but peer response is incredibly powerful, and peers are an important audience for young adolescents.

Do you need to publish class anthologies of writing? No, but frequent publication compels students to prepare pieces carefully, thus addressing editing and proofreading skills.

Do you need to to begin the year with poetry and music? No, but why not?

Do you have to do everything suggested in Part One, in sequence, to succeed? No, but it is useful to have a clear plan of how you are going to begin the year, how you are going to maintain what you have started, and how you are going to handle the following:

- creating a safe, trusting community of writers
- explaining the writing theory behind your writing program
- sharing your own writing
- assigning the first writing task
- establishing writing groups
- introducing the second writing task
- addressing the role (if any) of journals
- introducing the third writing task
- publishing student work

One key to success is seeing students as responsible learners. Jerie Weasmer and Amelia Woods (2000) write that "to develop and maintain an effective student-centered classroom, the teacher first needs to recognize students as decision makers and invite them to develop their abilities to collaborate on learning tasks . . . A trusting environment . . . invites students to take risks and think both creatively and critically" (pp. 16, 18).

By the end of the first month of school, after you have read a number of early drafts, polished pieces, journal entries, and in-class assignments all composed by the same student, you can make an honest assessment of that student's writing skills based on the evidence present in those several pieces of writing. That assessment, multiplied by the number of students in your charge, should provide some direction for what happens next in your writing program.

I saw my writing program as one of individualized instruction, where all students were exposed to a variety of writing tasks yet each student progressed at his or her own rate. I maintained conversations with each student through journals, individually responding to their questions and concerns. They had a choice of topics; this allowed them to celebrate their passions. Young adolescents gravitate toward their interests, and the flexibility I built into the writing program capitalized on that fact, which resulted in more engaged writing.

My attention was on the long term—the ongoing journal entries, the growing number of drafts, the increased complexity of sentences, the use of apt vocabulary, the growth of the writer, all over a period of ten months.

Now that the first five weeks were past and the community of writers was established, albeit tenuously, the students and I turned to activities that nurtured real writing and lifelong learning. The next two parts of the book suggest approaches for engaging young adolescents in writing once the school year is under way.

Part Two

Writing and Learning

Now that the snowball is rolling down the hill, what next? How do you maintain the momentum established during the first five weeks of school? In this part of the book I present strategies for your classroom writing community.

Chapters 9 through 15 describe a host of writing and learning activities. They are not necessarily sequential, although some connect with events on a school calendar. Students can write for the school newspaper before reading and responding to a play; they can create Letters to Self after composing Gifts of Writing. Nor do students need to do all of these activities, although the more they do, the more they develop their written expression.

During the year, my students wrote weekly letters to various recipients for a variety of reasons: to introduce themselves; to persuade the principal of a course of action; to voice an opinion; to acknowledge an author; to inform a parent; to apologize for a misdeed; and to honor someone special.

Chapter 10, "Anticipating the Unexpected," addresses the issue of how to respond to an unexpected event—the first snowfall, the death of a prominent personality, a school matter that cries out for attention, a terrorist attack. Also in that chapter, I explain an in-class writing activity called "Roominations."

In Chapter 11, "The Holiday Memory Piece," students gather at the last class before a significant holiday to celebrate by sharing family traditions and memories of holidays, birthdays, vacations, or early schooling.

Chapter 12 is entitled "Lessons Learned." At midyear, students reflect on significant lessons they have learned in class so far. Each student identifies three lessons, shares two of them at a class meeting, then revises and edits all three for publication in an anthology. What happens in the minds of other students when they see classmates publicly declare themselves learners? How are their attitudes about learning shaped by this activity?

Chapter 13 is concerned with the Letter to Self, the best writing activity of the year—so say the students. For this activity they do extensive writing, and the teacher *doesn't* read it. Students earn an automatic B as they write about themselves and their lives, creating personal time capsules that are returned to them at the end of their senior year. The Letter to Self may be the most developmentally responsive exercise in the book.

The second best writing activity of the year (again, according to my students) is the Gift of Writing, explained in Chapter 14. Each student creates a "gift of writing" for an important recipient and actually gives the gift to that person. This activity provides material for another class anthology.

Chapter 15 describes three different writing activities. Essay contests provide students with opportunities to write for specific audiences on specific topics—and possibly win cash prizes. Writing a news article on deadline is a meaningful challenge for young adolescents. During the school newspaper unit, each student becomes a reporter and learns the basics of journalism. The ideas presented on responding to a play may be used for any drama, not just *The Miracle Worker,* which I used in my class. Students read a play and write about it, answering any three of six general questions. They then select two of their three responses for publication in a class anthology.

All of these activities address the assertion *Volume + Variety = Fluency*.

9

Letters

Letters

Basic idea:	For the Letter of Appreciation and Acknowledgment, the student selects an important person in his or her life and writes a letter to that individual.
Assertions addressed:	1, 2, 3, 4, 5, 7, 9, and 10 (*see p. 17*).
Skills addressed:	Letter format, attention to audience, fluency in writing.
Class time needed:	Half a period.
Advance preparation:	Compose a model letter to a faculty member known to and respected by your students.
Time of year:	December.
Neat feature:	The letter is actually sent.
Assessment:	Give everyone an A and do not read any of the letters.
Journal entry:	"Three Important People." Identify three important people you actually know and explain briefly why each person is important to you.
Caution:	Do not read the letters your students write—they are personal.
Forms:	Distribute the following assignment to your students:
	Prepare an appropriate *Letter of Appreciation and Acknowledgment* for an important individual in your life. You will send your completed letter to that person. Your letter should make it clear to the recipient both why you are acknowledging and why you appreciate her or him. Your letter will contain several paragraphs, since there undoubtedly are several reasons why you appreciate and can acknowledge this important individual in your life.
Why do this?	To make writing real for your students; to enable students to honor others in their life via writing.

Early in my career I learned that young adolescents love to write—to each other. Hundreds, perhaps thousands of notes are passed daily in the halls and classrooms of a typical middle school. As I thought about ways to capture kids' natural inclinations to put their thoughts into writing I realized: notes can become letters, and letters seemed a promising possibility, since they are written for all kinds of purposes, on a host of different topics, to as many audiences as can be imagined.

On day one each of my students composed a letter of introduction. When the first anthology (containing free-verse poems, interior monologues, and personal essays) was published, I asked each student to write to two authors. When the first issue of the school newspaper appeared, I had students write to reporters commending their articles. In addition, as you will learn in subsequent chapters, students wrote Letters to Self, "secret" letters, and end-of-the-year acknowledgments to teachers.

Kids wrote other letters as well. Prior to the end of the marking period, I asked students to write to their advisors, describing their academic success, to whatever degree, in both English and social studies; advisors found these letters useful when conducting parent conferences. If a student fell ill or a relative of a classmate died, we composed sympathy notes. Inevitably, at some point in the year, a pressing school issue would arise, providing students with an opportunity to practice persuasive writing by lobbying the principal for more school dances, or more activity buses, or more sports teams, or more monitors at lunchtime, or fewer restrictions in general.

One year, we created a multimedia project and wanted to include testimonials from celebrities as part of the show. Students corresponded with—and received replies from—Joan Rivers, Michael Gross of *Family Ties*, and Billy Joel, among others. When a community issue reached the level of eighth-grade consciousness, we fired off missives to the local newspaper in praise or condemnation of a particular course of action. We even wrote to the President of the United States with specific advice on how to run the country.

A steady publication of class anthologies and school newspapers during the year resulted in each student composing at least twenty-four letters to peer authors and reporters. In all, the typical student wrote upwards of forty letters; all were checked for neatness, completeness, and accuracy (and rewritten, if need be), then sent to the intended audience. Through it all, students never asked about their grades on these letters.

Every year I organized a series of educational community service field trips to other school districts or middle level conferences. My students, budding "experts" in writing, using multimedia, handling inquiry, using heterogeneous grouping practices, organizing community service, and other middle school practices, spoke about their educational experiences. When we returned, each student wrote a letter thanking an individual who had made the field trip possible: the principal who approved the trip; the superintendent and the president of the board of education;

the educator who had invited us to present; my math/science teaching partner who prepared homework packets in advance for trip participants; and my substitute. At some point during the year, each student was invited to present at a conference; ninety percent of the students chose to go. I was not unmindful of the public relations value of informing the suits in the central office about our conference presentations; consequently I asked students to send letters touting the educational value of such experiences.

Letters of Appreciation and Acknowledgment

One of the students' favorite letter writing tasks, usually assigned in December, was the Letter of Appreciation and Acknowledgment (interestingly, our first two Distinctions). It took me a few years of trial and error to design this activity properly.

In January 1981, my first year using National Writing Project ideas, I wrote in my journal:

> 2nd period, Allyson asked a good question—"What is the purpose of this 'thank-you' letter due Wed?" I was able to point out two different reasons: (1) to bring joy to another person—a teacher, friend, relative, coach—by telling in some detail what that person did to help you; (2) to realize you don't do it on your own, and that you owe thanks to others, and that you have to recognize that as you go along in life. I am doing this exercise also, and I'm not sure to whom I'll write—let me think and rehearse.

My journal entry of February 2, 1982, noted:

> I want to have the kids do a letter of appreciation and really get into it. This is something that they have done in years past, but always I am looking for ways to increase the commitment of their writing. I was thinking about discussing the term "Thank you" in class beforehand, to get them to think beyond the mechanical response aspect and really search out someone who did something for them and tell it like it is. Too often I feel kids do not go deep enough into themselves, and their writing thus is not "impelled." Maybe no matter what they give me, I will want more. I guess I may never be satisfied—an interesting thought. At any rate, some rehearsal in class beforehand before giving out the assignment seems to be in order.

Two days later I reflected on the activity:

> The "letter of thanks" idea seemed to go over fairly well, although in some cases kids did not have an idea of who they were going to write to . . . I just wrote both of mine—to Sondra and [to] Bob Kaplan. They were fun to write

and made me feel good—I hope the kids get the same kind of feeling from them that I do. I was very aware when explaining the assignment that the task was meant to create "impelled" writing. I used the word "perfunctory" in class to describe the "Hi, how are ya" greetings people extend to one another as they pass in the halls, knowing full well that they are not seriously interested in the person stopping and running down exactly how they feel. So I hope that the kids will have a chance to really share something from deep inside themselves with another person, as I did.

Looking back on these journal entries, I can see that a crucial factor was missing: rehearsal—the need to identify the audience for the letter. Once I included that in the mix, the Letter of Acknowledgment and Appreciation assignment worked like a charm.

Identifying the Audience

"Open your English journal to a new page" I instructed one day in December. "The title is 'LAA.'" Students responded automatically, so ingrained by this point in the year was the practice of creating EJ headings.

"What does 'LAA' mean, Mr. B?" asked Dan.

"All in good time, Danny," I responded. "Kids, your homework tonight is to identify three people you actually know, then write a sentence or two about each of them, why you respect them, and why you feel they are important in your life. I'll collect your journals tomorrow."

My practice for all writing assignments was to begin with simple, introductory tasks that led to more complex activities. I have yet to meet an eighth grader who could not list three important people and say why.

The next day in class I asked, "How many mentioned your mom or dad in the journal entry last night?" Two-thirds of the students raised their hands.

"How many mentioned their best friend?" Every hand went up.

"What about grandma or grandpa, or an aunt or uncle, or a brother or sister?" Again, two-thirds of the hands.

"A teacher here in school, or a coach?" Half the hands this time. As they looked around the classroom, students were able to see that they had done the journal entry "correctly," that is, they had responded as had their peers. This brief exercise affirmed their choices and created solidarity.

"I'd like you to listen to something I wrote last night," I said. I then read a two-page typed letter to a staff member, in this case, Bob Kaplan, the library-media specialist, publisher of the school newspaper, and director of the school play.

Dear Bob,

The pace seems to get more hurried as the years go on. Each year I keep telling myself, one of these years I will slow down and try to do less but do it better. It doesn't seem to happen. Each year brings new challenges and new adventures, and I get stretched further and further. But through it all, I have certain people I count on, certain people who mean a great deal to me. You are such a person.

I want to tell you how much I appreciate your support. In so many ways over the past four years, you have encouraged me, aided me, consoled me, challenged me, helped me, and shared with me. It is a good feeling to know there is someone on whom I can depend, someone who will help out when help is needed. You are more than a professional colleague—you are a friend. I appreciate your friendship, Bob. It means a lot to me. Whether it is a brief chat in the morning before we start our days (and unfortunately we do not do this as often as I would like, our geographical realities in the building being what they are) or the loan of a piece of media equipment, or some such thing, I am always sure of your cooperation. I note with pleasure that we have philosophical disagreements on issues—we are not "yes men" to one another. This healthy interchange of ideas only adds to what I feel is a growing friendship.

So, my friend, thanks for just being you, for being the kind of person you are, and for being an important part of my life. I truly appreciate you, and I want you to know that.

Sincerely,

Ross

I intentionally wrote my letter to someone they all knew and respected; over the years I sent epistles to my teaching partner, the principal, a coach, the choral director, the technology teacher—always someone I knew my students held in high esteem.

When I finished reading I said, "Tori, would you please put this in Mr. Kaplan's mailbox?" The kids watched Tori leave the room with a letter and return empty-handed; they knew that a real letter had been delivered.

"That was a Letter of Appreciation and Acknowledgment," I explained; "or, as we're now going to call it, an 'LAA.' There are many important people in your life. Last night in your EJ you identified three of them and said something about each one. Your job this evening is to write a Letter of Appreciation and Acknowledgment to an important per—"

"Mr. B.," Lee interrupted. "Now that I know what the assignment is, do I have to write to one of the people I mentioned in my journal, because I really want to write to— "

"Yes, you may, Lee, and anyone else who wants to switch to a new audience," I replied. "What's more, your grade on this assignment is a guaranteed A, and I will *not* read your letter." That statement unleashed them; they were free to write to whomever, about whatever, for whatever reason—it was their choice, very real.

"If you don't read it, how will you know that I wrote it, Mr. B.?" Jessica inquired. Jess would not have dreamed of not writing her letter, but she was curious.

"Tomorrow when you come to class, Jess and everyone else," I replied, "I need to see a piece of paper with some writing on it and a 'Dear Mom' or 'Dear Uncle Joe' at the top. Your letter has to be substantive, as well. By the way, this is not a 'Dear Grandma, thanks for the five bucks and the socks' letter, as you can see by my letter to Mr. Kaplan."

That night, students composed letters of appreciation. Most enjoyed the letter writing exercise—and why not? They chose both audience and topic.

The next day, if I saw at a glance that a student had submitted a woefully brief letter, I initiated a dialogue.

"So Chad, do you really like your grandmother?" I inquired graciously.

"Yes, I do, a lot," Chad said nervously. He knew something was up, but he wasn't sure what.

"I *guess* you really do, since you picked her for your LAA. But is she really one of the most important people in your life? Because your letter doesn't suggest that, since she rated only three sentences. Tell me about her. Does she cook?"

"Yes," he answered softly.

"What does she cook? What's your favorite?"

"Rice pudding."

"What does she season it with? Cinnamon? Great! Did you mention that in your letter? No? Well, make a note of it in the margin. Good. Now, what else can you tell me about her?" In short order we learned that Chad's grandmother liked to sew, enjoyed watching pro wrestling on TV, and took Chad to New York City twice a year. Our reluctant writer, now armed with a slew of relevant details, was able to rewrite his Letter of Appreciation and Acknowledgment and have it pass muster.

The kids surely knew why the individual they selected was important in their life, and they were able to supply numerous details. Consequently, each letter earned an A, or it was considered incomplete. I reminded students that I did not select their audiences—they did, and they knew why, and they needed to celebrate the reasons in their letters. A brief conversation would elicit a host of missing information that enabled the student to transform an unacceptable note scribbled during the bus ride to school into a tear-inducing, three-hankie masterpiece.

Most letters, though, were wonderful at first writing. I know this because I watched students present them to their best friends, and the friends started laughing and crying and smiling, fully appreciating their tributes. I heard parents raving about the letters they received. Teachers showed me letters thanking them for an illuminating lesson on fractions or the opportunity to be in the school play.

Students wrote at length when composing Letters of Appreciation and Acknowledgment because they got to pick *who*, and they got to pick *why*. The assignment became personal, and very real, for them.

Amy wrote her Letter of Appreciation and Acknowledgment to her mother. They had been squabbling, as teenage girls and their mothers sometimes do. Amy showed me a four-page handwritten letter that eventually brought tears to her mother's eyes. In the letter Amy apologized for the fights she had thoughtlessly initiated.

A month later, when we did the "Lessons Learned" activity (see Chapter 12), Amy shared with her classmates the story behind her Letter of Appreciation and Acknowledgment:

> I remember when you told us about a girl who got in a fight with her mom, and then her mom died in a car accident that night. They never resolved their fight, and the girl's last memory of her mom was fighting with her. She never got to tell her mom how much she loved her.
>
> That made me think of all those times when my mom and I got in a fight. Some of them were in the car driving to school, and all those times my mom could have gone into a collision after dropping me off, but I'm so relieved it hasn't happened, and I hope it never will happen. But that's not all. My mom could have had a heart attack or I could have fallen down the steps and become brain dead.
>
> When I think of it I realize I'm the one starting most of the fights. Sometimes I just can't control my temper. Now, I try not to get in fights, but if I do I'm usually the one apologizing, and I constantly remind my family how much I love them.
>
> It's changed my life, and now I feel closer to my family. Thank you.
> —Amy Tanaka, age 13

Nine years later, I asked Amy to reflect on the letter she wrote as an eighth grader to her mom and the message it contained. She recalled:

> Throughout our middle school years, I think almost every eighth grader spent their time enveloped in conversations and worries over friends and crushes. For the first time, we had events like Teen Rec and dances to socialize with the other sex. In short, the effects of puberty and popularity were at the height of our lives. How could we think of anything else?
>
> Because of this constrictive perspective at that time, I distinctly remember the impact of the Letters of Appreciation and Acknowledgment assignment. Being so absorbed in my every day life, I easily forgot to thank and appreciate all the people who were supportive, especially my mother. I recall how difficult and rewarding it was to write that letter. Thanking my mother out loud would have been too difficult to do, so allowing me to write my feelings and thoughts down on paper was much easier to face.
>
> Working on the LAA assignment made me truly understand the concepts and effects of "appreciation" and "acknowledgment." Ever since then, these two concepts are at the forefront of my life, allowing me to appreciate and include my family, friends, teachers and everyone who has had an influence in my life.

All the Good Things

An activity that we did on Valentine's Day was not exactly a letter, but it advanced the cause. My teaching partner got the idea from a *Reader's Digest* article entitled "All the Good Things." We gave each student a list of all forty-seven students on the team with a blank line next to each name. We asked them to write one affirmative sentence about each of their peers. After twenty-five minutes, my partner and I collected the forms and moved on to another activity.

That day after school we read through the completed sheets, selected twenty-five descriptive comments per student, did some minor editing, and typed them up. The introduction to the booklet noted:

> The reader will discover a host of observations by members of Team 8-1 about members of Team 8-1. When one reads them, one gets a clearer understanding of how we on Team 8-1 see each other, how we appreciate one another, and how we communicate with and about each other.

We deliberately did not identify which classmate wrote which comment, so that when a student read a line describing herself, she could only speculate as to who had written it. As students read through the booklet, they gained insights into fellow team members and simultaneously discovered the positive ways in which they themselves were perceived by their peers. A twenty-five-minute, in-class writing activity strengthened the bonds of this community of writers.

Assertions Addressed

The Letter of Appreciation and Acknowledgment addressed all but one of the assertions (we did not read them aloud). During the year, students wrote letters almost weekly, which forced them to continually think about audience, purpose, and topic; the letter writing added to the volume that leads to fluency in writing. In addition, the letters were a form of publication, since they went to real audiences.

Closing Thoughts

If your goal is writing for real, consider the following: the Letter of Appreciation and Acknowledgment doesn't cost any money; students affirm actual people in their lives; you don't have to read any of the letters or spend time evaluating them (everyone gets an A); letters are not accepted until

they are substantive; two of the key Distinctions of the year—acknowledgment and appreciation—are reinforced; and many of the assertions about
writing are addressed.

Not every writing assignment should be awarded an automatic A, of
course, but in this case it is appropriate; the letter is a personal communication not intended for a wider audience. The A encourages volume. I felt that
if I could get student hands moving across the page, regardless of what they
were writing, it was a worthwhile activity.

10

Anticipating
the Unexpected

I t's snowing," a voice whispered. Heads turned toward the windows; white flakes were floating against the gray-black trees edging a nearby field.

"Quick, everyone to the windows!" I instructed. As the kids moved from their seats, I put a cassette tape in the sound system. Robert Frost's gravelly voice filled the hushed classroom:

> Whose woods these are I think I know.
> His house is in the village though;
> He will not see me stopping here
> To watch his woods fill up with snow.

In less than a minute, Frost intoned his elegant, mysterious fourth verse ("The woods are lovely, dark and deep . . ."), my students experienced a poetic moment, and we resumed the task we were engaged in before snowflakes beckoned.

Too often, teachers resist what is happening with their students, creating dissonance in the classroom. But where I taught on Long Island, it snowed every year, and I was ready.

A teacher can count on several unanticipated events during the school year. Each provides an opportunity for students to explore ideas and events through writing. The daily newspaper gives you every lesson you need; you just don't know the curriculum in advance. But when disaster strikes, or victory occurs—in the school, or the community, or the nation, or the world—it may be time to set aside the lesson plan of the day and focus on the compelling event. Put another way, should it be business as usual when the unanticipated happens?

In-Class Writing

On regular occasions during the year, I invited students to open their journals and begin writing. My three purposes in doing so were:

- to assess each student's ability to compose on the spot and obtain a benchmark against which later writing could be measured;
- to give students practice with instant composition, a skill they needed for state tests and examinations;
- to learn more about my students from their responses.

Often I supplied a series of prompts. One in-class assignment, given in November just prior to parent conferences, read as follows:

Consider the following "events" of the fall:
    The United States timeline, PEEC (the field trip to the Poconos), journal entries, the Distinctions, the Cold War, free-verse poems, interior monologues,

personal essays, letters to authors, Thursday reading period, drafting and revising, our student teachers, school visitors, team publications (three anthologies and the school newspaper), computers, Open House, advisory, fall sports, music, arts, foreign language, science, gym, lunch, Team 8-I.

In your journal, respond to the following questions:

- What observations and reflections do you have on the first ten weeks of school?
- What learning experiences have proven most worthwhile for you?
- What comments and coaching do you have for me? for the student teachers?
- What other comments do you have?

For an assignment such as this I allowed students twenty to twenty-five minutes of writing time, then collected their journals, read and commented in them that evening, and returned them the next day.

On this particular assignment, I included the homework on the same sheet:

For Friday, November 10, write a letter to your parents about your growth as a learner this fall. Include specific references.

I wanted students to consider the learning they had done during the first quarter as well as build on the thinking and journal writing they had done in class that day. The in-class assignment "primed the pump"; the letters they composed that evening were, as a result, more detailed and thoughtful than if the students had not been prompted in class to write about their year so far.

Dealing with Death

A reality in teaching is that you can count on coping with tragedy on a regular, albeit unexpected, basis. Students die. Their parents, siblings, or relatives die. Teachers die. We know this will happen; we just don't know when. The death of a teacher or a student can shake a school to its roots. On occasion we have advance warning. A colleague develops cancer; students and staff endure several painful months watching a friend waste away. That happened in 1991.

Cliff Lennon was my teaching partner, the math/science teacher on Team 8-I for four magical years. He initiated a beginning-of-the-year field trip to the Pocono Environmental Education Center (PEEC); he organized a whitewater rafting trip and took kids to Maine. He coached varsity basketball, chaperoned the Madrid exchange for Spanish students, and started the lacrosse program at the middle school. He was loved by his students, their parents, his players, and his colleagues.

The year we began teaching together, Cliff and I developed the Distinctions as a philosophy for the team. Our second year, Cliff suggested transforming the individual magazine project (see Chapter 18) into a four-subject interdisciplinary project. He came to me one day and said, "Ross, we have a problem. The kids have stopped doing their science and math homework. They're too busy writing their magazines."

"I'm sorry about that, Cliff," I responded, "but I can't ask them to stop doing something they're enjoying."

"No, I don't want them to stop—I want in! Can we make this assignment an inquiry into math and science as well?" Cliff saw an opportunity and wanted to seize it.

We did, the kids loved it even more, and for the next six years the Inquiry Project, as it came to be known, represented the best teaching I ever did in my thirty-five-year career.

In March 1991, Cliff was diagnosed with liver cancer. He died ten months later, in January 1992. Although we all knew it was coming, his students were devastated, as was I, by the tragedy of it; this wonderful human being was gone forever at age 49.

The morning after his death, as our students came into school, I met them at the door and told them the sad news. One student went immediately to the computer lab and typed a moving tribute to Cliff. In class that day, I invited students to write farewell letters to assuage their grief. Some letters were sent to Cliff's mother; others were buried on school grounds in a special time capsule filled with memorabilia related to Cliff's life.

The day after his funeral we held impromptu gatherings at the middle school for Cliff's former students on Team 8-I, now high school students: the freshman came at one o'clock, sophomores at two, and juniors at three. We shared poems and passages and invited the high school students to write letters about Cliff to include in the time capsule. In May we organized a memorial service. Over three hundred people—students, parents, teachers, administrators, and members of the board of education—honored Cliff's memory with their presence. Music groups performed, his former students served as ushers and escorts for Cliff's family, and a small group of students worked with me to organize the service in the high school auditorium.

Eighth grader Perri Chinalai, who was in Cliff's advisory that year, was the final speaker on the program. I remember thinking how difficult it must have been for this slender wisp of a girl to speak through her grief about her favorite teacher. She rose to the challenge:

> I knew Mr. Lennon as my teacher, my advisor, and I also knew him as a great friend. Mr. Lennon's name was usually found in the same sentence as friend. He was wonderful to all of us. He treated us with kindness, respect, but mostly trust, and as a result we treated him the same. He never gave up on us. Even if we were struggling because we were absent or having trouble, he would take his personal time to be with us and help us.

As I look through pictures of him and the letters that I received from him, each shows his great personality. He always had a smile but was able to help us with the most serious problems.

I don't think any of us will forget our individual relationships with Mr. Lennon, the nicknames he gave us, the money he lent us, and the after school activities that were spent together.

I love Mr. Lennon as many of us do, and I'll never forget him. He had such a tremendous impact on all of us, and he will live forever in my memory.

"To live in hearts left behind is not to die."
—Perri Chinalai, age 14

Roominations

One day in early December I silently handed each student an instruction sheet as they walked into the classroom. At the top in bold letters were five words: "Follow the Instructions!! No Talking!" Students took their seats and began reading the instructions, glancing occasionally at the plethora of posters adorning the walls, ceiling, and furniture:

Read the instructions below, then follow them. No questions. If you don't understand what to do, read the instructions again. And again.

Your Task: This is a test of your ability to read, write, and follow instructions. You are to create a piece of writing during this class period. Use the entire period—don't rush, but be finished by the time class ends. Base your writing on a picture or poster visible in this room.

Instructions:
1. Sit somewhere comfortable. Do not communicate with others. Do not ask questions. Extra paper is available on the round table if you need it.
2. If you write me a question, I may write a response. Basically, everything you need to know about this assignment is on this sheet.
3. Pick a poster or picture in this room. Then do the following:
   - Think about what that poster or picture communicates and what you want to say about it in your piece of writing. React to it.
   - Plan, or pre-write, or rehearse your piece of writing. Make a list of ideas you may include in your reaction to the poster/picture.
   - Write a first draft. Use any mode (form) that you like—poem, narrative, letter, essay, journal entry, whatever. Be creative.
   - Revise your first draft, and then create draft 2. Make your reaction as good as you possibly can make it. Do your best!
   - Edit your draft—check for spelling, punctuation, etc.
   - Write your final draft neatly. Put your name and today's date on top for the heading.
   - Staple your final draft on top of all other sheets of paper that you used.

- Hand in your paper. If you finish early, sit quietly at your seat and read your book.
4. You will be graded on: (a) how well you follow the instructions; (b) the quality and correctness of your writing; (c) how well you explain/react to/comment on the poster or picture you select.

What I liked about "Roominations," as I called this exercise, was that there was no way the student could prepare for it, at least the first time I used it. Although students had been studying the posters since day one, they did not know that this in-class writing activity was on the agenda. It was truly a surprise to them; they had to make quick decisions and get started on their writing.

I also liked the fact that if they wrote me a question seeking guidance (more "volume" on their part), I said only that I "may" respond. My intention was to force my students to be as self-reliant as possible. There are instances in life when one has to make a series of decisions solo; Roominations was such a time. Naturally, this experience provoked anxiety in some students, but they muddled through. In most cases, the novelty of the activity captured their attention; a student could write about a poster that sparked his or her interest using any mode of expression; there were no limits other than time. Because I never did this activity earlier than November, students had already explored a variety of modes and could draw on experience to select the most appropriate form.

My classroom contained more than a thousand visual images, quotations, and other messages, giving students ample material from which to select a starting point for their writing. The classroom became a teaching tool; posters that had been part of the background suddenly moved forward into student consciousness.

A month later, during our "Lessons Learned" activity (see Chapter 12), Sami Southard recalled her experience with Roominations:

> A final lesson came from the assignment where we had to choose a poster in Mr. Burkhardt's room and write about it. Contemplating Martin Niemoller's strong words ("They came for the communists—I did not protest—I was not a communist . . . Then they came for me and there was no one left to protest.") assisted me in finding what my meaning of life is. The statement echoed the Golden Rule, and I believe that it was the perfect way to state it. And, as I read it over and over again, I realized just what freedom was.
> —Sami Southard, age 13

Josh Silverstein vividly recalled the poster-filled classroom eighteen years years later:

> I loved that room. I loved the myriad, blizzarding onslaught of quotations and imagery, like being in a giant evolving brain . . . "Life is unfair," "There is no try, there is only do," "There's a little of me in all of youse (Archie Bunker)," "Keep

on truckin'" . . . It was a room that felt connected to the outside world and made you feel the potential of your life, inspired you, challenged you to participate, connect, and try to understand what WE all were doing here, in that school, in America, in the world . . . what does it mean to be thirteen? . . . and why?

As a writing activity, Roominations stood in marked contrast to the many other occasions where students had opportunities to draft, revise, consider, reflect, edit, draft and revise some more, and labor leisurely over a piece of writing. This exercise was a "done deal" in less than forty minutes, a useful measure of each student's ability to compose on the spot.

Often, students being tested are asked to respond in writing to this type of prompt. Such test situations call for students to make quick decisions, write against the clock, and create coherent text. Roominations, though not intended only as test preparation, provides students with a similar experience.

As a follow-up, if you use this strategy two or three times, you can ask your students to select their best Roomination for yet another class anthology.

The Petition and Peer Pressure

One year, an ugly incident in early December led to considerable journal writing. Jack (all the students' names have been changed in this section) began circulating a petition on a Wednesday morning. The petition denigrated Sharon, another classmate. Essentially it said, "I don't like Sharon and refuse to be her friend." Jack spent the morning inviting team members to sign; many did.

When she learned about the petition just before lunch, Sharon went to the nurse's office in tears. Jack, realizing what he had done, immediately destroyed the petition. That afternoon, my teaching partner and I set aside our social studies and science lessons and called a team meeting.

Periodically during the heated discussion that followed, during which we asked why so many nice kids had ganged up on one of their teammates, students wrote in their journals as a way of thinking through their responsibility regarding what had happened.

That evening as homework we asked students to consider all that had been said in class, and their role, if any, in the incident; they were then to write about it. In journals, students struggled with the immediate issues of fairness and friendship. Here are several unvarnished excepts (Burkhardt 1988, pp. 11–15):

> I have quite strong reactions to this discussion. I did sign the petition. In fact I was the third one to sign it & am willing to take responsibility for it. I spoke to

Sharon last night and I didn't apologize. To be honest, I thought you [teachers] took it a bit too far.

And I didn't sign it because of peer pressure. I signed it for a reason. A while back I told Sharon something. And what did she do? She let it out! I couldn't belive it. I got in trouble and she didn't apologize. This happened on several other occasions & that's why I signed the petition. And anyway, if she wanted the people who signed to be her friends, she should have given us the respect and appreciation & treated us like friends.

—Sally

I was anxious to discuss this subject. I was so disgusted, so disappointed in most of my classmates that I was about to burst. I felt a need to air my feelings, to *show* my classmates this anger. I wanted them to know the sheer anguish that they were putting Sharon through. That's why I'm glad that our team had this discussion. I truly believe that each and every one of my classmates wanted and needed to share their viewpoints on this.

This whole thing has really been bothering me—perhaps more than it should. I lay awake last night, feeling Sharon's anguish and pain rip my heart apart. Didn't these people realize what they were doing? . . .

I am not only ashamed of those who put their signatore on that list, though I am ashamed of myself. I wasn't there when that "petition" circulated the classroom, and I am afraid that I would have signed it if I had been there. I am afraid that I would have bowed down to peer pressure—that I would have been swept along.

—Lynn

Today in the discussion, I felt guilty because I signed the petition. Later in the day I appalogized to her and spent lunch with her in the nurse's office. The person I was most mad at, (besides myself) was Jack. How could he do this to her? To anyone? I later told him my feelings . . . It just reminds me how nasty Yvonne, Sally, Jessica and Meryl can be. I am still friends with them, but I don't trust them. Yvonne, Sally, Jessica and Meryl, (and the rest of them) are the meanest girls I know. You can never tell when they are going to turn on you. What happened with Sharon was she thought that Yvonne, Meryl, Sally and Jessica looked nice. She got suckered into being friends with them. They told her things about Crystal, which made Sharon hate her. Then, they got Jack to start the petition. Jack did it because it drew attention to him. No one knew it was going to go this far, except maybe Sally, Jessica, Yvonne and Meryl. I think of "Yvonne's friends" as people who talk about each other all the time and who use people to get whatever they want. Sharon is a snob, though. She may have deserved a good talk, but no one deserves a petition. Sally, Jessica, Meryl and Yvonne don't believe they should forgive her. At night they call Sharon up and tell her off on the phone.

—Amy

I do admit that I signed the petition about Sharon. When someone asked me to sign the petition my first reaction was to sign it. I didn't even know what it was about. I admit I was very wrong but even when I knew what the petition was about I signed it. The thing that makes it wrong for me is that I have nothing against Sharon. I like Sharon. I guess I really didn't think about what Sharon would feel like. After I signed it and before Sharon saw it, I began to feel real guilty about signing it. I knew I was wrong. I think that everyone is to blame. Its not fair for just one person to take the blame. The fact is I am sorry and I know I made a mistake.

—Bill

These refreshingly honest, sometimes awkward, and always thoughtful reflections on the tangled social relationships that led to the petition incident underscore the ability of young adolescents struggling toward maturity to tell it like it is when asked to do so.

Two days later, after things had settled down, I used my weekly poem to reflect on the petition incident, move past it, and encourage students to do the same. Distance often provides clarity.

Questions of Growth

do we join the mob
and say hurtful words
gang up all on one
use signatures as swords

do we go along
emboldened by the crowd
and when we look back
do we feel sure and proud

do we ever take
another person's view
do we recall times
when we were victim too

when the questions come
and we cannot hide
will we do what's best
how will we decide

life provides the lessons
soon another turn
tomorrow and tomorrow
as we grow and learn

Assertions Addressed

When my students engaged in unexpected writing, they addressed several assertions:

- *Every student a writer:* Each student had ideas that he or she wanted to communicate about the topic because it was of such magnitude in their lives; the death of a teacher, a school fight or argument, or a national news event created a stir that needed to be addressed.
- *Ability level:* When I read my students' in-class writing, I learned about their ability as writers.
- *Topic selection:* The unanticipated, in-class writing exercises often involved choice, allowing students to write about topics of interest to them.
- *Writing process:* In the Roominations activity, students had to plan, draft, revise, edit, and finally "publish" their pieces.
- *Volume + Variety:* A student's ability to write was enhanced by being asked to do so spontaneously on regular occasions during the year.

Closing Thoughts

There are many ways to teach writing. One is through those unexpected events that you know will occur during the year, even if you don't know when. But if you plan for them, you can take advantage of real situations and help your students cope with and understand them better by writing about them. This is an appropriate strategy for, after all, "Young adolescents enjoy novelty and spontaneity. How often in our teaching do we provide such occasions? Effective teachers incorporate a variety of learning experiences into the classroom. Repetitive activities numb the soul and chill the spirit" (Burkhardt 1995–96).

11

The Holiday Memory Piece

The Holiday Memory Piece

Basic idea: Students write about a family tradition, memory, or celebration and share it with the class the day before a vacation.

Assertions addressed: 1, 2, 3, 5, 6, 7, 8, 9, and 10 (*see p. 17*).

Skills addressed: Sentence structure, paragraphing, sequencing ideas, listening, reading aloud, drafting, and revising.

Class time needed: Two periods: (1) introduce the activity and assign homework; (2) have students share their holiday memories.

Advance preparation: Prepare a model memory piece to read to the class.

Time of year: Just prior to a major school vacation.

Neat feature: Students are engaged in an academic activity on a day that is usually given to nonacademic pursuits.

Assessment: None needed; the public sharing and reaction from peers is sufficient.

Follow-up: Students may create a class anthology of traditions or memories.

Journal entry: None.

Caution: Do several "reading your writing aloud" activities with students prior to doing this one.

Forms: Here is a generic description of the assignment, which you may hand out to students.

For next Friday, prepare a Holiday Memory piece of writing that you will share in class. Earlier today you heard an example of a holiday memory—a family tradition. Consider all the holidays that your family celebrates. Select one activity, memory, or tradition, and celebrate it through a piece of writing intended to be shared with others. Practice reading your piece aloud before Friday's class. A prop may be useful when you share your Holiday Memory. Remember, accurate details create interesting writing.

Why do this? To celebrate writing; to enable students to know more about one another; to provide an academic activity on a day that might otherwise not be very productive.

Every year on Christmas Eve we go to a place called Quogue Wildlife Refuge. It is a home for sick and injured animals that might have been shot at by hunters or just hurt real bad somehow. We used to live in Hampton Bays which is right by Quogue, so when I was one my dad started taking me there, probably because my mom wanted us out of the house to wrap presents.

We've been doing it now every Christmas Eve, and my younger sisters love it. Our favorite animals there are the deer. We bring carrots and celery for them to eat, and my dad tells my younger sisters how maybe these reindeer will be on the roof tonight bringing presents.

It's sort of sad seeing the animals caged up. I think they should be out in the forest, but it is better for them here because the people who run Quogue Wildlife Refuge feed them more food than they'd get out on their own. And, besides they eventually set them free. This has been a tradition for 13 years now, and I hope we always do it.

—Holly Galla, age 13

It may be different at your school, but at mine, the last day before Christmas vacation was not an occasion for significant academic achievement. With visions of sugarplums dancing in their heads, many of the kids did not project a focused, studious demeanor. Teachers, succumbing to the inevitable, scheduled class parties and movies; by last period, the halls were filled with litter from the festivities, students were gliding along the walls, and a pervasive feeling—"If we can just make it to the bell, we'll be okay"—permeated the school.

So when the principal poked his head inside my classroom door halfway through last period, his jaw dropped. What he saw was a group of students, dressed in reds and greens, seated on the floor in a circle, listening politely as peers read aloud, and applauding when each student concluded.

"What's going on? Why is it so quiet?" he inquired. The din of a school nearing the edge of chaos could be heard from the hallway behind him.

"Oh, we're sharing family traditions," I informed him.

Christmas Eve Exchange

The Holiday Memory Piece had its genesis in a story I wrote while in the Peace Corps. I knew that my family would be gathered at the Buccaneer Lodge in the Florida Keys on Christmas Eve 1962, so I typed a tale of how we used to celebrate when we were kids. I sent it to the owner of the Buccaneer Lodge and asked him to read it to my family that evening. He did. Later, I learned from my sisters that Mom burst into tears and headed straight for the ladies' room fifteen seconds into the story.

Five days before vacation, I began class by asking my students to settle back and relax.

"I'm going to read you a true story," I said. "This actually happened to me. When I'm done, I'll have some questions for you, so listen carefully."

I didn't actually have any questions for them, but saying so seemed to be a good way to get them to focus. With that modest introduction, I began reading:

Christmas Eve Exchange

Somehow, Dad always seemed to get me when our family exchanged names for Christmas Eve. My twin brother Robert and I celebrated our birthday on December 9. And when my older sister Robin brought home the idea of "Secret Santa" from her third-grade class, we began a Burkhardt family tradition of exchanging names for Christmas Eve gifts on Robert's and my birthday.

The "exchanging names" present was supposed to be a small token, a simple gift serving as a prelude to the following day when the tide of presents reached flood stage. We agreed on $1 as the spending limit, and each of us attempted to choose something both special and appropriate for the person whose name we drew. . . .

As Christmas Eve approached, my father began his annual lottery litany—"I wonder whose name I drew? Where is that slip of paper? Mom, have you seen it?" Each of the four of us shuddered when Dad said that, because we feared we were this year's holiday victim. Although his eventual "exchanging names" present was indeed wonderful, its recipient went through a special kind of hell to earn it. . . .

Traditionally Dad sat at the head of the table, Mom at the other end closest to the kitchen. I sat to Mom's left, next to Robert. Robin sat opposite Robert, and Valerie was across from me. Since presents covered our plates, we had to open them before we could eat. Dad went first, making a very big deal over a box of two-inch nails, an "exchanging names" gift from Valerie. Mom said she really liked the large economy size box of Morton's "When It Rains, It Pours" iodized salt that I carefully selected just for her. Robin got a horse calendar from Robert, who then opened his gift from her: a rolled tube in red wrapping. Robert's howls of laughter at finding Alfred E. Newman staring goofily from the cover did not improve my mood.

"I don't have a present yet," I observed calmly. Dad slapped his forehead—a gesture not unfamiliar to any of us on Christmas Eve—and declared, "Oh, gee, I must have your name! Mom, do you think Wright's Drug Store is still open?"

"Bob, don't you have anything for him?" Mom asked hopefully.

"Wait a minute," Dad replied, and quickly left the table. He returned with a paper sack twisted shut and secured by a rubber band. The bag rattled as he placed it before me. "There! Boy, am I glad I was able to find that. You'll just love it, son."

I eyed the bag, removed the rubber band, and peered inside. The rattling was caused by eight peanuts.

"Let's eat," said Dad, passing the potatoes.

After grace, I said, "This isn't fair. Everyone else got nice presents. Where's mine?"

"Okay," Dad answered. "Go look under Mom's pillow."

Quick race through the hall, doorway, bed, pillow . . . a red box!

"What's in it? Open it!" siblings clamored as I returned to the table, smiling. And then, lifting the lid, under layers of white tissue paper, I found an even whiter pair of my mom's underwear. Laughter from the others. Red cheeks on my face.

"How'd that get in there?" asked Dad. "And who wants more gravy?"

I pushed at the mashed potatoes on my plate, ignoring the cheery conversation around the table. Dad noticed my sullen silence.

"Try the top shelf of the medicine cabinet in the upstairs bath—," but I was already through the dining room door across the den up the stairs down the hall into the bathroom open the mirror, and there it was, a small box wrapped in shiny blue paper with a green bow on top. *This is it! This is the one! I wonder what it is!*

I proudly carried my "exchanging names" present to the dining table, lording it over my brother and sisters, knowing that while Dad had his fun, he always produced the best gift of the evening. I carefully untied the ribbon, neatly unwrapped the blue paper, slowly removed the lid, and cautiously lifted the small blanket of white cotton to find . . . a used cork.

Tears welled up in my eyes.

"Bob, don't you think you've gone far enough? Stop torturing the poor boy. Give him his present."

"Okay, dear. Ross, this is it, I promise. Look in the desk drawer. No tricks this time," Dad vowed.

Reassured, I galloped to the living room again, pulled open the top drawer and seized an envelope with my name on it. Ripping it open, I found a note that said, "GO TO THE BACK DOOR." Racing back through the dining room and kitchen to the rear of the house, I spied a note scotch-taped to the back door handle: "LOOK IN ROBIN'S BOOTS." I sprinted to the hall closet, grabbed my sister's black winter galoshes, turned them upside down and shook furiously. Another white note floated out. "LOOK UNDER YOUR PLATE." *This has got to be it. It's been there all along. Why didn't I look there first? But what's small enough to be under my plate and still be something good?* I flew back to the dining room, spilling cold mashed potatoes as I lifted my plate. Another note, "LOOK IN THE HAMPER." *Rats.* Into the kitchen, onto the back porch and there, finally, in the wicker hamper on top of a week's worth of dirty laundry, sat a plain cardboard box. My "exchanging names" present, at last.

Time is the great healer, but also the great eraser. The pain of being Dad's Christmas Eve victim has disappeared. I realized later how deeply he loved me to play with me in that way. Mom also confessed that some Christmases she traded my name to Dad if after several tries he didn't draw me.

I don't remember any of the presents he gave me, although at the time they were just what a young boy wanted and, more importantly, the envy of my brother and sisters. What I do recall is racing madly through our Roselawn Road home on Christmas Eve, upstairs and downstairs, year after year, thinking, *This is it! This has to be it!* And even though it wasn't most of the time, the joy and excitement of the search stays with me.

"Oh, Mr. Burkhardt, that was so beautiful," said Holly, sniffling. She and a few other girls were visibly moved.

"Thanks, Holly. I'm glad you enjoyed it," I said. "Now," I continued, turning to the class, "that's what happened at my house on Christmas Eve, my holiday memory. What are yours? In five days you begin a two-week vacation. For this Friday's class, I want you to share a family memory. Before we go away for the holiday, we're going to have a celebration of writing at which we share our traditions. As you know, Christmas Eve and Hanukkah will soon be here. Kwanzaa and New Year's Eve are next. Martin Luther King's birthday is celebrated in mid-January, and Groundhog Day falls on February 2. Don't forget Valentine's Day and St. Patrick's Day. Then we have Easter, Ramadan, Mother's Day, Memorial Day, and Father's Day. There's also the Fourth of July, Labor Day, Halloween, Thanksgiving, and some others I probably forgot to mention. Oh, yes, each of you has a birthday every year, as do your brothers and sisters and parents. Your parents may also celebrate wedding anniversaries. So the question is, what does your family do on a holiday? What are your traditions, and how do you celebrate?"

"What do you actually want us to do, Mr. B.?" asked Dani, slightly overwhelmed by the list of possible holidays.

"Well, Dani, I just shared one of my family traditions, the story of how we exchanged names for a Christmas Eve present. I'd like you to share one of your family holiday memories with the class. We are going to celebrate writing this Friday. You are invited to wear holiday dress, if you so choose. The piece of writing you create will be a public piece that you will share with the rest of the class. You might want to practice reading it aloud once you've written it. Any questions?"

Usually there were none. The students understood the assignment, both from the model provided and the simple instructions. I allowed them a few minutes to jot down tentative ideas in their English journals, and we turned to a different activity for the reminder of the class.

Students spent the next few days preparing short pieces to share at the "Holiday Memory" celebration. In the ten-year history of this assignment, no student ever asked his or her grade. Why not? Probably because they thought that sharing writing with an important audience—their friends—was more significant than any grade.

How do you grade such writing, anyway? The finished product was beyond grading, because it was writing for a public event. The affirmation from classmates and the joy of sharing one's self with friends was sufficient reward.

Sharing Family Traditions

On the appointed day, students gathered excitedly in my classroom. They were relaxed; the mood was jovial. They knew that this was their last academic task before the vacation; in fact, they did not really see it as an academic task.

I read first, sharing a poem I wrote especially for the occasion. Entitled "'Twas Four Days Before Christmas," with apologies to Clement C. Moore, it managed to mention every student's name, as well as teachers, subjects, and other touchstones of the year. By the time I was finished reading, the students had settled comfortably next to their friends, and we were ready to begin celebrating traditions.

I asked for volunteers. Zach, ever dependable, raised his hand.

Christmas Tradition

Every year my whole family would drive down to Florida before Christmas. My brother and I would get to the back of our van before everybody else to be able to lie down, but Mom would always make me sit up where the cooler was because my legs were the shortest. My brother would start laughing at me because I had to sit there. My dad would start off driving. After a while he would start dozing at the wheel and my mom would scare the living daylights out of him by screaming and we would all wake up.

Spencer and I would always open up the back windows while we were lying down; it would be really fun and cold. Soon we would get really bored and I would start asking, "How much longer do we have?", "When are we going to get there?", and "I have to go to the bathroom." So we would pull over and have a rest.

When we finally got to the Florida border, we would stop at the Welcome Center. My brother and I would play frisbee and have fresh squeezed O.J. But we still had several hours left to get to Sanibel Island and those were the most frustrating hours since we had already been in the car for nearly 30 hours. Sometimes we got to our condo in the middle of the night and sometimes in the afternoon.

On Christmas Eve we would always go to the candlelight service on the beach near the Sanibel Lighthouse. It is a beautiful service with everyone singing Christmas carols on the beach. The service would end with everyone holding a lighted candle and singing "Silent Night." Afterward we often would ride our bikes back to the condo along the bike paths and look at the many beautiful lights. We would get to open one present Christmas Eve and it would be pajamas.

In the morning I would wake up at 6:00 but we didn't open the presents until 8:00. The kids would line up in height order to go into the living room so I was always first. One person would be the 'Santa' to hand out the presents and stockings. The stockings always came first and soon the room was filled with wrapping paper.

For dinner we usually had turkey and potatoes and always dessert. If it was a warm day we would go for a swim in the afternoon.

—Zach Poole, age 13

Applause filled the room as Zach finished.

Danielle described the time when she was six years old and walked into her parents' bedroom on Christmas Eve, just in time to catch her Uncle Bill donning a red suit and white beard. Her innocent confusion drew warm smiles.

Chester shared his family's New Year's Eve tradition:

Pots N' Pans

When I was six, my family started a tradition. On New Year's Eve, we would stay up until the ball fell at midnight sharp, signifying the New year, then we would grab a bunch of pots and pans and line up on the stoop and clash them together and yell "Happy New year" at the top of our lungs, in our pajamas, on a cold winter's night.

This activity usually started another tradition, that of visiting our friendly druggist to replenish our supply of head cold medication.
—Chester Guala, age 13

Dani, who was Jewish, offered a different holiday memory.

A Kutsher's Moment

Once a year around the fall season my family takes a four hour trip up to Kutsher's in the Catskill Mountains. Kutsher's is a family oriented hotel type place where many family's go to be together. When we go we allways meet the rest of my family up there. Almost all my aunts, uncles, cousins go and grandparents on my mother's side.

It's a beautiful place surrounded by gorgeous scenery. There is a lake outside and many trees. The rooms inside are also very lovely. The walls are wallpapered with nice scenes of trees and it's carpeted. It has two full size beds, a foldout couch, table, desk, and dresser. There is also a bathroom with a large mirror and plenty of supplies. Attached to the bathroom is a walkin closit with a mini refriderator!

Up there there are plenty of things to do. They have an indoor swimming pool, a workout gym, a swedish massage area with a steamroom and wirlpools. Also there are places to play tennis, volleyball, racket ball, and go ice skating. In the dinning room they serve breakfast, lunch and dinner with almost anything you want. At night they usually have a show with singers, dancers, and comedians, too. One night they have something called "a night at the races" where you can bet money on what horse wins in a real race (on filmstrip).

This is a great place to go with your family and friends to spend an exiting weekend with the people you love most!
—Dani Marx, age 13

Not every memory was sunshine and happiness. Natascha wistfully shared a poignant family tradition that ended because of the death of her mother's friend. D.J. related the story of his parents announcing their divorce on New Year's Eve. Jen, a Jehovah's Witness, informed her peers that her family did not celebrate holidays.

A caution: Make sure that the sharing of these holiday traditions is not the first time your students read aloud to one another. We had done similar activities on a regular basis since school began, so students did not feel as threatened as they might have had I not worked to make the classroom safe for reading aloud.

Of course, I learned this the hard way. At the very first holiday memory celebration, a student laughed inappropriately at another classmate who was reading aloud. The reader became embarrassed and upset and could not continue. I immediately took the disrespectful student out of the room and had him sit in the office for the rest of the period, as he had violated the safe space of the writing classroom. This incident taught me the importance of making the room safe for reading by making my expectations for behavior very clear.

Other ideas for sharing memories include "My Favorite Grade School Memory," "My Best Vacation Ever," "My Best Birthday Blast," and "My Favorite Family Story." The idea is to have students write about something important to them, then share with the class.

Teaching Tolerance

On the surface, the Holiday Memory Piece appears to be simply about celebrating traditions, yet underneath are lessons of tolerance and acceptance. As students shared holiday memories and traditions, they saw their peers more completely as a result of listening to Jake explain how his family chopped down their own Christmas tree, or Joanna describe how she opened her presents during Hanukkah.

What happens in the kids' minds as they learn more about their classmates? What impressions of the reader do they gain, informed by the writing? Anonymity breeds disrespect; when kids share their traditions, they become known to their peers, and respect for one another increases.

If we wish to teach tolerance, there is no better way to do it than to minimize anonymity. If a student feels known in school, he or she is less likely to act out. One wonders: in the spate of school shootings during the 1990s, did those students feel invited and welcomed and respected?

Holly Johnson and Lauren Freedman (2001) have noted the social nature of young adolescents, their need for community, and the benefits they derive from sharing themselves with one another:

Because young adolescents—as human beings—are social by nature, they actually benefit from being members of a community. By talking and listening to each other, students learn to connect with others. Their interests, ideas, and preferences become part of the learning, and they develop support for each other around those interests and ideas. Through their interactions, students come to realize how their similarities and differences create a rich diversity in their lives and classrooms. (p. 36)

The writing strategies that we employ in our classrooms can and should address not only the intellectual but also the social needs of our students.

Assertions Addressed

One of the most appealing aspects of the Holiday Memory Piece is that it can be done at any time of the year. But whenever you do it, your students will address a number of the assertions about writing:

- *Publication:* This activity promotes oral tradition.
- *Audience, purpose, and topic:* Students knew they were going to read to peers and shaped their tales accordingly.
- *Reading aloud:* As they read their holiday memory pieces, some students changed their text on the spot, realizing that they could say it more eloquently.
- *The teacher as writer:* From my "Christmas Eve Exchange" to the parody of "'Twas the Night before Christmas," the teacher as writer went first.
- *Topic selection:* Every student chose his or her own tradition to honor and share via writing.

Closing Thoughts

Fourteen years after she composed it, I contacted Holly Galla, seeking permission to use her holiday memory at the beginning of this chapter. She reminded me once again of the ability of a particular piece of writing to remain vivid years later. Holly, now a sales representative for a computer company, had come full circle as she recalled a family tradition:

> OK, so now you are making me feel all nostalgic and teary!! I completely remember writing about the Quogue Wildlife Refuge . . . and you know, it seems so appropriate that this is resurfacing in my life right now. This past Christmas was literally the FIRST Christmas that my Dad nixed the idea and I couldn't bear the thought of not going, so I made my husband come with me and we walked around and fed the deer. It was so special and almost like a "new" tradition that my husband and I will continue to do every Christmas. My Dad was so happy when I told him we went b/c he was beginning to feel like my sisters and I had outgrown it.

12

Lessons Learned

Lessons Learned

Basic idea:	Students celebrate learning and share lessons they have learned with their peers.
Assertions addressed:	2, 3, 7, 9, and 10 (*see p. 17*).
Skills addressed:	Reflection, public speaking, listening, writing for publication.
Class time needed:	Ten minutes of introduction, then a double period four days later.
Advance Preparation:	The Lessons Learned assignment sheet.
Time of year:	January and June.
Neat feature:	As one student shares, others realize how much they have learned—affirmation!
Assessment:	No grade need be given. Self-assessment occurs in reflection, preparation, presentation, and discussion of the various lessons learned.
Follow-up:	Type and post all Lessons Learned in the hall outside class. Create a Lessons Learned anthology. Share the anthology with parents; discuss parent reactions.
Journal entry:	"What I Learned from 'Lessons Learned'" a. What did you realize about your own learning? b. What did you realize about other students and their learning? c. What do you wish you had shared at the Lessons Learned meeting? d. What else do you have to say?
Caution:	Do not do this activity if you have a thin skin—your students might not tell you what you want to hear, and tell you what you do not want to hear.
Forms:	"Lessons Learned: An Opportunity to Reflect" assignment sheet (Figure 12.1).
Why do this?	This activity is a reality check for teachers. You discover if the important lessons you are striving to teach are actually getting through to your students. This activity also reinforces the concept of a community of learners.

The one important thing I learned from Mr. Burkhardt is to never underestimate the power of writing. Things are always there that you don't see. [Writing] also gives you new perspectives on different things in life. And each piece of writing always has a lesson and a story about life to tell.

—Lee Jarit, age 13

One of the things I learned in English and Social Studies is a better system for writing. The drafting and revising helped me a whole lot because I knew what I could do to make that particular piece of writing better. It also helped me improve my typing skills. The silent reading did more for me than I expected it would. It gave me a chance to read, which I don't do much of. Reading expands your vocabulary and nourishes the mind.

—Matt Dougherty, age 14

Do you remember the social studies lesson I taught last fall about barbed wire shutting down the western frontier in 1873?" I asked the class one day in early January. Some nods, some murmurs, some blank stares.

"I thought so," I continued. "Well, my real question is, what important lessons have you actually learned so far this year? Ten, twenty years from now, what are you going to remember about what you learned in this class?"

Following that introduction, I distributed an assignment sheet titled "Lessons Learned: An Opportunity to Reflect" (Figure 12.1).

"For Thursday," I said, "your homework is to determine three important lessons that you have learned so far this year as a result of being a student on Team 8-I. You will be expected to share two of your lessons at a team meeting. We plan to publish your lessons in another class anthology. Any questions?"

"Mr. B., can these be any kinds of lessons?" asked Mark.

"No, they can't," I replied. "It's quite possible you learned something important when you were on the soccer team this fall, Mark, and that's great. But what we are talking about here," I explained, "are lessons you learned because you are on Team 8-I. One of your lessons should come from English and social studies. Another should come from math and science. The third lesson can be anything that you learned as a member of the team since September. Is that helpful, Mark?"

"Thanks, Mr. B."

When my teaching partner and I initially created the Lessons Learned activity, we were somewhat nervous. *What would they say?* we wondered. *How would they respond?*

Student Learning

As students entered class on Thursday, I stood at the door checking to see that each had three lessons written out. One student didn't; I asked him to

Figure 12.1 Lessons Learned: An Opportunity to Reflect

This assignment is due at the afternoon team meeting on Thursday, January 11.

The beginning of a new year presents an opportunity to look back and to look ahead. We invite you to reflect on the past four months of our "simultaneously shared journey." Much has happened since September when we first introduced the Distinctions. Even more lies ahead during the next six months.

What important lessons have you learned so far this year?

Select three (3) significant lessons and describe each in a paragraph (total = 3 paragraphs). One lesson should come from English/social studies. A second lesson should come from math/science. The third lesson can come from any experience you have had as a member of Team 8-I.

Explain *why* each lesson is meaningful to you. *Type and double-space this assignment,* and be prepared to share your "lessons" in class on Thursday, January 11, at the afternoon team meeting.

This assignment addresses the Distinctions of *Communication, Responsibility, Acknowledgment, Contribution,* and *Commitment.*

---

sit in the hall and complete the assignment before entering; he did. Meanwhile, the other forty-six members of the team filled my classroom, some seated in chairs, others on the window ledge, still others on the floor. I sat on one side of the circle; Cliff, my teaching partner, took a chair opposite me.

"We're very interested in what you say you are learning," I began. Then I asked for volunteers. Jason raised his hand.

"Yes, Jason?"

"I learned you guys are serious," he began.

"What do you mean, Jason?" I prodded.

"Well, remember in the beginning of the year when you talked about the Distinctions? I thought to myself, 'Okay, there they go, the rules again, but I'll bet by next week these things will be gathering dust.' I was sure you were going to put those Distinctions aside and start in with the homework. But you kept referring to them again, and again, and again. You guys are really serious about the Distinctions, aren't you?"

"Thank you, Jason, and yes, we are indeed serious about the Distinctions and about learning," I confirmed.

With that, we were off and rolling. Student after student rose to the occasion, recalling lessons old and new. Each student in the circle shared a lesson; using a class list, Cliff kept track of who spoke. Once we had gone all the way around, both asking for volunteers and calling on reluctant students, we invited students to contribute a second lesson learned. We heard some amazing things.

Kristen learned about drafting and revising:

One of the lessons I learned is how to revise and edit pieces of writing. I have been learning to revise and edit because Mr. B gives us back our first drafts with corrections and suggestions. Then we are given the opportunity to improve the first draft. Rewriting a piece more than once lets you see how to use better techniques to make a better piece of writing.
    —Kristen DeBenedetto, age 13

Christine noted something that I had unwittingly taught her:

One of the many important lessons I have learned was written to me by Mr. Burkhardt. In past years my confidence in question asking was not high. On September 8, 1992 while writing in my EJ, I said, " . . . sometimes I feel my question is dumb." A couple of days later when my EJ was returned to me I quickly flipped through the pages to find my grade (as many students on Team 8-1 do). While looking through I read a comment that Mr. Burkhardt had written to me in response to the statement I made earlier. He wrote, "The only dumb question is the question you don't ask." I thought about that comment for a while and realized how very true this was. Now I never feel as though I will be made fun of or feel stupid when I ask a question. What he said has stuck in my head, and I remember it each time I go to raise my hand with hesitation.
    —Christine Love, age 13

Jean remembered the impact of my critique of her poetry, reinforcing the notion that time spent responding to student writing is a worthwhile investment:

At PEEC, and in school, Burk showed me that a teacher can also be your friend. I never believed that a teacher as busy as Burk could find time for one student. When Mr. Burkhardt took his weekend to write me a two-paged typed letter on my poems, I was blown away. I felt top priority. My other teachers let my poems collect dust, and when I finally asked them what they thought (after months of waiting) the typical answer was, "They're very nice"!
    —Jean Schantz, age 14

Bobby recognized that his ability to speak in front of people had improved:

The first lesson I've learned, and still am learning, is to speak in front of people. I've always gotten very nervous about talking in front of people, but things like doing the poetry memorizations has helped me with speaking a great deal. It has even helped me in Spanish class when we are doing oral work. I have also gotten a much better sense of participation. The discussions we have about poems, the team meetings, have all helped a great deal.
—Bobby Unterstein, age 13

Adam underscored the importance of friends, something he realized on the field trip to PEEC, in the Poconos, early in the school year:

At PEEC, I realized many other things. Being hundreds of miles away from your home, parents and your own bed makes you think about more than just material things. You begin to forget about the unimportant things and start to feel closer with everyone . . . and realize that's what's really important. This happens even with people who you didn't even know one month ago. Putting things like friendship and concern for others above your other needs makes you a better person and a better friend. So I also learned at PEEC, among many other things, that people should never get upset about the unimportant things they worry about, because friends are really what's most important in life. And I learned never to forget this. And, hopefully, I never will.
—Adam Silver, age 14

Tom took two important life lessons from *The Miracle Worker:*

I learned that no matter how hard the odds are against you, you should never give up. You can overcome anything if you put your mind to it and try hard enough. Even if there's something that seems impossible and no one believes that it can be done, you can do it, if not by yourself, then with the help of someone who cares for you. In other words, I learned two things: never say never, and nothing is impossible.
—Tom Mooney, age 14

David commented on the impact of the Distinctions on his everyday life:

The other lesson that has affected me in the past 4 months of our "simultaneously shared journey" is how these acknowledgments fit into my everyday life.

In the beginning of the year when we defined the Distinctions I began to realize how often I don't do these things. Now I'm trying to use these Distinctions with my family and at home and with teachers and friends at school. It makes me feel like a nicer person.
—David Szymanski, age 13

Not every student spoke about academics. Jen, a social butterfly, addressed the pernicious issue of gossip:

A lesson I have learned from my friends is not to talk behind each other's backs. I know that my friends can all admit to that we have done it to each other. It's kind of like that song, "What goes around, comes around." I have decided that I'm not going to do it anymore.
—Jen Levy, age 13

Jessica emphasized the importance of being a member of a team of students:

The third and probably the most important thing that I have learned this year does not have to do with any teachers or academic classes. Instead it deals with the kids on Team 8-1. This year I've discovered the group of people that I have been with for three years are all nice, fun, and interesting people. I am now friends with almost everyone on the team, even though a year or two years ago I could have been their worst enemy. Thanks to them this will be a year I [will] never forget.
—Jessica Cepelak, age 13

Perhaps the greatest compliment of all came from D.J., who told his classmates:

Over all this year I have learned maybe the greatest lesson of my life. That's that a group of totally opposite people can get together and form a sort of family. Thank you. . . .
—D.J. Kaczmarczyk, age 14

Reflections

In all the years we did this activity, no student ever asked his or her grade on the assignment; the sharing with peers of personal lessons learned was valuable in and for itself. Also, no student ever did the assignment incorrectly, for there were no right or wrong answers. Each student's lessons were honored.

As student after student spoke to their peers, I realized that we were engaged in a powerful experience. I thought about what might be going on in the minds of the listeners—probably many different things: "Hey, I learned that lesson, too." "We're supposed to be learning?" "Oops, I didn't learn that." "Wow, I've learned a lot of stuff so far!" Of course I don't know what they were thinking, but I do know that all learners need affirmation. When students realize how much they have learned, they gain confidence and become better learners.

That evening as homework, students did a journal entry reflecting on the lessons learned, both their own and those of classmates.

How often do teachers take class time to ask students what they have learned, and do it formally, allowing their students to say what they really have learned rather than explain three causes of the Civil War? How often do teachers ask students to be responsible for their learning by declaring publicly what they have learned and subsequently publishing those reflections in a booklet?

The Lessons Learned activity is excellent middle level practice if you are working on building a community of learners. If Nick hears Allison say that she learned how to draft and revise, he may realize, "Oh, I learned that, too." The student who says, "I didn't learn anything" has to confront the reality of peers standing up and declaring that they have learned something. Kids begin to grasp the fact that their job in school is learning.

Each time we did the Lessons Learned activity, Cliff and I came to know our students better as learners. We understood the results of our efforts in the classroom more clearly, and we found out what worked and what didn't. We adjusted our instruction if more than a few students brought to our attention a lesson that wasn't productive. Conversely, we also learned which lessons to keep when, year after year, students lauded them. Seeing students declare themselves learners—and watching them as they listened to their peers and realized how much they all had learned—was very rewarding.

A caution: don't do this exercise if you have a thin skin. You might have a special lesson that you think is wonderful, but no student mentions it. That can be disappointing, but it is also useful feedback if it happens. You may learn that what you see as crucial is not necessarily viewed that way by the learners. If everyone mentions your special lesson, that's also feedback. When given the opportunity, young adolescents will tell you what's so.

Publishing the Lessons

After students completed sharing their Lessons Learned, they typed and edited them for publication, and we created another class anthology, a practice that Beth Ann lauded:

> I think getting my writing published is really fun. It is fun to know and see that your writing is in a book, even though it might be really bad or really good. It is fun to have the books, and I will be able to read them in a few years and know that I wrote something. It is meaningful to me because I like to write and see my writing in a book. I also like to get the letters from other kids.
> —Beth Ann McEnany, age 13

Once the anthology was published and distributed, Cliff and I asked students to take it home and share it with parents. We posted a complete set of lessons on the walls outside our adjoining classrooms. For the next several weeks, sixth and seventh graders walking by would stop and read a lesson or two that an eighth grader learned, reinforcing the concept of a community of learners throughout the school.

The evening after the students shared their lessons, I leafed through my tattered copy of *Poems for All Occasions* and, wonder of wonders, found "Lessons Taught, Lessons Learned," a poem I read to the class the next day, punctuating the conclusion of our group reflection.

Assertions Addressed

As they worked through the Lessons Learned activity, students reinforced several of the assertions about writing.

- Students wrote their Lessons Learned at their own, varying levels of ability.
- Because students could select any lessons that were significant to them, they had ample choice. The result was that as they shared, we recalled a range of teaching and learning experiences.
- When we published the Lessons Learned booklet, we had a record of what students said was meaningful; students could see what classmates said were the significant lessons.
- As they shared, students directed their reflections on learning at classmates as much as their teachers.

Closing Thoughts

The Lessons Learned activity made students engage in metacognition—thinking about thinking. They learned what they had learned, not only by reflection, but also by listening to peers. The entire community of learners was strengthened as a result of thinking about the learning process, then publicly writing and sharing their insights.

Why should you conduct this activity with your students? Essentially, to help them understand both what they learned and that they learned.

13

The Letter to Self

The Letter to Self

Basic idea:	Each student writes a five-part Letter to Self (LTS), a personal time capsule.
Assertions addressed:	1, 2, 3, 9, and 10 (*see p. 17*).
Skills addressed:	Reflection, thinking, writing at length, sequencing, recording history.
Class time needed:	Six periods.
Advance preparation:	Obtain a large envelope for each student. Label a cardboard box (LTS plus graduation year) for storing the envelopes. Prepare an assignment sheet explaining the LTS.
Time of year:	January.
Neat feature:	Secret letters; map of the community; returning the LTS at high school Senior Breakfast four and a half years hence.
Assessment:	You don't read it, and students earn an automatic B if each two-page part is done on time. If the student does an extra page per section, he or she earns an A. If any part is late, the student earns a C for the project.
Follow-up:	Near the end of the school year, ask students to do an LTS appendix, because a lot happens in the life of an eighth grader from January to June.
Journal entry:	"Doing My LTS" a. How did you feel about doing your LTS? b. What part was easiest for you? Why? c. Which part was most difficult for you? Why? d. What did you learn about yourself by doing your LTS? e. Extras—how did you "enhance" your LTS? f. What else do you have to say?
Caution:	Do not read any student's LTS, tempted though you may be.
Forms:	LTS assignment sheet; map of community; favorites; appendix.
Why do this?	Because it's the best writing activity they will do all year—just ask them!

Your grade on this next assignment is a B, and I will not read it," I announced to my students one morning in mid-January. That piqued their interest. "All you have to do to earn the B is meet the deadlines and submit two pages a day for the next five days."

The hands went up.

"How do we get an A?" Bobby wanted to know.

"Easy," I responded. "Submit three pages each day instead of two."

"You're really not going to read what we write?" asked Heidi incredulously.

"Do you remember the Letters of Appreciation we did last month? I didn't read them. Same here. The only people who will read your Letter to Self are you and the people you show it to."

"What's a 'Letter to Self'?" Jessica asked.

"My older sister said this was the best," Danny interjected.

"She's right, Dan. I suspect you will enjoy this assignment. Here's a sheet explaining it all," I continued, asking Jessica to distribute the assignment sheets.

"The Letter to Self is a letter you write to yourself about who you are now, halfway through eighth grade. There are five parts to it, and you can start with any one of them. The first part of your LTS is due *mañana*."

"If you're not going to read it, how will you know we did it?" Mike inquired.

"Good question, Mike. I'll be standing at the classroom door tomorrow, and before you enter, you'll have to show me your two LTS pages, each marked with one of the five code letter combinations. There's a different code for each of the five parts. That way I'll know which part you did as homework."

"What if we don't meet the deadlines?" inquired Magda. (The possibility of Magdalena missing a deadline was slim to none.)

"Your grade drops irrevocably to a C," I replied. "No second chances on this one. When you walk through the door tomorrow, I need to see at least two handwritten pages."

"What if, later on, we want to add on to a part we already did? Can we?" asked Ben.

"Absolutely, Ben. In fact, I encourage that."

I held up a 9x12 clasp envelope.

"Here's a large envelope in which to keep all five parts of your LTS," I explained, asking Ben to distribute one to each of his classmates. "See that cardboard box there in the corner, the one marked '2nd Period LTS'? You can store your LTS in there until it's done. That way you won't lose it."

"But," asked Tori, "what if I write something personal that I don't want you to read and don't want to keep in class?" Tori voiced a concern shared by other students, as indicated by several heads nodding in agreement.

"If you want to keep any part of your LTS until we're all done, you can," I replied, "but be very careful, and don't lose it. Also, I will need to see that you've done at least two pages as homework, so you'll have to bring your LTS in for me to check each day."

"Can I type mine?" queried Adam. "I don't like to write by hand, and the computer is totally faster."

"Yes, Adam, but be sure to make a back-up copy. I'm not interested in any 'The computer ate my homework' excuses on this one," I said.

Narcissism Rampant

And so we began working on our Letters to Self. What impressed me most about this project was that even with a guaranteed B for composing ten pages and an A for doing fifteen, students submitted an average of twenty pages per LTS; some pushed way beyond thirty!

Why did students write twice as much as they had to? What was it about the Letter to Self that captured their imagination and engaged them in serious, reflective writing? In his seminal book, *A Middle School Curriculum: From Rhetoric to Reality*, Jim Beane (1993) asserts that "[t]he central purpose of the middle school curriculum should be helping early adolescents explore self and social meanings at this time in their lives" (p. 18). The Letter to Self did just that.

One of youth's enduring questions is "Who am I?" The Letter to Self assignment allows students to delve deeply into that question, then fashion a response, albeit from the eighth-grade perspective. Narcissism is alive and well in middle school; for this assignment my students received credit for looking deeply into the mirror and recording what they saw.

Five Parts

As class went on, we continued to review the assignment sheet; the kids asked questions and I came up with answers on the spot. For the LTS, students were asked to write at least two pages on each of the following five general topics:

- *Me, now:* My hopes, fears, dreams, intentions, goals, problems, concerns, likes, dislikes, joys, frustrations; what I like about myself; what I don't like about myself; what I'm proud of; what I think about; what bothers me; who I am; etc.
- *My world:* A description of my home, bedroom, school, neighborhood, town, favorite places to go, chores, allowance, pet(s), possessions, clothes, religion, current events; favorite books, music groups, movies, TV, etc.
- *What I do:* My hobbies, pastimes, sports, school activities; what I do when I'm alone; what I do with friends; favorite snacks and foods; how I spend my weekends and vacations; special activities I do; organizations I belong to; etc.
- *People in my life:* My family, siblings, friends, best friend(s), teachers, the opposite sex, people I like, people I'd like to know better, people I admire and respect, important people in my life, people who annoy me, etc.

- *My future:* Predictions, what I want to do, what I'm looking forward to, what I'm dreading, my goals, my hopes and fears for the world, the second half of eighth grade, summer vacation, high school, college, marriage, employment, etc.

Once I responded to students' preliminary questions, I pointed to four cardboard boxes sitting on top of a bookcase in the corner of the classroom. The cartons, somewhat obscured by posters hanging from the walls and ceiling, had been gathering dust since day one in September.

"See those boxes up there?" I asked. "Can you read what is written on the outside of each box?" Students looked more intently and saw that each box had the initials 'LTS' and a year, beginning with the current one and advancing into the future.

"Are they what I think they are, Mr. B?" Carolyn asked.

"Yep. When you complete your Letter to Self, Carolyn and everyone else, I will keep it for the next four and a half years and return it to you at Senior Breakfast, just before your high school graduation."

Murmurs around the class; students had just been transported into an unknown future. Most eighth graders cannot conceive of a time four and a half years hence; four and a half months, four and a half weeks, sometimes even four and a half days represents the outer edge of their projected existence. Yet suddenly, they existed in the future. They found this aspect of the LTS extremely appealing.

"But what if I move?" Kevin wanted to know.

"I'll track you down," I assured him. "Schools keep addresses of where they send your records. I'll find you."

Maps, Favorites, and Secret Letters

On the second day of the LTS project, students brought in Polaroid cameras, video cameras, and tape recorders to capture the sights and sounds of their eighth-grade lives. They showed classmates clippings of current events, taken from the daily newspaper, before placing them in their packets. I supplied neighborhood maps, and they began locating the treehouse, the hill where they broke their arm, the intersection where their dog got run over, and the homes of their friends. On another form that I distributed, they compiled lists of favorites: music groups, TV shows, foods, books, places visited, and the like. They brought in photographs, old homework assignments, Broadway show programs, magazines, candy wrappers, and birthday cards. If an object was small enough to fit in the envelope, it usually wound up in someone's LTS.

I walked about the classroom, checking off which of the five parts each student had completed as homework, praising their work, recommending enhancement activities ("What if you had everyone sign the outside of your envelope?"), and enjoying their enthusiasm as they became absorbed in a search for self.

On the third day of the LTS project, I invited students to compose "secret letters." I had their attention instantly; they didn't know what it was, but it sounded cool.

"I know," I began, "that many of you admire others in this class from a distance, and you may not have the courage at this point in your life to say what you want to say to them. You admire classmates for their courage, their deeds, their talents, their beauty, and their personality. Well, here's your chance to tell them so. I invite you to write a secret letter to anyone in this class. Keep it secret. I've got plenty of envelopes, and you can take as many as you want. When you have written your secret letter, put just the recipient's name on the outside of the envelope, and as I walk around the classroom with my hands behind my back, place your letter in my hands. Even I won't know who wrote it. Or you can put your secret letter in my mailbox in the office. Use the initials *SL*—secret letter. I'll attach it to that student's LTS, and he or she will open it four and a half years from now at Senior Breakfast. Go for it."

"Mr. B., can I have two envelopes?"

"I need three!"

"Gimme ten, please."

I was not surprised when a team of forty-seven students generated sixty-eight secret letters voluntarily, with no expectation that this additional writing would affect their grade in any way. Talk about volume!

The Appendix

"Mr. Burkhardt, I wrote four pages last night about people in my life, and I'm not even up to my mom yet," Jessica announced as she walked in on day four of the LTS project. By now the classroom was a bustling workshop; students were deeply engrossed in creating personal time capsules. Looking around the room I saw kids engaged in writing, rereading what they had written, sharing passages with close friends, preparing materials to put in their packets, interviewing one another, and enjoying it all. They recognized, as I did, that something special was happening. Contagious laughter, unfeigned excitement, and purposeful energy permeated the atmosphere.

On the last day of the LTS activity I asked students to reread everything they had written and create an appendix—two additional pages, based on what they had discovered through rereading that they had left out. As they reviewed what they had written, I heard comments such as, "Omigod, I left out my brother!" and "My dog, I forgot my dog!" Thus a sixth section was added to each LTS.

Holding Back the Aging

The Letters to Self far surpassed my expectations; as previously noted, most students went significantly beyond the minimum needed for a B. The all-time record for the longest LTS was 39 pages, typed, single-spaced.

What was it about the Letter to Self that so captured the imagination of the students? Student journal entries written after they completed the assignment shed some light on this question. Dan allowed:

> This project was of incredible value to me. The whole idea of sort of holding back the aging. You change so much as the years go on that it's nice to just sit and read what you thought in the past.
> —Dan Brickley, age 14

Heidi confessed:

> I learned that sometimes I can be really judgemental about people. When I read it over I noticed I can be really mean sometimes. I have added my views on everything such as gays, drugs and alcohol, and smoking. I wrote a secret letter to someone that I like and now I feel much better that I told him. [Note: "He" would not receive Heidi's letter for four and a half years.] I think the secret letters are a very good idea.
> —Heidi Lipinsky, age 13

Meghan noted:

> By the time I got to doing my last section I noticed I could write more about the way I feel and it came easier for me. I began to write like the way I realy speak because I thought to myself that I wanted this LTS to be a lot like me so it would be more valuable to me. So I learned to always express the way you realy are when you do an assignment like this.
> —Meghan Carey, age 13

The Appendix Redux

Just before the school year ended, I asked students to create a second appendix to their LTS. Much happens in the life of a middle schooler in five months; I gave them a sheet suggesting a variety of topics on which they might consider commenting:

the Super Bowl
the NCAA Final Four
the new baseball season
the Oscars
recent current events
summer blockbuster movies
romantic trials and tribulations
high school next fall
plans for the summer

And so they added even more pages to their Letters to Self. As with some earlier writing activities, no student ever asked what his or her grade was for this second appendix.

Senior Breakfast

Four and a half years later, at the high school Senior Breakfast just a week before graduation, I distributed the Letters to Self to my former students, now mature young men and women, and listened to them laugh out loud as they rediscovered who they were back in eighth grade.

"Look at my handwriting! It's so young-looking."

"I can't believe I was in love with *him*!"

"Look at what I wrote," Jen said to Nicole. "I hated your guts in eighth grade, and now you're, like, my best friend!"

More than a few students realized the immense growth they had undergone since January of eighth grade.

The Best Assignment of the Year

Year after year students voted the LTS the best writing activity of the year, primarily because it celebrated and affirmed who they were while simultaneously enabling them to address immediate personal concerns.

Lauren's journal entry spoke directly to this:

The Letter to Self is one of the best, if not, the best writing assignment that I have ever been assigned. I had a total of 39 typed pages, but the grand total, maps included (not letters), came to 47 pages. I was kind of surprised . . . I never realized how long it was . . . I guess there's just so much to tell, I know I could have said so much more. Sometimes, I think that I started to ramble, because I would think about one thing, and as soon as I thought of it I would write it, but my thoughts would drift totally off the subject of the thing that I was supposed to be writing about—and I would end up writing about my thoughts and feelings on bagels and dishwashing liquid, instead of MY WORLD. But I would snap out of it, and get myself back on track. I did have one fear about the project as a whole. That was that someone would read my project. I have the file on my computer under a password that only I know, and I would be wary of leaving my envelope on the couch in Mr. B's room . . . I guess I was a little paranoid . . . But when you think about it, if anyone did decide to read it, they would literally be reading my thoughts, which is scary.

I'd say that the easiest section was ME NOW, only because it was the most general. It would seem perfectly logical in that section for me to drift of into no where, and write about Tight Purple Sweatpants, and then suddenly snap myself back into reality, and talk about how I talk to myself. Really anything about myself could be in there . . .

The hardest part was probably PEOPLE IN MY LIFE. I ended up with 12 pages on the subject, but I also coined the phrase—"So much to do, so little time." My bedtime is 10:00, and I GOT HOME AT 4:30. I wanted to include and talk about so many other people in my life, but I just didn't have the time! . . .

I've learned by doing PEOPLE IN MY LIFE how many real friends and companions I have. I've become really good friends with Jessica Cepelak. When I am with her, I don't have to worry about saying the wrong thing or looking stupid— I can just be my wild, wacky, loony self, and Jess will (usually) go right along with me. As Humphrey Bogart said in "Casablanca" "I think this is the beginning of a BEAUTIFUL friendship." I've also learned my feelings on certain people who have left my life, people who have entered it, and that I have definitely entered the realms of computer geekdom.

Extras . . . hmmmmmm . . . 35 pages? Nah! I added my relationship chart from health, one of my neighborhood, one of my house, and one of the middle school auditorium. (A lot of important stuff happened to me there, I never realized that) I included 5 pages of printed out E-mail from Petersen and Matt, important stuff, and a secret letter that Fallon gave me, a letter from Jessica, and my audio Letter to Self, which I got a lot of my friends to talk into, and say who they think they'll be sitting next to, who they'll be going out with, and who they'll marry. I also promised each of them that even if the two of us have gotten into a HUGE fight in 10th grade, and we hate each other's guts, I promised them that as soon as I hear their voice on my tape, I will go over to them, and give them a hug . . .
—Lauren Thogersen, age 13

Granted, Lauren was an exceptional student, and her journal entry was significantly longer and more detailed than those of most of her classmates. Yet what she wrote—the quality of her reflections on an assignment that had great personal value to her—were representative of the insights and passion that other students shared about this project. Quite simply, year after year, students said that the LTS was the best writing project they ever did.

Expecting the Unexpected

As with other assignments, I learned to expect the unexpected when I assigned the Letter to Self. I was invited to give a writing workshop in Hawaii in June of 2000. Brooke, who had been my student in 1993, was by then a college student on Oahu, studying to become a teacher; she had moved away from the school district during her ninth-grade year.

I e-mailed Brooke and invited her to help me present the workshop. I still had her LTS and brought it along as a surprise. When she and I started explaining Letters to Self to the workshop participants, Brooke complained to the audience, "Yeah, they were great, but I never got mine back."

"Well, Brooke," I rejoindered, having anticipated this moment, "your waiting is over. Here it is." I handed her a dusty packet covered with scribbles.

"Omigod!" Brooke exclaimed, tears filling her eyes. She looked at it, then at me, smiled, and then looked at her LTS again.

"Omigod, I can't believe this. Look, it says 'I love Brad' all over the outside. I was so crazy about him then." She paused, then added, "He's in jail now!"

Matt's Letter to Self was also memorable. Matt, a quiet, unassuming student with a cheery smile for all, spoke of everyday things in his LTS. Some excerpts:

My World

"Hello Matt. I am a phsycic. I know all. Here is what you were like in 8th grade, in your point of view: I love my neighborhood. Almost all of my friends live in it with me. I like to ride my bike around my neighborhood because I know my way around. There is a Pizza Parlor and a bagel shop in it. I can just walk down and have a slice of pizza or a bagel. I also love my room. I have a stereo, a desk, some posters, a model, and my CD's. But I really love my bed, and my comforter. It's so comfortable. I have a lot of stuffed animals from when I was little lying on my bed. Every week I either get the newspaper and mail every day, or take out the garbage and recyclables. My brother and I switch every week and we each get $7. $1 for each day. Sometimes I do the dishes or the laundry. I've read so many good books that I don't have a favorite. . . Hello Matt. It's me, that guy that knows everything. ~~I know you would never admit this, but in 8th grade, you were not popular. Most kids think you were a total geek. Actually, they still do. The only people that like you are your friends, who aren't popular, either, so don't feel left out.~~ Well, I must go, and tell the other people that don't even know me all about them. Bye." "Wow! That guy was cool! That's exactly what I was going to write! Exept for the geek part. It's a good thing I wrote all that down. Let me just cross out the geek part. Well, that's better. Hey, I never wrote anything like this in a report! Here we go: mug butta beans potatoes mushroom orange red blue steak spoon spoon spoon tree loghouse Abraham Lincoln mony school is stupid school is stupid!

People in My Life

Let me start with my Mom. She is really nice. Most kids are telling me that every day, like "Your mom helped me at the Library yesterday!" and a whole bunch of stuff like that. Even people that don't like me. My Dad is really nice to, and funny. A lot of people say I look just like him, but I don't. I don't see any resemblance . . . My brother A.J. is, I hate to admit it, probably my best friend. I can tell him anything. Almost. I see him every day, and I know a lot about him, and we have a lot in common. Sometimes when he does something dumb, I'm like, Duh, but he kind of reminds me of, me. There is also someone else in my life. You! Dum-bass! Freak! I am you! Wait a minuet. How the hell does that make any sense!

The Appendix

Oh, my God! How could I forget all that juicy stuff about me that only I and a few other people know and if this information falls into the wrong hands I would be dead meet and every body would hate me or think that I'm stupid or get scared of me because they think I'm so wierd? . . . There was one time when I cried on the bus, and the reason was because I got in a seat and then Losky sat in it. Everybody was yelling at me to get out of the seat, and it made me feel bad, so I kinda started to cry. I don't know why I would cry for such a stupid reason. It's dumb. That afternoon at home I got a bad cut, and I cried because of that, so the next day I

told everybody that that as the reason, and then showed them the scar. . . . There was my first girlfriend in 6th grade, Lorraine. Then in 6th there was Jessica Schechner. I dumped them both, but, they always said, "Uh, um, no! I dumped you first!" That is so, stupid. Can't they just get over it and admit it? My first kiss, was with Jessica, in the old gym, at the end of the spring dance. After that at Andrew Haber's house, I couldn't stop thinking about her. Then, 6 weeks later, on that beautiful day, when we got back from Mystic Seaport, at teen rec, I dumped her, then my friends made me realize that I should go out with her again, so I said yes. Then it was like a couple of days later when I dumped her for good.
—Matt Blend, age 13

During his sophomore year in high school, Matt developed leukemia. Aggressive treatment, including relocating him to Seattle for experimental procedures, proved fruitless. Matt died halfway through his junior year. His family and friends were devastated.

At Senior Breakfast a year later, one of his buddies collected Matt's LTS and delivered it to his parents, for whom it was a bolt out of the blue. A year later, Matt's mother sent me the following e-mail:

I can't begin to tell you how much we appreciated the gift of LTS! One of Matt's classmates brought it to me after the annual Senior Breakfast. Not all of the kids thought that it should be passed on, after all, it was confidential. I waited until I felt "ready" to open the envelope. I was ready to cry. What a delight, instead of tears, we laughed and laughed! Matt's unique sense of humor was gifted to us in this package! He wrote about the music he loved, his friends, how sad he felt when he witnessed another student being teased on the bus (this particular kid just stopped in with a Briermeire Pie over Christmas holiday). He wrote that it was weird, but his little brother was his best friend . . . he wrote how he will take care of him and help him out when they are both in the high school. He wrote that you lived in the neighborhood and he thought that you might end up being an "OK" teacher. We read about how much he loved his town, his neighborhood and home. He even wrote about his bedroom, and how much he loved his old red quilt (we are going to use this old quilt to make a new quilt with pieces of his clothing patched together). Inside were a few odd items, a menu from an evening out, drawings, etc. All in all, it was just so wonderful! It felt a lot like a visit with Matt! We will treasure the package. Thank you, Ross.

She also let me know that inside his LTS were the following items:

- sheet music for a NYSSMA [New York State School Music Association] music solo
- place mats from a restaurant we visited on vacation—we used to always play Hangman on the back while we waited for our meal
- the bib that comes with the juicy Florida oranges that Grandma sends every Christmas. He must have taken it to bring to school.
- a map of the school to which he added where he was when he got his first kiss . . . Also his favorite toilet was starred! Very important info!

We cannot anticipate every eventuality. No one expected Matt to die. But the law of averages suggests that some of the members of the current seventh grade will not be alive at graduation five years hence. Matt's family cherishes his Letter to Self, and I am glad they have that memory of him.

Assertions Addressed

In creating Letters to Self, students reinforced several of the assertions about writing:

- Every student was a writer and explored important personal issues, often at great length.
- Each student wrote at his or her ability level; four and a half years later, when they were given their letters back, they could see considerable growth in their written expression.
- Because the five parts to the LTS offered wide latitude (any topic was fair game), students could write about whatever they wanted to and still receive credit; this encouraged many to go beyond the minimum expectations.
- Their audience was an imagined future self some four years in the future; most had not written to or for this audience before.
- The volume they created enhanced their fluency as writers.

Closing Thoughts

For every writing activity I had multiple goals. In the Letter to Self project, I was interested in having students:

- develop writing fluency
- explore the chronology of their lives
- engage in sustained reflection
- create a treasured heirloom
- construct a time capsule
- do a fun project
- participate in a shared experience (everyone else did it; students watched others and borrowed ideas from them)
- record an overview of one's life
- focus on self-awareness

As a developmentally responsive classroom activity, the LTS served young adolescents while meeting their social, emotional, and intellectual needs. And it was extremely easy to grade!

14

The Gift of Writing

The Gift of Writing

Basic idea: The student prepares a Gift of Writing (GOW) as a public piece of writing but intended for a special individual, then presents it as a gift to that person.

Assertions addressed: All ten (*see p. 17*).

Skills addressed: Attention to audience, drafting and revising, writing group participation, preparation of writing for publication.

Class time needed: Five periods:
1. Review EJ entry, share model, explain assignment.
2. Writing groups review draft 1.
3. Writing groups review draft(s) 2+.
4. Type up final draft and prepare it for publication.
5. Submit final typed draft for class anthology.

Advance preparation: Create a model GOW to share with your students.

Time of year: February—it makes a great Valentine's Day gift!

Neat feature: Students compose dedications and plan special ways to deliver their gifts.

Assessment: Students are evaluated on their drafting and revising process, their writing group participation, and the final version of their Gifts of Writing.

Follow-up: Delivering the Gifts of Writing to the intended audiences. Publishing a class anthology that is shared with parents. Discussing parent reactions to the anthology. Having students write letters of acknowledgment to other authors in the anthology.

Journal entry: Two separate entries:
"Three Important People, and Why"
"Doing My GOW":
a. What did you learn by creating a GOW?
b. What was the hardest part of the GOW?
c. How did your writing group function?
d. What was the best part of this assignment?
e. What else do you have to say?

Caution: Remind students that the Gift of Writing is meant to be a public piece and will appear in a class anthology.

Forms: GOW assignment sheet and planning form.

Why do this? To enable students to honor important people in their lives through writing.

ake out your English journals," I instructed my students late in the period on a cold day in February. "The title of this entry is 'GOW'—gee-oh-double-you." I could hear pages turning as students repeated a familiar practice: creating a heading for a journal entry.

"What does GOW mean, Mr. B.?" Carolyn inquired as she completed the journal entry heading.

"All in good time, Carolyn. Just follow the instructions," I said, pointing automatically to the sign above and to my left. "Now, for homework tonight, list three people that you actually know, and tell why each of them is important to you."

"Didn't we do this last December with those letters?" asked Chad.

"No, this is a different assignment, Chad. That was the Letter of Appreciation. This is the GOW."

"Are you sure?" Chad persisted. "It sounds like something we already did."

"I'm sure, Chad," I replied.

To the class I said, "You may use the remaining minutes of class to get started." And they did.

Modeling a Gift of Writing

The following day I asked students whom they had listed in their journals. "How many mentioned mom or dad?" Half the hands went up. "What about your best friend?" All hands. "Anyone mention an aunt, uncle, or grandparent?" A third of the arms moved toward the ceiling.

Students looked around and saw other hands in the air; they were reassured that they had done the assignment "correctly." I then asked them to get comfortable.

"I'm going to read you a piece I wrote called 'Tears on the Turnpike.' Listen to it carefully. I've got some questions for you when I'm done." This time, I actually did have some questions in mind.

I began to read aloud:

Tears on the Turnpike

If you had asked me beforehand, I would have guessed that my father would be the first one to cry. Old Weepy, we used to called him. He was about as hard as a soft-boiled egg. It got so bad, he even cried when he had to spank one of his children, so the four of us agreed to feign tears on such occasions and allow Dad to complete his paternal obligations faster. This time, though, it wasn't he who cried.

June 12, 1962—a warm, late spring afternoon. I remember it clearly for many reasons. First, it was the day my twin brother Robert graduated from Princeton. I had received my diploma from Dartmouth just two days earlier, coincidentally on Old Waterworks' 46th birthday. In his youth, Dad enrolled at Purdue, but he was excused from the rigors of higher education because of, as he put it, "too much wine, women, and song." For him to celebrate his birthday by seeing both sons receive sheepskins was just overwhelming. And when Robert surprised us all by leading his class into the elm-shaded courtyard in front of Nassau Hall, Dad almost burst with pride. Princeton tradition has it that the head cheerleader walks alongside the valedictorian to lead his class in one last "locomotive" for old P.U. Robert, needless to say, was not the valedictorian.

The sunlit morning grew cloudy and dark, and the rain began falling in earnest when Dr. Robert Goheen stepped to the podium to address the graduating class. A man of keen perception, President Goheen noted the drenched seniors, faculty, and parents vainly holding up umbrellas, newspapers, and graduation programs against the downpour; he quickly decided to forgo his speech to the Tigertown Class of '62. At which point, naturally, the sun burst forth. We had our pictures taken in black robes standing next to a half-buried cannon painted with orange '62's, bid farewell to friends of the past four years, then piled into the Oldsmobile and headed north on the two hour drive to our Hudson River home in Central Valley, N.Y.

Dad drove, Mom dozed next to him, and I rode shotgun. In the back seat, Valerie sat directly behind me, Robert dominated the middle, and Robin, or Puss, as we affectionately called her, sat behind Dad.

Puss, my older sister, always kept her feelings to herself. It was hard to read her face. I wondered how she reacted to seeing both of her younger brothers graduate from college before she did. Puss had emulated Dad's Purdue performance by flunking out of Vassar after a year; she was currently enrolled in her third college, as a sophomore.

The cumulative effects of the festivities in Hanover two days earlier, the six-hour drive south from New Hampshire, the Sunday night graduation celebration for Robert and me, and the many activities at Princeton had all taken their toll. We lounged in our seats, catatonically counting the cars on the New Jersey Turnpike as we headed back north. Everyone was going home except me; I was headed for Newark Airport to catch a plane for Bloomington, Indiana, to begin my Peace Corps training as a phys ed teacher in Tunisia. As I said, it was a memorable day.

Just before Newark Airport, visible on the right from the turnpike, stands a landmark our family calls the "ghost eyes" church. The twin steeples have numerous circular openings, and the alignment of the openings is such that as you drive past, you seem to see a pair of eyes in each steeple opening, and closing, in a slow blinking process. As I rested my head against the window and watched the "eyes" open, then close, then open, I heard sniffling from the back seat.

"Well, if it isn't 'Nails' Burkhardt," my mother exclaimed. Her declaration prompted me to turn around and see who 'Nails' was. I assumed that my younger sister, Valerie, was crying; after all, her not undeserved family nickname was "Baby." To my surprise, however, the sniffler was Puss. This was most unexpected. Puss never, ever cried. When Elvis got drafted, Puss laughed. When Bambi's mother was shot by the most dangerous creature in the forest, Puss sat dry-eyed. But now the tears streamed down over her cheeks. The runways of Newark were visible on the left.

"What's the matter?" I asked softly. "What's wrong?"

"It's . . . it's just that you're leaving," she sobbed, her chest heaving involuntarily, "and I won't see you for two years, and that makes me sad."

I didn't know what to say. Honest expressions of love from my older sister were something to which I was not accustomed. Mumbling that I was only going away for two months and would be home for ten days in August before I flew to Tunis, I turned frontward and stared straight ahead. The car was silent save for the back seat sniffles; the roar of tractor trailers groaning past the Oldsmobile filled the interior space as we slowed for Exit 14.

We six had been together as a family for nineteen years. Within the hour, one son would depart, and two days later the other son would leave for his Peace Corps training in Utah: my brother Robert was headed for Iran.

I understand it all more clearly now. I see Puss's tears for what they were, and the embarrassment I felt then has turned to appreciation. I never did thank her for the love she expressed through her tears. That moment, however, has stayed with me.

Dad cried at the airport. Predictably, so did Mom and Val. Robert gave me the "Hail fellow about to venture forth into the world" routine; we were both very taken with ourselves then (and even now, I suspect). Puss hugged me silently just before I boarded the plane, her red eyes downcast.

I didn't cry until later.

After I had finished, Perri complimented me on my piece.

"Thank you," I said. "Now, what happened in the story?"

Various students recalled various details—black gowns, cannons with orange numbers, the "ghost" church, and Puss's tears. Perri said the story made her feel sad. Another student said it reminded him of the time his brother left for the army.

"It's clear to me that you understand the story," I said after a while. "But I have a question: how do you think my sister Puss would react to it? And how would her reaction be different from yours?"

You could actually see the kids' faces light up. In an instant they became keenly aware of the concept of audience.

"Well, she was in it. She was there," Rebecca offered. Nods of assent around the room.

"Exactly," I said. "This piece of writing was actually a gift that I gave her. All of you understood it, but she got more out of it than you did because she was part of the story. She was the intended audience, and she loved it.

"Last night for homework," I continued, "you identified three important people in your life. What I want you to do now is to select one important person in your life—you may already have identified him or her in your EJ—and write a public piece, a GOW, for that person. GOW stands for Gift of Writing. Eventually you will give your Gift of Writing to the person for whom you write it, and it will also be published in a class anthology. Your GOW should celebrate that person and your relationship with him or her. If you look back at what you wrote in your EJ, you might find that you have already started on—"

"Mr. Burkhardt," interrupted Danny. "Now that I know what the assignment is, can I change one of the names in my EJ, because I really want to write my GOW to—"

"Yes," I answered.

"Mr. B.," Josh shouted, "can I do my GOW for more than one person? I have three really good friends, and I need to—"

"Yes," I interrupted, smiling.

What I liked best about this project was that writing became the gift; students actually gave something of themselves, something they created, to important people in their lives. Is there anyone who wouldn't treasure such a tribute?

The Assignment Sheet

The assignment sheet for the Gift of Writing from a typical year stated:

Your assignment is to create a piece of writing to be given to a specific audience. The audience might be a parent, a friend, a teacher, a neighbor, a relative, an advisor, a brother or sister—someone or ones with whom you have shared or experienced significant events.

The form you select for this piece can be a poem, a narrative, an essay, a fable, an interior monologue, a dialogue—whatever form best fits the purpose of what you are trying to say.

You should select an event that has happened that you want to capture in writing, or a shared feeling, or a realization you now understand but didn't then, or a tradition that you appreciate, or some words that were spoken to you that meant a great deal, or a memory you want to arrest in time—some part of your experience with that audience that has meaning for you. Then, through writing, create a piece that that audience will appreciate because of that shared experience or special understanding.

Think of the pieces I shared in class: the story about exchanging names at Christmas that I wrote while overseas and had a friend read to my family on Christmas Eve; the eighth grade farewell kiss poem for a specific group of eighth graders last year; the booklet of poems I wrote for my family and close friends last Christmas. All of these pieces can be read by a general audience and be appreciated, but the ones who get the most out of them are the ones who were the intended audience.

You might want to create a series of poems for the members of your family; write about something that happened a long time ago with your parents and you that you remember and want to share with them as a way of letting them know your feelings; write a fictional version of something that actually happened, knowing that your intended audience will really understand the piece; create a mini-diary of entries sharing feelings about a person and tracing your relationship with that person; write an essay in which you take a position that brings a smile to the intended audience; satirize something.

There are many ways to do this piece of writing, and many forms it can take. Most important are the following:

(a) you need to select a specific audience for whom you will create the piece;
(b) you need to know why you are celebrating this relationship;
(c) you need to write about a topic, person, or event that has meaning for you and for your intended audience.

Please have a first draft of this piece ready for Thursday. Also, do a journal entry after you complete your first draft telling how you composed the first draft, what you noticed, your difficulties, etc.

On the back of the GOW instruction sheet, students found a planning form to assist them in mapping out their Gifts of Writing (see Figure 14.1).

Creating a Gift of Writing

We usually did the Gift of Writing project in February, just in time for Valentine's Day. Earlier in the year, writing assignments such as free-verse poems, interior monologues, and personal essays were introduced, giving students a variety of forms from which to select the most appropriate for their gifts of writing. Students worked in writing groups for three days, drafting and revising their gifts. As they neared the end of the process, I invited each student to consider a dedication to the individual (or, as in Josh's case, individuals) for whom the GOW was intended.

In composing their Gifts of Writing, students came to understand the difference between writing "to" someone—such as a letter of acknowledgment to one individual—and writing "for" someone—a public piece of writing meant to be understood by all but particularly appreciated by the intended audience.

A caution: the first year I did this activity I neglected to stress to my students that the Gift of Writing was to be a public piece and would be published in an anthology. Diana balked; she didn't want to share her GOW with me or anyone else except the individual for whom she wrote it. Earlier in the year, she had thoroughly enjoyed creating both the Letter to Self and the Letter of Appreciation and Acknowledgment, neither of which were public pieces. Her protestations helped me understand that I had not made my expectations clear.

The following year when introducing the Gift of Writing, I emphasized, "You're going to create a public piece."

Jake responded, "Then I can't write the story I want to."

I replied, "Well, Jake, there might be a way for you to do it, and we can discuss that after class. However, this assignment, unlike the Letter to Self and the Letter of Appreciation and Acknowledgment, is about public writing. I invite you, on your own, to compose a GOW for a friend, and only that friend, if you want to. Meanwhile," I continued, "I suggest that you start working on your GOW for our class anthology."

Figure 14.1 GOW Planning Form

Who (audience): _____
_____

Why (purpose): _____
_____
_____
_____

What (topic): _____
_____
_____
_____

Form (poem, essay, interior monologue, etc.): _____
_____

Details to include:

After students typed up their final drafts, they took them to writing groups for final proofreading. When Matt typed six pages for his GOW, and when Cindy went through eight drafts before being satisfied, they had my attention. Why, I wondered, did students go so far beyond the norm on this assignment? I suspect it was because they were wholly invested in the audience, the purpose, and the topic; they had made choices for all three and were honoring them.

When the GOWs were finally edited and printed, a volunteer group of students stayed after school to number and sequence the pages for publication. I then sent the packet to the central office for duplication.

Reflections

Tori did three related journal entries while composing her GOW. Her thought process during the project is revealing:

Three Important Persons

One person in my life that is really important to me is Bean [Eileen Wind, a best buddy]. I can tell Bean everything. We have this thing called "Trusters."

Whenever either of us has something to tell the other, and it's private, we say "Trusters" and we vow never to tell anyone else. Bean is always there for me.

Another important person is my Dad. My dad always makes me feel better when there's something wrong. Dad is so patient with me, and he always helps me when I need it.

One other person is you, Mr. Burk. I really admire, because you let me be me, and you make everything so fun. Also you let me see that there's two sides to everything. And you make me feel important. Thank you, Mr. Burk. I didn't write this so I can get brownie points, it's how I really feel.

—Tori Schappert, age 13

Having identified three important persons in her preliminary entry, Tori selected someone she had not mentioned before in her journal as the recipient of her GOW. After completing a first draft and before taking the piece to writing group, Tori wrote:

My GOW Audience

I picked my best friend Marisa. I couldn't believe how much I remembered about our relationship. I enjoyed writing about the good points. I wrote an essay. I'm pretty much satisfied with my piece, but I think I could add a little more. It was really easy to start it but I had a little trouble ending it.

Right away I picked who I was going to write about, but then I changed my idea because I thought it might be better to write to someone else.

I basically wrote how we met and what we've been doing in the past years, and we are still friends now so I could continue writing a lot more.

—Tori Schappert, age 13

Once her GOW was complete, Tori looked back on the entire process:

Doing My GOW

I really enjoyed writing my piece. At first I had no idea who I was going to write to. Then I figured I probably have a lot to write about if I wrote about one of my close friends. So I was deciding between Bean and Marisa, and I figured since Marisa doesn't go to this school I'd write about her. Right away I thought about a specific event in our relationship and started writing.

The writing group really helped me. I don't realize my own errors, or I don't see what's not clear to other people. It really helped me to improve my piece. It was a good experience for me to hear what other people thought of my writing.

I'm not really sure how I'm doing to deliver it. I was thinking if it's finished by this weekend, I'd wrap it some how and just hand it to her, because she's coming out this weekend. Or I'll just send it to her and explain in another letter what it's all about, like you did with your sister.

I really think that Marisa will appreciate reading it, and seeing how I feel about our friendship.

—Tori Schappert, age 13

Acknowledgments

After the anthology came back in bound form from the district office, I distributed one copy to each student, then asked them to compose two letters of acknowledgment to other authors in the anthology. To ensure that each student received an acknowledgment, the names of all students whose writing appeared in the booklet were placed in a paper sack. I walked around the room with the sack as each student drew out a slip of paper. One letter went to the classmate selected by lottery, and the other went to any other author. This process forced students to read several GOWs.

As an author in the anthology, one year I received a letter from Annie which said, "I feel like I experienced the moment with you and your sister Robin. Your story made me feel like crying. I appreciate the fact that you create pieces of writing along with your students. Your writing helps me in getting started with the assignments."

The Meaning to Recipients

The Gift of Writing assignment elevated student composition from a mundane task to a gesture of great significance; students imbued their pieces with personal commitment, they celebrated writing, and they nurtured a lifetime skill.

One compelling aspect of the GOW was that the intended audience didn't expect it. Students had the opportunity to design the delivery, then eagerly anticipate that moment.

Carolyn's gift of writing for her grandmother proved to be a pivotal episode in her eighth-grade year, and I learned once again that when giving writing assignments, expect the unexpected.

> *"Two Birthdays in a Row to Remember"*
>
> This is dedicated to my grandma and Bob,
> two people who mean so very much to me,
> also the ones I love so very much.

The summer of my 12th birthday was warm and nice outside. My grandma was staying with us. She came up from Florida and was visiting us for my birthday. I was happy she would be with me for my birthday because my grandma is sick. This is a birthday that I will remember forever because my grandma is someone I love very much and care about a lot. My grandma means a lot to me. Not only was this the best birthday because my grandma was with me but also because a lot of family came to see my grandma and me. What else could a twelve year old girl want for her birthday than to be with the people I love, and people that I don't often see.

Last summer when I turned 13 years old, the day was great. It was warm, and there was a nice breeze in the air. Later on that day after I opened all my presents from my parents and sister, we got ready and went to my grandma and grandpa's house for dinner. We had fish from a restaurant. We had a lot of fun, but what made this a birthday to remember was not only having my family there but also a good friend of the family, Bob. Bob was sick and was very weak. Bob was like a grandfather to me. He came to see us all even though he was very weak. He gave my sister and I a "Silver Dollar". This may sound like a funny gift, but it was the best gift of all. This "Silver Dollar" means a lot to Lauren and me because Bob died on October 28, 1993. This is something that we will have for the rest of our lives to remember him by.

These two people, my Grandma and Bob are very special to me. Even though my grandma is sick, but still alive, and Bob is no longer with us, I keep telling myself that I am very lucky to have known them. I'm glad they were two people who meant so very much to me. For as long as I live I will remember my grandma and Bob as people I care about and people who meant the world to me. I will love and remember them for the rest of my life.

—Carolyn Makar, age 13

A week after Carolyn sent her gift to her grandmother, she burst into class proudly bearing a letter.

"Mr. B., look what I got yesterday!" she exclaimed, a huge grin on her face. Excitedly, she read me a letter she received from her aunt Doris:

Dear Carolyn,

Your beautiful letter about your Grandma & Bob is something I'll cherish for life. You have been blessed with a fantastic mind and a heart as big as the entire world. How lucky you are! You will always have love, because you think love.

[Your mother] was here with the children when I opened your master-piece. She started to read it and like me, half way through, she started to cry. [Your sister] Lauren said, "Mom, why are you crying?" Her answer was, "If you could read this letter you would cry, too." It is just so beautiful.

Carolyn, many thanks for sharing your letter. God bless you always.

Love,

Doris

And then, barely a week later, Carolyn walked into my classroom in tears. Her beloved grandmother had died the night before. I held her as she sobbed uncontrollably, devastated by her loss. When she calmed down, I said, "Carolyn, she knew—your grandmother knew. She knew you loved her, because she read your Gift of Writing." Carolyn looked at me and smiled through her tears.

Over the years Gifts of Writing have taken many different forms. Chris Waldemar wrote five rhyming poems, one for each member of his family, and published a booklet, *Waldemar Family Poems,* to be read at dinner on his father's birthday. Chris illustrated the poems with drawings of his mother, father, two brothers and the dog, and placed booklets on each dinner plate just before the birthday celebration. His father, who had scolded him earlier in the day for not taking out the trash, was in tears that evening when Chris joyously acknowledged him by reading the last poem in the booklet:

> **Dad**
> You put food in the table
> And wish we had a maid named Mable
> Who could cook good steaks
> You help with homework
> And usually make no mistakes
> Sometimes you drive us to school
> Even though Nana calls you a fool
> So we thank you Dad for your time
> 'Cause you make our lives shine ! ! ! ! !
> —Chris Waldemar, age 13

The unexpected power of a Gift of Writing can also be seen in what happened to Rebecca, who wrote the following piece for her father.

> *A Child*
>
> When I was eight years old my dad took me to New York City to see "The Nutcracker." During the intermission we went outside into the lobby and looked at the stores. I asked if I could buy something and my dad said yes and showed me the things that I could buy. I asked for something that he didn't point to and he said he didn't have enough money for it. I felt really bad for the rest of the day, and I still do when I think about it. I still have the sticker that I bought instead.
>
> That same year around Christmas, I went to get my dad a present. I already had all the presents for the rest of my family. We were at some kind of a mall and there was a store that sold pins. I saw a pin that was fluorescent green, and I really liked the color so I bought it. It said "Yuck Fou," but I didn't know what that meant. Then later that week I found out what it meant at school, and I felt really bad. I didn't want to give it to my dad, but I didn't have the time to get him something else, so I gave it to him. I still remember how well he took it. He smiled and said thank-you. That was the last I saw of it until about a week ago when I saw it on his shelves in the basement, and it all came rushing back to me.
>
> I just wanted to say thank-you for being a great dad, and I'm sorry for the times that I messed up.
> —Rebecca Siddons, age 12

Later that spring I invited Rebecca and three other students to assist me at a writing conference for language arts teachers. One of the topics about which she presented was her Gift of Writing. The following week Rebecca handed me a letter:

> Dear Mr. Burkhardt,
>
> Just the other day at the Merrick-Bellmore conference something happened to me while I was in the Writing conference. When we started to talk about the

GOW's I got over something that has been bugging me for half my life. Whenever I used to think about the 2 things I wrote about in my GOW I would get huge pangs of guilt, so in result I didn't think about them often. Then when I had to give my GOW to my dad I was very nervous, I didn't know how he would react. But after I gave it to him I didn't feel the guilt pangs anymore. The first time I realized this was on Friday at the conference while we were talking about them, I thought about mine and I could actually laugh about them. At the beginning of the year I would have felt terrible thinking about them. So, I want to thank you for helping me get over this, whether you realize you did it or not, because now I am closer to my dad and I have gotton over 2 painful memories!

Thanks,

Becky

I was struck by Rebecca's comment "whether you realize you did it or not." We cannot anticipate every repercussion from a given assignment. Unbeknownst to me, Rebecca used her gift of writing to overcome feelings of guilt regarding her father. Her letter suggests that writing can be therapeutic. I wonder how many other students have made use of an assignment for their own, real reasons.

Learnings

What does a student learn when creating a gift of writing? What skills are developed? Each piece presents a myriad of opportunities for learning. For example, to set up a dedication, a student may need to learn how to create a box on a computer screen and how to use different fonts. He or she would also have to understand the concept of a "Dedication." In relating an event, writers must be able to sequence events, recall significant details, and insert them in appropriate and effective places in the text. In addition, consistent verb tense is important in telling a story. In this way, skill development is individualized and addressed in the context of a student's writing.

Year after year, students chose the Gift of Writing as the second best writing activity. (The Letter to Self was always number one.) Why was the GOW so popular? First, the students had choice—they could pick the recipient, form, and topic for their gift. Second, they were creating real writing for real reasons. Students actually gave their writing to the intended recipient; they were able to both honor a relative or a friend and get academic credit for it. Creating dedications and publishing an anthology added to their enthusiasm.

Recently I asked my sister Robin to tell me what she remembered about both the "tears" incident in 1962 and my Gift of Writing about it more than twenty years later. She responded:

I was impressed when you made a big deal about a moment which had embarrassed me. That sob I let out came from deep within, I never saw it coming.

And I guess it shows how deeply I love you and how sometimes I didn't know it. I can't say we were best friends as kids, I was a poke and not exactly light, but underneath all that were the values and positions I now hold more boldly. Things are closer to the surface. I think you liked that story because it showed that you mattered to me, maybe you didn't know that, maybe neither of us did. But in your writing you have found an event that is singular in either of our experiences so far as I know.

—Robin Burkhardt

Why have your students create "Gifts of Writing" for important people in their lives? Among other reasons, to celebrate writing and relationships.

Assertions Addressed

The Gift of Writing assignment reinforced all ten assertions. Students selected their own topics and audiences and modes of expression; I modeled a gift to inspire them; they worked in writing groups as they drafted and revised their pieces; we published a class booklet, and everyone received a copy; the booklet reflected the varied abilities of the students, each of whom wrote at their own level; they added to the year's volume of writing through their multiple drafts and a reflective journal entry, all the while engaged in writing for real.

Closing Thoughts

Summing up the experience, Garrett, whose Gift of Writing honored the sensitivity of his mother and her counsel just before a big math test ("As long as I did my best, then she would not be mad at me if I got a bad grade") wrote the following journal entry prior to giving his gift to her:

I have had a lot of fun doing the gift of writing activity. I have spent a lot of time writing this. I think that my mom will be very happy to know that I appreciate her so much. I can't wait to deliver it.

I have made six drafts on my gift of writing. Every time I read my gift of writing piece [to my writing group], I found more and more corrections and many more things that I wanted to say. The two groups that I was in the people have really helped to make my piece of writing better. They have given me many good ideas.

I dedicated this piece of writing to my mom who is always there for me. I plan to deliver my piece of writing to my mom by putting it on her pillow right before she goes to sleep.

I have really enjoyed this activity. Because I have finally said what I wanted to say.

—Garrett Genova, age 14

15

The Essay Contest, the School Newspaper, and Responding to a Play

Three other challenging activities—taking part in an essay contest, putting together a school newspaper, and responding to a play—also engaged students. Each activity was an individualized exercise with specific time limits; all were supported by journal entries.

In most classrooms, students compose essays; many schools publish student newspapers; language arts teachers frequently include plays in their literature curriculum. The activities presented here are not new, but all have interesting motivational devices—prize money, an inflexible deadline, a set of six choices—that engage young adolescent writers in very real ways.

The Essay Contest

Most of the writing tasks I assigned allowed students significant choice of topic, form, audience, or some combination. In that regard, the annual essay contest was significantly different.

In 1975, the Ladies Auxiliary of the American Legion at a nearby senior citizen retirement community approached the principal of our middle school with an idea: they wanted to sponsor an essay contest, and would our middle school be interested? The Auxiliary suggested a $25 prize for the winner. We agreed, and for twenty-five years the contest was a fixture in our eighth-grade writing program; the prize money increased significantly over the years.

The assignment sheet announcing the contest (the theme changed every year) read:

Since 1975 the Ladies Auxiliary of the American Legion at Leisure Village has sponsored an Americanism essay contest for eighth graders at Shoreham–Wading River Middle School.

This year, the theme of the American Legion essay contest is:

"Good Citizens = A Strong Democracy"

We all have roles to play as citizens of this country. We have duties to perform and jobs to do. What makes someone a good citizen? How does being a good citizen strengthen democracy in this nation of ours? And what about young people? What can a middle school student do to support and promote democracy?

In your essay you should explore the topic of a citizen's responsibilities to our democracy, with particular emphasis on what you and your peers can do. Illustrate your points with specific examples and anecdotes from past or present times.

Entries in this year's Americanism essay contest are due no later than Thursday, February 16. Your essay should be typed (double-spaced), or neatly written in ink, and contain no more than 500 words.

In June, three SWR students will be awarded prizes of $150, $100, and $75 each for their winning essays.

As a writing assignment, the essay contest, with its fixed topic and unmovable deadline, was unique. Since Shoreham–Wading River Middle School was the only school in the contest, I emphasized to my class that a student from our school was sure to win. We had winners every year! (One facet of the reality of American capitalism is that money talks; the promise of prize money was a great motivator.)

I used the essay contest as a writing assignment for my students. We discussed audience: what could students assume about the nature of the judges, senior citizens who were members of the American Legion? What kind of essay would appeal to them? The 500-word limit leveled the playing field a bit—all students had a chance to win. Once students completed their essays, I asked, "Who wants to enter the contest?" Most did—they had nothing to lose.

Another positive aspect of the essay contest was that the winners were invited to read their essays aloud at a meeting of the sponsoring organization. Proud parents were invited as well; they saw their children speak publicly, receive awards, and be honored for their writing.

You may want to start an essay contest for your students. I invite you to use the sample form below or adapt it to a local civic organization in your community:

The _____ Historical Society announces its annual essay contest on local history. The contest is open to any middle school student in the school district. First prize is $100, second prize is $50, and third prize is $25. The first-prize winner will be invited, along with his or her parents, to the annual banquet of the Historical Society to receive the award, and the winning essay will be published in the Historical Society newsletter. The topic for this year's Historical Society essay contest is: "_____ [topic] _____."

Requirements: Entrants must be students enrolled in the local middle school. The essay must be between 500 and 1,000 words, double spaced with standard margins, and in blue or black ink whether handwritten, typed, or computer printed. List sources consulted (select a proper bibliographical form and be consistent). Attach a properly formatted cover sheet. Deadline for entries is _____.

Scoring will be based as follows: 55% on content; 20% on sources and bibliography; 20% on use of English; 5% on the cover sheet. The cover page must include the following information: title of the essay; student's name and address including zip code; student's phone number; school name; name of supervising teacher; grade level; names of student's parents. All essays should be mailed or delivered by _____ to:

> _____ Historical Society
> Street Address
> City, State, Zip

If you have any questions, please contact _____ at [phone number].

Ask your local Rotary, Lions, Elks, Kiwanis, Moose, American Legion, Garden Club, Sierra Club, or any other civic organization to sponsor the contest. These organizations are often looking for community projects, and promoting writing among young adolescents is a natural.

When students write about a real topic not of their choosing, for a real audience of adults whom they do not know and who will judge their work, for real reasons (again, money talks), they grow as writers.

In general, students found the essay restrictive both in length and subject. They chafed at these restrictions, but I believe it was good discipline for them to write inside established, inflexible parameters (even as I also understood the limited value of the five-paragraph essay as a life skill).

The School Newspaper

Many schools sponsor student newspapers. A distinctive feature for ours was the fact that publishing the newspaper was part of the curriculum. Every eighth grader, not just a few talented writers, became reporters and wrote articles on deadline.

Each team took a turn doing the four-week journalism unit. Four or five issues of the newspaper, with a press run of 800 copies, were published each year. We gave each student a copy; we also sent copies to the elementary schools for every fifth grader, giving those students a sense of the school they would be attending the next year. Copies also were sent to the high school journalism class.

Bob Kaplan, the library media specialist, acted as publisher, I served as editor, and students were reporters, doing the leg work as they chased down stories.

The students on one team began their articles on the day another team published its issue. I distributed copies of the newspaper and asked the kids to take fifteen minutes and read as many articles as they could. We then had a brief discussion about the strong points and weak points of the issue, and I assigned homework.

First, the students had to compose Letters of Acknowledgment to two reporters. As we did for similar activities, we made sure that every reporter received at least one letter; the second letter went to any other reporter on the newspaper staff.

Second, I assigned a journal entry to get students thinking about their task ahead:

a. What are the best aspects of this edition of the school paper?
b. What areas for improvement do you see?
c. What suggestions do you have for future editions?
d. Please give a general critique of the newspaper, including your observations and comments.
e. What else do you have to say?

The next day we held the first meeting with the publisher, the editor, and the reporters. Students shared journal entries as we critiqued the latest issue of the newspaper in greater depth. I announced that we were scheduled to produce the next edition of the paper four weeks hence.

We brainstormed ideas for articles, clarifying and expanding on students' suggestions as a way of introducing what a news article looks like. We explained the difference between objective and subjective reporting, differentiated between first-person writing and third-person writing, and emphasized the importance of having a good lead to engage the reader. The publisher explained to students that certain articles had to appear: a review of an upcoming school concert, a report on the fall sports season, an interview with a new staff member. Before the end of class, the publisher informed the students, "Tomorrow you will select your topics."

Then I assigned a second journal assignment, "Three Ideas," in which I asked students to propose three possibilities for articles and to describe each in a paragraph.

Adam, never a slacker, listed six:

1. Interview with a teacher
2. A poll about kids' favorite teacher
3. Taste test
4. Gift ideas
5. Kids opinions on (politics) the President + who they want
6. Why we have no honor roll
   —Adam Silver, age 14

There was a buzz of excitement in the air when the publisher arrived in class the next day. Bob began asking for suggestions, and in the space of ten minutes, he covered the chalkboard with over fifty different ideas.

Bob then asked students to raise their hands. As he called on each student (the reporter) in turn, they selected a topic to write about. As much as possible, he (the publisher) honored their choices. If a student was dead set on writing about the soccer team and had to settle for cross-country because soccer had already been taken, Bob suggested two possibilities: the students could switch topics if both parties were willing, or the second student could interview the soccer coach while the first focused on the team. We tried to accommodate student interests, because we knew that our reporters would be more invested in their articles if they were excited about their topics.

That evening, students composed a third journal entry, "My Article," which involved the following:

a. Describe your newspaper article in one sentence.
b. Who are the people you need to talk to for this article?
c. What questions do you need answered in your article?
d. What do you already know for certain regarding your article?
e. Write the introduction (the lead) to your article.
f. What else do you have to say about your article?
g. What else do you have to say about anything?

All three journal entries were assigned in the space of four school days; we wanted our reporters to think about their task: writing an article on deadline for the newspaper.

Inflexible Deadlines

"If your article is not complete by December 14," I announced to the class the next day, "it will *not* appear in the paper, and you will fail this four-week unit. 'Complete' means typed on the computer in Times font ten, spell checked, free of grammatical and punctuation errors, and approved by both Mr. Kaplan and me. We go to press on the evening of the 14th," I told the kids, "and we cannot wait for you." The silence in the room told me that I had their attention.

"You have no choice in the matter. I can cut you slack on other assignments, and I have, but on this one, no way. We have a deadline that we have to meet. Once they start printing, we will not yell 'Stop the presses!' as they do in the movies."

I gave each student a list of deadlines:

11/18: List of interview questions due
11/29: First draft due
12/2: Second draft due
12/7: Third draft due
12/14: Final draft due

Of course, if every assignment had such tight deadlines, that would not serve kids.

Since most articles depended on information gathered through interviews, we also discussed how to conduct a successful interview. Students were taught different ways to gather information. We shared models of good interview questions (those that would not elicit simple "yes" or "no" responses). Some kids created surveys or polls to collect short-answer information. Students needed help in both scheduling interviews and rehearsing their questions.

One challenge that some students faced was writing text that would be read two or three weeks in the future about events that had not yet occurred. Since the paper was scheduled to appear on December 15, if a student was reporting about the Winter Concert on Thursday, December 14, for example, that reporter had to write, "Last night's music extravaganza . . ." prior to the event actually taking place.

We gave each student a checklist:

_____ In your article, do you answer the following questions: WHO, WHAT, WHERE, WHEN, WHY and HOW?
_____ Do you use the third person (as opposed to the first person)?
_____ Does the action in your article take place in the past, present, or future? Do all your verb tenses agree?

_____ What alternatives to "said" do you use?
_____ Do you use direct quotes in your article?
_____ Do you identify each person you quote?
_____ Does your article have a good lead?

After students were under way, but before they completed their final drafts, we set up writing groups of three or four students. In their groups, students shared drafts of articles in progress. Each reporter read his or her article aloud twice; group members offered response guided by the following prompts:

What is good about the article?
What is missing from the article?
How would you improve the lead?
How would you improve the closing?
Comment on the overall interest level of the article.
Offer other suggestions for improvement.

Aware that the newspaper would reflect on our team when it was distributed to the entire school (as well as to many people outside the school), each student wanted to make the publication as interesting as possible; they worked with enlightened self-interest when assisting peers in writing groups.

A week later, we assigned a fourth journal entry, "Doing My Article." I gave kids the following questions:

a. What are you doing to complete your article?
b. What problems are you encountering?
c. What successes are you having?
d. What are you learning as you create this newspaper article?
e. What else do you have to say?

Bobby responded:

The article I'm doing is "Cuts in Sports." Should things stay the way they are, or should we bring cuts into our sports program? That is just one of the questions I hope to answer with my article. Within my article I'm going to include as many different opinions as there are, except mine. I'll do this by interviewing teachers and students, grades six through eight, teams one through four, boys and girls. That should about cover it. Then I'll compare opinions, and generate suggestions & new ideas.
        —Bobby Unterstein, age 13

Bobby was headed in the right direction; he had thought about the steps he needed to take next.

Adam shared what he had learned:

It is hard to interview someone when you can't write very fast! I had a little trouble with this and tried not to misquote someone, but hey, I tried as hard as I could (yes, I know there is no try). And I learned that writing an article is a lot more than writing off the top of your head. It requires a lot of interviewing, thought, and time put in to make the piece worth publishing. I also learned to use my time wisely; no really, I did; I learned the hard way, though.
    —Adam Silver, age 14

As the students worked on their articles, we found the following guidelines useful:

- One author per article; no coauthors.
- Two teachers, one of whom is the English teacher, must sign off on a student's final draft before it is considered done.
- Students, save all drafts!

The principal read every article and signed off on each of them before the newspaper went to press. On occasion he exercised administrative authority and requested a rewrite; other times he clarified issues and provided missing information.

After completing their articles, each student wrote a letter to an adult who had helped in some way (for example, a coach interviewed about a team or a teacher featured in a profile), acknowledging their assistance.

Once all the articles were done, Bob, the publisher, used a desktop publishing software program (Pagemaker) to put them in newspaper form. He then delivered a disk containing the formatted newspaper to a local printer.

Publication Day

The day the newspaper came back from the printer was a day of celebration. Four students volunteered to come to school early and deliver the paper; every language arts teacher received a class set; other staff members found copies waiting in their mailboxes.

In class, students read the paper cover to cover, praising peers and enjoying the fruits of their collective labor. Some students expressed a sense of letdown, noting how tiny their articles seemed after four intense weeks of work interviewing, drafting, revising, and proofreading. We also were aware of the fact that elsewhere in the building, another eighth-grade class was reading and critiquing our edition, starting the process all over again as they prepared to become reporters. Later, the publisher stopped by to congratulate the kids; his reporters gave him an ovation for all his efforts.

That evening students completed a fifth journal entry on the newspaper. In this entry, called "Being a Reporter," they reflected on the entire unit. I asked them to consider the following:

a. What did you learn?
b. Briefly describe your completed article.
c. What was the value of this learning experience?
d. Describe the specific actions you took to write your article.
e. What else do you have to say?

Adam responded, in part:

a. Being a reporter is one tough job. I think I appreciate newspapers and articles much more because I think of how much work must have gone into them. I mean, the drafts, the names, the quotes, the spelling, the hyphenation and the grammar, it's enough to drive anyone crazy. I also learned the correct way to write a newspaper article, and the numerous drafts and correcting you must go through before the article is considered "done."

b. When I first started the article, I decided to do it in a question-answer way. But as the article progressed, it didn't sound or look right. Just questions and answers made the article seem dull. So I changed my article and added much more interpretation of the quotes. And that made all the difference in my article, along with the common grammatical and spelling corrections.
—Adam Silver, age 14

Summing Up

Writing a news article on deadline for publication is a useful challenge for young adolescents. The journal entries forced them to plan ahead, think things through, and commit themselves to a course of action. The entries also allowed Bob and me to monitor student progress; if we read a journal entry containing a cry for help, we could respond.

Our goals for the newspaper project were:

- To help students develop and enhance their interviewing, reporting, writing, and word processing skills;
- To enhance students' self-esteem (we expected that even the weakest writer would have an article that he or she could be proud of and that everyone in the school would read);
- To foster a positive group feeling as students contribute to a project larger than any one individual.

We met our goals every year.

For me, the newspaper project was a high point in the year's writing program, for several reasons:

- Newspaper articles were a new form of writing for most students.
- This was a real writing exercise that resulted in a tangible public product.
- The activity was inclusive: every student participated.

- Students got a taste of journalism while providing a service to the school.
- Students learned the six basic questions of journalism: who, what, when, where, why, and how.
- Reading was encouraged; all language arts classes stopped what they were doing to read the newspaper.
- The student reporters were proud that the entire school was talking about "their" newspaper.
- By creating a newspaper, students become producers of knowledge.
- Inevitably, controversies arose with some articles, enabling us to discuss issues such as censorship, fact versus opinion, balanced reporting, and libel.
- The high school journalism program benefited as well, because all eighth graders were given this experience, which they could later draw on.

Brooke's Interview

Brooke's experience provides a good example of how useful such an activity can be for all students. An average student, Brooke exploded with energy, engagement, and academic accomplishment during the newspaper unit. Her interview questions were excellent, and her article was among the most widely read in that issue of the school newspaper.

What happened? Ten years later, Brooke recalled:

One day Mr. Burkhardt overheard Rachel Moskowitz and me talking about this cute guy named Paul Rudd. Paul Rudd starred on the NBC television drama *Sisters*. Mr. Burkhardt told us that his son Théo was friends with Paul Rudd. My mouth dropped to the floor. I had never met anyone who knew any famous people! This was BIG!

Before I knew it, Mr. Burkhardt walked in to class with two 8 x 10 head shots of Paul, each autographed for Rachel and me. Attached to Paul's photo was his resume. I noticed a few things about Paul and started poking around for more information. Mr. Burkhardt asked me if I wanted to interview him for the school newspaper. Of course, he had to see if he could set it up first, and if I was up for the task.

Paul lived in California at the time, so the interview was conducted by telephone. The time arranged happened to fall during one of our many school trips. I remember being very nervous on the bus ride upstate. I sat in the front of the minibus with Mr. Burkhardt as we went over my interview questions.

When the time came to make the call, we were at a steak house in upstate New York in the middle of our presentation to teachers. It wasn't the most appropriate of places to be conducting such an important interview, but that wasn't going to dampen my day. For all Paul knew, I could have been at home.

The interview went very well. As nervous as I was, I don't think Paul suspected a thing. I sat in the kitchen of the restaurant on a little wooden stool, talking [for] about an hour on the phone with my new "actor friend," and when we were done I almost cried. I couldn't believe that it was over. I secretly smiled, though, knowing that I still had his home phone number! (girls will be girls . . .)

Compared to other writing assignments of that year, I know that this one is the most memorable. They were all memorable, but this was the biggie. I enjoyed many of the assignments. I think the reason was because we published everything! If it was in a book for everyone on the team to read, then we all just worked a little bit harder to make it just that much better.

From time to time I hear about Paul Rudd. He's starred in movies such as *Romeo and Juliet* and *Cider House Rules,* as well as on Broadway. I often wonder if he remembers me. After all, during our interview he did call me his "first fan"!
—Brooke Berlickij Caputo

Rarely does writing get as real as it did for Brooke.

For further information about the school newspaper project, contact the publisher at: mediamanbob1@yahoo.com.

Responding to a Play

In my class, students read two plays: *The Miracle Worker* by William Gibson and *Inherit the Wind* by Jerome Lawrence and Robert E. Lee. I assigned parts, and we acted out each play. I was interested in what students understood, so I assigned journal entries in which they described a favorite character or commented on a twist in the plot. When we finished a play, I wanted to know more about what they had learned, so I gave them a test.

Robert Rubinstein (1994) addressed the issue of testing for learning with two analogies:

We know that to learn a skill you must first experience failure. When a child sets out to learn to ride a bicycle, we expect that child to fall several, if not many, times before mastering that skill. The same applies to a young athlete learning to bat or to shoot a basketball. For some strange reason, however, we expect students to do well on tests—all tests—from the beginning. We penalize them heavily if they "fall off the bike," or "miss the shot."

If, however, teachers believe that learning should be a positive, success-oriented process and experience for students, then we must give a wide variety of types of tests. (p. 79)

The Test

For *The Miracle Worker,* I designed a set of six questions as a take-home test; students were asked to respond to any three. I had designed the questions in such a way that, no matter which three questions they answered, their understanding of the play would be revealed. My aim was not to trip students up but rather to allow them to reveal their learning under ideal conditions; I wanted them to succeed. The assignment sheet read:

> As a summary of your understanding of *The Miracle Worker,* select three (3) of the questions below and write about each of them.
>
> A.   Keys and water: Keys and water were used as symbols throughout the play. Describe three instances where each was used (a total of six) and tell how the use of water and keys in each of those instances advanced the play.
>
> B.   What I learned: Describe and explain three (3) significant learnings you now have as a result of reading *The Miracle Worker.*
>
> C.   Essay: "On Being Disabled"—Write an essay on this theme. Include specific examples from the Helen Keller story in your essay.
>
> D.   Quotes: Select two (2) significant quotes/passages from the play and write about each of them. *Explain fully* their importance to the play.
>
> E.   Design your own question/exercise that allows you to write about your understanding and experience reading *The Miracle Worker,* and then respond to that question/exercise appropriately.
>
> F.   Creative writing: Select only one (1) of the three activities below—scene, poem, or interior monologue.
>
> > 1. Create a new scene in the play involving at least two characters. Include dialogue and stage directions. This scene can take place during the time of the play or after Helen acquires language. Submit all drafts.
> > 2. Write a poem of at least 16 lines that relates to the play and/or the characters in it. Submit all drafts.
> > 3. Write an interior monologue from the point of view of one of the characters in the play. Include setting (who, where, when). Submit all drafts.

Students enjoyed responding because of the wide latitude I gave them; they could select questions they felt were easiest and use forms that most appealed to them. All of the forms of expression suggested in this assignment had been required assignments earlier in the year; in this activity, they were options.

Note that choice E placed responsibility squarely on the student. At times students complain that the questions on a test do not really measure what they learned. In this instance, not so. A girl who selected choice E decided to wear a blindfold for twenty-four hours and report on her experiences.

As a concluding activity, we showed the 1962 black-and-white film version of the play, starring Anne Bancroft and Patty Duke. The kids loved it!

A Student's Response

Bobby's *Miracle Worker* response revealed what he had learned from reading the play. He selected choices B, D, and F:

For choice B, "What I learned," Bobby's main point was:

There is such a thing as too much love . . . I never thought love could ever be a bad thing no matter how it was used. But I guess there should be a fine line set between love and pity.

Bobby said that the play "reinforced how hard a time blind and deaf people have trying to communicate." He continued:

The final thing that I learned from [reading this play and] watching this movie is how much I take my senses for granted. Anyone with five functional senses doesn't even think twice about being able to run up a flight of stairs or get to class on time . . .

For choice D, "Quotes," Bobby wrote in part, "This quote, 'Helen is a treasure just waiting to be found,' is important because it explains how, even though blind and deaf, Helen is still very smart and has much to say."

For choice F, "Creative writing," Bobby used an ABXB, ACXC, ADXD, AEXE, AFXF rhyme scheme to compose a five-verse poem that summarized the play:

" . . . And there was light . . ."
Helen Keller
deaf and blind
First a brat
But now so kind

Helen Keller
Daughter of the Captain
With proper teaching
Folded her napkin

Helen Keller
Daughter of Kate
Not communicating
But no sign of hate

Helen Keller
Student of Annie Sullivan
"She can never learn"
Oh yes, it will happen

Helen Keller,
A treasure to be found
Once revealed
Is the sweetest of sounds

   —Bobby Unterstein, age 13

As with earlier activities, when students completed their *Miracle Worker* summaries, I asked them to select two of their three responses and prepare them for publication in another class anthology.

Assertions Addressed

As they composed essays, wrote newspaper articles, and reflected on *The Miracle Worker*, students addressed the assertions about writing again and again.

- *Every student a writer:* Each student communicated ideas through writing.
- *Ability level:* Both the published newspaper and *The Miracle Worker* anthology included writing from every student, regardless of ability. If you were a member of the class, your writing was published.
- *Topic selection:* All three activities included some level of student choice.
- *Peer models:* Students examined previous copies of the school newspaper before composing their own articles.
- *Reading aloud:* In writing groups, students honed the text of their news articles.
- *Publication:* Students published in all three activities.
- *Writing process:* Students drafted and revised during all three activities.
- *Audience, purpose, topic:* Students had to consider all three when writing essays and news articles.
- *Volume + Variety = Fluency:* By the time students completed all three activities, they had composed a minimum of thirty pieces of writing, including drafts, revisions, journal entries, letters, lists, and sets of interview questions.

Closing Thoughts

Essays, newspapers, and plays can be used to advance students' writing skills. In the heterogeneous classroom, all students participate in these activities as they respond to one another in writing groups, compose letters to reporters, and assume parts when reading a play. The central point here is that a writing strategy can be adapted to all kinds of learners. Our job is to provide as rich and challenging an experience as we can for all students who enter our classrooms.

Summary

Teaching writing is a complicated task, and there is no one way to do it. At once demanding and rewarding, it is rarely easy. You have to think on your feet and respond to myriad requests while nurturing the fragile spirits of youth. And you have to respond sensitively to the embryonic ideas of your students while simultaneously maintaining control of a room full of active young adolescents. That is why I used as many techniques as I could, many of them "hands-on," to engage my students. Forms mastered earlier in the year, such as poems, personal essays, interior monologues, and first-person narratives, were revisited in assignments that came later.

The seven chapters in Part Two describe many different writing strategies for young adolescents. While each strategy has its own attraction, it is the cumulative effect of all of them, and the multiple drafts required for several of them, that move students toward fluency in writing. A student who wrote a letter of introduction on day one, defined three Distinctions on day two, then composed free-verse poems, interior monologues, personal essays, and related journal entries during the first five weeks of school, had barely begun to write. The same student went on to write about *The Miracle Worker*, be a reporter on deadline, enter an essay contest, honor a relative or friend with a gift of writing, prepare a Letter to Self, consider lessons learned midway through the year, share a holiday memory, and render a Roomination.

While doing these things, this same student wrote over thirty journal entries, composed and revised countless drafts, sent numerous letters of acknowledgment to other students or teachers, and continually addressed the assertions about writing.

What was the impact of all this writing? What happened next?

These activities were a prelude to the culminating activities that ended the year: the poetry booklet, the parent writing conference, the individual magazine, and writing for closure.

Part Three

Culminating and Reflecting

How do you conclude a year of intense writing? How do you draw upon everything taught thus far and present it in a new way, guiding students to revisit past practices while simultaneously exploring writing challenges with new levels of demand? What activities can you do to tie the year together while concurrently encouraging students to reflect on the journey? This concluding section responds to these questions.

Chapters 16 through 19 describe four writing activities, each capitalizing on the skills taught earlier in the year even as they advance students toward what's next. The final chapter offers reflections on the writing activities described in this book and what I have found to be their lasting impact on young adolescents.

When students create individual poetry booklets, they use the skills of drafting, revising, and editing. After choosing several poems from those crafted during a two-week poetry writing unit, they prepare their poems for three increasingly refined levels of publication. Writing groups provide response opportunities, deadlines inspire industriousness, and publication reinforces editing, proofreading, and sequencing skills. All of these activities are familiar to the students at this point in the year, yet they take on new resonance as the disparate pieces come together. The poetry booklet also anticipates the individual magazine.

At the Parent Writing Conference, students reflect on the reams of writing they composed during the first seven months of the school year. Students teach writing philosophy to parents by explaining the ten assertions. They also select representative writing samples for their portfolios. In doing so, they consider the gains they have made in writing, then discuss their portfolios with parents; no teacher is present.

The individual magazine is the culminating experience of the year. All skills introduced earlier in the year are addressed once again as students write about self-selected themes using many forms of expression. They respond to one another's writing in groups, prepare pieces for publication, and generally celebrate the written word.

The activities presented in Chapter 19, "Writing for Closure" bring the year to an appropriate conclusion. Letters of appreciation are prepared for teachers, and students say farewell to classmates through Memory Minutes, a closure ceremony.

Finally, there is reflection. What lasting value did all the drafting, revising, journal writing, letter writing, publishing, listening, and thinking have on students? What enduring values did they take away? The final chapter explores these questions.

16

The Poetry Booklet

The Poetry Booklet

Basic idea: Over nine days each student composes twenty-two short poems based on models provided in class; then selects ten for an individual booklet, five of those for a class anthology, and three of those for submission to the school literary magazine.

Assertions addressed: All ten *(see p. 17)*.

Skills addressed: Word choice, descriptive language, poetic forms, listening, reading aloud, drafting, revising, preparing writing for publication.

Class time needed: Twelve periods: one for each of the eight poetic forms; one for returning all poems and explaining the poetry booklet assignment; two for writing groups; and one computer lab period for typing.

Advance preparation: Determine specific models for each form of poetry. Also, review several other poems using the OBQUIN (see p. 196) method to get students thinking about how poems work.

Time of year: Any time after January.

Neat feature: Students work simultaneously toward an individual booklet and a class anthology.

Assessment: The completed poetry booklet can be assessed as a major writing assignment.

Follow-up: Each student selects one poem and writes an explanation of it for a class or hallway display, "Our Best Poems."

Journal entry: After students complete their booklets, ask them to reflect on the experience of selecting poems for publication and producing a booklet.

Caution: When presenting model poems, proceed from simple to complex. Do not start, for example, with metaphor.

Forms: Poetry booklet assignment sheet.

Why do this? To tap into the poetic abilities of your students; to give each student a mini-publication experience in anticipation of the individual magazine.

I send students to their homes
where they've the task of writing poems.
—RMB

The emphasis on poetry in my classroom—from "The First Day" and frequent poem memorizations to my weekly poems and repeated references to Robert Frost—culminated in the poetry booklet project, usually done in late March. This activity was many things: an exercise in crafting several forms of poetry, a vehicle for publishing student verse, and a harbinger of things to come—the individual magazine.

I deliberately did not introduce the poetry unit in any formal sense; I provided no overview, nor did I say to the kids at the outset, "You're going to write twenty-two poems over the next nine days." That might have scared off some of them, particularly students who felt inadequate when composing verse. We eased into the poetry booklet project gradually.

OBQUIN

As a lead-up activity, I introduced students to a strategy for interpreting poems I call OBQUIN: OBserve, QUestion, INterpret. Each day I presented a new poem for consideration: "Mending Wall," "Stopping by Woods on a Snowy Evening," and "Birches" by Robert Frost; "My Papa's Waltz" by Theodore Roethke; "Not in the Guidebooks" by Elizabeth Jennings; and "anyone lived in a pretty how town" by e. e. cummings.

As homework, students studied the poem, wrote five observations about it, raised five questions, then offered five interpretations. In class the following day we gained insights into the poem as student after student contributed; they improved at OBQUINs as they did more of them.

Adam's OBQUIN for "anyone lived in a pretty how town" was typical:

OB:
1. The poem is called "anyone lived in a pretty how town."
2. The poem is written by EE Cummings.
3. No one cared about anyone in this "pretty how town."
4. "He" (in the poem) had a loving wife.
5. When he died, no one stopped to kiss his face.

QU:
1. Why didn't anyone care for anyone else in this pretty-how town?
2. When "he" died, why did no one stop to kiss his face?
3. What is the significance of "sun moon stars rain?"
4. Why are children apt to forget to remember?
5. Why does the order change in verse 21 of the poem?

IN:
1. Because everyone had only concern for themselves.
2. Because no one cared about anything.
3. The passing of time.
4. Because that's the way kids are!
5. Because something drastic has changed.
   —Adam Silver, age 14

Having raised student consciousness about the internal workings of those six poems, we moved to the next step: crafting verse.

"The Red Wheelbarrow"

One Monday in March, students walked into class and found William Carlos Williams's "The Red Wheelbarrow" printed on the chalkboard; I asked them to copy it into their English journals, then study it.

After a few minutes of quiet time building on their OBQUIN experience, I asked, "What do you observe about this poem?"

"Not too many words," said John.

"How many are there, John?" I pressed. "See any patterns?"

"Sixteen," John replied.

"Great. What else?"

They looked again. A hand went up.

"There are three words in the first line and one word in the second line of every verse," Melanie observed.

"Very good, Mel," I said. "What else can you see?"

"Hey, he split the word," Seth remarked. "In the title, 'wheelbarrow' is one word, but he broke it into two. Why did he do that, Mr. B.?"

"Why do you think he did, Seth?" I responded.

After a few minutes of discussion, students agreed that the poem was quite descriptive, conjuring up a strong visual image of a farm in a scant sixteen words. I used the term "still photograph" to describe "The Red Wheelbarrow" to the students.

"This evening," I said, announcing the homework, "instead of interpreting poems, I'd like you to write a couple. Do each poem on a separate sheet of paper, and use a repetitive word pattern the way William Carlos Williams did. Your task is to create two 'still photo' poems using just a few words. See what you come up with. And remember: save—"

"—all drafts," they chorused back.

The next day we shared our still-photo poems. I began with my own:

Sight
so much depends
upon

a pair of
glasses

resting on my
nose

helping me to
focus.

Students read their poems; we acknowledged everyone who contributed. Then I walked to the chalkboard and raised a map. Behind it was a poem.

"Copy down that poem, then study it," I instructed. Another William Carlos Williams composition, this one about a cat stepping gingerly into a flower pot, met their glance. They copied. I waited. They studied the poem. I waited some more. Five minutes passed.

"What do you observe?" I inquired.

The discussion, similar to that of the preceding day, elicited a variety of observations and perspectives.

Finally, I asked, "How does this poem differ from yesterday's about the 'white chickens'?"

They pondered the question. After a moment someone suggested that this poem had a little more action in it. I volunteered that the poem reminded me of a slow-motion replay on TV; the kids understood the analogy instantly.

"For homework this evening," I told them, "your task is to create two 'slow motion' poems. Remember, these are different from the still-photo poems you wrote last night. While you are drafting your slow-motion poems, think about word choice, patterns, and brevity. You can use the rest of the period to get started."

As I walked around and collected their still-photo poems, they began.

Slow-Motion Poems

We fell into a pattern: during the next two weeks I introduced a new poetic form each day, we discussed its salient features in class, and students wrote two or three in the same form as homework.

Bob, who loved basketball and admired my poster of Michael Jordan photographed in midair as he flew towards the basket, crafted a slow-motion poem entitled "The Poster" using a three-two word pattern for each verse:

Jordan frozen in
mid-air

Sweat glazed body,
tongue hanging

White Nike sneakers,
tongue hanging

muscles bulging but
never moving
　　　　—Bob Mullaney, age 13

Fast Action Poems

In class that day we looked at "fast action" poems, using another William Carlos Williams creation, "The Great Figure," as a model. Students copied it in their journals, we discussed it, and I asked the obvious question: How does this poem differ from "The Red Wheelbarrow" and the slow-motion poem?

Following the discussion, I held up a large color poster I had borrowed from the middle school library: Charles DeMuth's 1932 painting *The Figure Five.*

Surprise swept around the room; they knew instantly what it was: a painting of a poem.

Students observed the telescoped numeral 5 in gold, receding (or emerging?) in the center of the painting; the diagonal slashes of rain; the headlights of a red fire truck; the initials "W.C.W."; and the word "Bill." We enjoyed the melding of art and literature.

(Suggestion: show students the painting first, ask them to write a poem about it, then share Williams's "The Great Figure.")

Shattered Shapes

The following day, after students had read their fast-action poems to peers, I introduced them to the poetry of Arnold Adoff. At first glance, Adoff's poems appeared to be nothing more than random words scattered across the page; we dubbed them "shattered shapes."

The kids became excited about Adoff's free-form treatment of the English language. When I announced that the homework was to create three shattered-shape poems, they didn't blink. They were looking forward to experimenting with this new form; few noticed that I was asking for one more poem than the two previous assignments.

The next day we shared Adoff-inspired poetry. Greg constructed an intricate "puzzle":

Puzzle
     built of many p ece
              i s
          a
   w   n
each one interlocking
      t   t
      h   h
        e
        r

like a mystery

you will piece it together one
                   by one.

        —Greg Megara, age 13

List Poems

On Friday, day five of the poetry unit, I collected the shattered-shape verses, then introduced "list" poems. List poems are just that: lists of dreams, events, feelings, actions. We studied Walt Whitman's "There was a child went forth" from *Leaves of Grass.* Then I read something that I discovered the night before in my copy of *Poems for All Occasions:* it summarized much of the poetry unit to date:

There Was a Poem Went Forth

There was a poem went forth every day
And the students made observations on them,
   those observations they became,
And those observations became part of them for the day,
   or for a certain period of the day,
Or for many years or studying cycles of years.

The patterns of words became part of those students,
And the red wheelbarrow, and the white chickens,
   and the glazed rainwater,
And the figure 5, and the gong clangs,
   and the siren howls,
And the careful cat, and the right forefoot
   then the hind, and the empty flowerpot,

. . .

And the Third-month lambs,
    and the Fourth-month field sprouts,
And the content and the form,
    interesting and appropriate,
And all the events of the week in the school.

All these became part of those students
    who went forth every day,
    and who now go forth for another week,
    and who will continue to go forth until June.

I asked my students to compose three list poems as homework that weekend. No one complained; they were too busy enjoying the creative process and, of course, sharing poems with peers. We had truly become a community of writers.

Érica found the list poem a useful form to explore a very real issue that bothered her. On Monday she submitted "Everything of Mine":

Everything of mine, you say is yours.
So you can take my stereo that eats tapes,
and skips CDs.
You can have my messed-up drum set
that rattles in places it shouldn't
when you beat upon it.
You can keep my dirty socks lying on the floor,
the ripped up posters on my walls,
the TV with the broken color tube,
the VCR with the video tape that melted on it,
the other videos that got worn out from over-use . . .
Heck! Take the whole damn room. I don't care anymore!
Everything of mine, you say is yours,
even including my art.
But does that mean that you now own
my heart?
       —Érica Piteo, age 14

When I asked Érica about this poem six years after she wrote it, she explained:

The poem was a mixture of fact and fiction. I wrote it, as I remember, after a fight with my parents over my possessions. A young teenager fighting about his or her thing with the parental units, and the parents say, "You don't own anything—this is our house, and all the stuff in it is ours!"

The things I mentioned were all broken as a symbol of some bad things that were happening in my personal life at the time. I may have only been 13 or 14, but I had my own troubles.

After I wrote the poem, I looked over it. It sounded okay at the time, but something wasn't falling right on the ear, so I changed a lot around and decided, instead of making it between parents and a child, it should be a dispute between lovebirds. It just sounded better with that last line.

Haiku

After collecting the students' list poems, I introduced Japanese haiku. Several students already knew the form, having experimented with them in sixth grade. I put some examples by Basho on the chalkboard, students copied them in their journals, and we noted the inflexible structure:

three lines;
five syllables in the first and third lines;
seven syllables in the second line;
seventeen syllables total.

Before students began crafting their haiku, I offered one of my own as a model. Since I spoke of my family often, they appreciated this tribute to my sibling:

Twin Brother
Experiences
shared in youth create a bond
that lasts a lifetime.

On Monday, some students said that the rigid haiku form constrained them; others thought it a worthwhile challenge to compose in such a restricted format. Every student shared at least one haiku; because they had composed three as homework, they had choice as to which one they read.

Garrett hinted precociously at the "senior moments" of a later age:

The Search
I sit at my desk
looking for something that is
not there any more.
        —*Garrett Genova, age 14*

Larissa drew on her love of skiing to issue this warning:

Double Diamond
Beware: ski with care
If you don't you will suffer
So please be aware.
—*Larissa Figari, age 13*

Rhymed Couplets

I collected the kids' haiku and put them in a bulging folder of poems, then I introduced the rhymed couplet. Robert Frost has composed many provocative examples: "The Secret Sits," "The Span of Life," "An Answer." The kids enjoyed discussing and comparing them. We talked about meter and end rhyme, and we revisited "Stopping by Woods on a Snowy Evening" to examine its brilliant AABA, BBCB, CCDC, DDDD rhyme scheme. I explained trimeter, iambic quatrameter, and iambic pentameter. Shakespeare was mentioned.

We discussed what constituted a couplet ("a couple of lines that rhyme," Jake volunteered) and agreed that a couplet needed end rhyme and consistent meter in each line. I assigned three as homework.

The next day, few students were satisfied with their couplets; the strict requirements of meter and rhyme challenged them.

Dan shared a couplet that looked to the future, with a nod to mom and dad:

I might venture high or low
Please protect me but let me grow.
—*Dan Brickley, age 14*

Melanie understood the demands of the couplet; she captured my fancy with "A Teacher's Poem":

A teacher's job is to teach and tell,
but more than not they learn as well.
—*Melanie Fraine, age 14*

Metaphors

Year after year students found metaphor to be the most difficult poetic form of the ones they attempted. I saved it for last because of its demand for abstract thinking. We used Ezra Pound's "In a Station of the Metro" as a model. In two lines (actually three, since the title sets the scene), Pound limned the ghostly images he imagined while waiting for a subway train in Paris.

I shared my own metaphor, celebrating the joy a teacher living in snow country might experience on occasion:

Snow Day

Five a.m. phone call;
the Liberty Bell!

That evening, the students wrote their metaphors, most of them struggling. In class the next day I explained again that a metaphor was a simile without the use of "like" or "as." A few more understood it after peers shared their efforts. Bob demonstrated mastery:

The Dirty Look

The glare in his eyes;
a bitter cold day.

—Bob Mullaney, age 13

After collecting the students' metaphors, I announced the homework: two more poems using any of the nine forms of poetry we had studied. Then I read a verse of my own:

Poetry Workshop

Still photo, slow motion, fast action, list,
rhymed couplet, metaphor, shattered shape (twist),
free-verse poem, Japanese haiku:
twenty-two poems created by you.

They applauded.
"See you tomorrow," I said. "Have fun writing your two poems."

The Poetry Booklet

On day ten of the poetry unit, a Friday, I pulled it all together. First, I commended the students for having written twenty-two poems in the past nine days. Then I gave them their assignment for the weekend. I distributed an instruction sheet that listed the nine poetic forms they had learned in class thus far. As a class we reviewed the two-part assignment:

After completing today's homework assignment, you will have written two or more of each of the following kinds of poems during the past two weeks, for a total of at least twenty-two (22) poems:

> still-photo poem
> slow-motion poem
> fast-action poem
> shattered shape poem
> list poem
> haiku
> rhymed couplet
> metaphor
> free-verse poem

Your two assignments:

A. Create a poetry booklet of your ten (10) best poems using at least four (4) of the poetic forms listed above.

B. From these ten poems, select the five (5) best and type them up for a class anthology. Put each poem on a separate sheet; put your name on each sheet. You will have time in the computer lab on Monday to type your five poems.

Your poetry booklet and your typed poems for the anthology are both due by the end of school on Monday.

When creating your poetry booklet:

- Write or type each poem (and title) on a separate sheet of paper.
- Spelling and neatness count.
- You can create brand-new poems or revise existing ones.
- Illustrations are optional and encouraged.
- Create a cover with your name, date, and a title.
- Include a one-page introduction in which you:
  — tell what you learned by studying poems in class;
  — share your experiences writing these ten poems;
  — explain at least three (3) poems in your booklet (where the ideas came from, what worked, etc.).

I handed back the original drafts of the poems I had collected. Several students were amazed at how many they had created; two or three verses a day had not seemed like a lot of writing, but suddenly they were swamped with twenty-two sheets of paper (or more: some students had multiple drafts of poems, others had done four or five of a specific model) to sift through in search of the ten best for their booklet.

"Remember," I advised, "you need to have at least four distinct forms of poetry in your booklet. Choose your ten poems wisely."

Poetic License

Occasionally during the poetry unit, a student said that he or she could not write poems. As a countermeasure, I distributed a "poetic license" to each student, complete with the official signature of the Poet-in-Residence (yours truly), telling them they were now free to create poetry. And they did.

One of the reasons I chose March for the poetry booklet activity was to enhance the possibility of having my students' poems selected for publication by *Contemplations,* our middle school's literary magazine. I asked the kids to select their three best verses from the five they ultimately submitted to our class anthology and submit them to the magazine for consideration. The faculty advisor for *Contemplations* was always on the lookout for material, and she was overjoyed when, at the end of March, my students gave her almost 150 edited poems.

Melanie's Poetry Booklet

Melanie called her eleven-page poetry booklet, "My Book of Poems." She included two still-photo poems, three rhymed couplets, two fast-action, two haiku, and a slow-motion poem. Six of the poems were illustrated.

Melanie's introduction alluded to the recent poetic outpouring:

Af first, I had no idea we were going to accomplish so much in such a short time. Now looking back, I realize it wasn't that difficult. Writing two or three poems each night wasn't too much to expect.

I've learned a lot by studying the different types and styles of poetry. First of all, I never realized how many type of poems there are, especially when you categorize the poems by what they are describing. Plus, there is a lot to creating poems.

Before we started writing poems we interpreted poetry. We did this by observing the poem first. Then we would ask ourselves questions about the poem, which ultimately made us interpret the poem. Using this method, we got the full understanding that the poet was trying to convey. Actually, this method gave me a new look at both reading and creating poetry . . .

By doing this project I've realized that to write poetry, you don't have to be some student that gets extraordinary English grades. You just have to be able to express what you want to say or feel.

There are many ways in which you can begin forming your ideas for a poem, as for example, my poem "Dreams." This idea came from another poem that I wrote in the beginning of the school year. Both poems contain the same basic idea. All I did was simply shrink the ideas down into haiku poem form.

Another example would be "Sun Shower" and "Lightning Bolt." These two poems were meant to fit together because they are the total opposites of each other. This makes the subject more interesting. After writing the two poems, you can compare and contrast them, and see how they may be similar. I thought this was a neat method.

The last example of creating a poem was demonstrated in the poem "The Eagle." This is a very basic method. I got the idea for this by first thinking of the idea or subject I wanted to write about. After doing this, I thought of ways to describe that subject, which depend on the type of poem I was writing. "The Eagle" was inspired by my bird, but whose not exactly an eagle. This method is probably the easiest, and the one that is widely used.

Now you can read ten poems I have selected to put into this book. They are my personal favorites. Enjoy!
—Melanie Fraine, age 14

One of Melanie's haiku, "Forgiveness," raised an important question:

Why is it that we
ask for forgiveness only
when we need it most?

In "The Hard Way Out," Melanie honored a central fact in the lives of young adolescents:

When you're going through life's hardest bends,
you find and realize your closest friends.

"The Road to Utopia"

John created a memorable poetry booklet, "The Road to Utopia." A prolific writer possessed of a vocabulary advanced beyond his years, John relished fantasy, as reflected both in his verse and e-mail screen name, Earthdwarf.

The introduction to John's seventeen-page poetry booklet explained:

One of the first things one needs to understand before reading this book is that these poems are not connected, although they are bound together in this volume; but rather are from three distinct chronicles. I use the word chronicle instead of series because every poem in this book does stand alone, despite some being continuations of others. These chronicles are: The Wanderers, Abyssal Day, and Spirit of the Fallen Lands.

The first chronicle presented, the Wanderers, follows the exploits of a band of travelers through the enchanted forest of Evergrove. During the course of their journey they meet many kinds of people, each with a history and past that represent a portion of humanity. This book tells of only four days in their journey, but rest assured a more complete collection will follow.

Abyssal Day, the second chronicle, features four poems about exile, emptiness, cruelty, and finally escape, hence the title. Unlike the Wanderers, they do not all feature the same characters or the same setting. They are only bound by the general topic itself.

Finally, the last chronicle, Spirit of the Fallen Lands, contains several poems in various forms discussing nature, the universe, and eternity. These wonders of the natural world which we no longer sustain the interest in that our ancestors did are most likely the key to comprehension of the ancient past. All of them have true hidden meanings, but discovering them may take several readings.

To better enjoy these poems, achieve a temporary open-minded state of thinking. Be less concerned with realism than with perspective. The same was required in order to write them.

—John O'Brien, age 14

The first chronicle, "The Wanderers," contained four "shaped" poems. "Lost Souls" resembled a peaked tower; "Endlessly Challenged" presented the outline of a fish; "Brothers of Fire" suggested both a tent and a tongue of flame leaping up; "Evergrove" was typed in the shape of a pine tree:

Evergrove

On
day one
they came to
a dense grove of
tall pine trees older
than the human race that
looked as pure and unharmed
as young saplings just planted. They
asked the trees, "How is it you have eternal
life and we do not?" The forest had the power
to speak; but chose not to as to instill mystery in
them. The elder
spruces then went
about their job as
always, to provide
a guarded haven
for all the world.

The second section of poems, "Abyssal Day," concluded with "Leap of Faith," written in free verse and employing a pattern of two-line stanzas in which the first line contained four words and the second line three. John observed the maxim "In poetry, every word counts." (His romance with the semicolon is apparent as well.)

Leap of Faith

They told him he'd
never make it;

but at the time
when he left;

he decided not to
worry about it.

But as he stood
at the edge;

of the final obstacle
the infinite chasm;

he could not ignore
it any longer.

When the wind came
he backed up;

then ran up to
the chasm's edge.

Then he leapt, hoping
for the best.

John's third section, "Spirit of the Fallen Lands," included "Golden Sunrise," another free-verse poem crafted using a four-words-per-line pattern.

Golden Sunrise

As he looked out
the old tower window;
the golden sunrise behind
the tall green hills;
seemed to pause despite
the flow of time;
to allow the onlookers
a view of eternity.

John submitted three "shaped" poems to *Contemplations:* "Evergrove," "Lost Souls" and "Endlessly Challenged." All were selected and published.

Six years later I asked John what he remembered about his days as a young poet. He responded:

> Until recently, I always had a problem with sticking to specific assignments and strictly emulating models. Back in fifth grade I actually failed an important writing assessment test because the topic was limited. I believe "The Road to Utopia" was a one-of-a-kind item born out of a rather general poetry exercise. It remains my favorite of the pieces I did in eighth grade, one which I have never revised, revisited or expanded and whose format I never recycled.

Assertions Addressed

In the poetry unit, students addressed every one of the ten assertions about writing:

- Each student became a poet and communicated ideas in verse.
- Each poetry booklet reflected the writing ability of its author.
- Each poet chose the topics for the twenty-two poems.
- Because each class began with the sharing of poems written the previous evening, students learned from one another by example.
- I became the teacher as poet, sharing my verse with the community of poets.
- When they read poems aloud in class and later in writing groups, these young poets discovered possibilities for revision.
- Three opportunities for publishing occurred: the individual poetry booklet; the class poetry anthology; *Contemplations,* the middle school literary magazine.
- The writing process—drafting and revising—helped students craft verse.
- Because we shared poems each day, students began writing with their peers in mind.
- Composing twenty-two poems in nine days added to each student's fluency as a writer.

Closing Thoughts

The poetry booklet, a major piece of independent work, grew in complexity over the years as students reached new levels of excellence. They had to master the task of creating a coherent, connected booklet with a cover, an introduction, the body of text, and supporting illustrations (I required one illustration; many students designed several). Because they created the text for the booklet piecemeal over nine days, students were not overwhelmed by the task of composing almost two dozen poems all at once. They also found that creating the booklet was a relatively easy task because it focused on one form of expression: poetry.

The process of winnowing down twenty-two poems to ten (for the poetry booklet), then to five (for the class anthology), and then to three (for consideration by *Contemplations*) was a great exercise in selective editing. Each student had to decide which were his or her best poems, then live with the results of those decisions in print.

17

The Parent
Writing Conference

The Parent Writing Conference

Basic idea: In the Parent Writing Conference (PWC), the student conducts a half-hour writing conference with his or her parent, without a teacher present.

Assertions addressed: 1, 2, 3, 6, 7, 8, and 10 *(see p. 17)*.

Skills addressed: Organization, preparation, presentation, analysis, reflection.

Class time needed: Four class periods:
a. explanation of assignment
b. portfolio preparation
c. more portfolio preparation
d. follow-up discussion

Preparation: Each student needs a classroom folder in which to save all drafts and revisions created during the school year. Filing of student papers should be ongoing.

Time of year: March/April

Neat features: The Parent Reaction Form provides direct feedback from parent to teacher. Students observe their writing progress over time.

Assessment: Journal entry; Parent Reaction Form. No mark goes into the teacher grade book—use Complete or Incomplete.

Follow-up: Class discussion about writing after students complete their PWCs.

Journal entry: "Doing My PWC"
- What did you learn by examining your writing with one of your parents?
- What questions did your parent have about your writing?
- How has your writing improved since the school year began?
- What are your current writing strengths?
- What areas of your writing need improvement?
- What else do you have to say about your writing this school year?

Caution: Make sure the parent knows that the PWC is meant to be a positive experience for the student. If a parent is not available, enroll an aunt, uncle, grandparent, or trusted teacher.

Forms: PWC: Letter to Student; Letter to the Parent; Writing Portfolio Checklist; Parent Writing Conference: Appointment Form; Parent Writing Conference: Directions for the Student; Parent Writing Conference: Guidelines for the Parent; Parent Writing Conference: Reaction Form.

Well, first when I told my mom the idea about a writing confrence she thought it was one of those stupid things you could have in the middle of the civil war. She wanted to have this confrence with me either when she was gardening or when she was putting Lydianne to sleep. So I finally I got upset and started to yell at her that this was important to me and I didn't want any interuptions and that she should for once do something the way I wanted it and to my convini- ance and pay attension to me. So finally she agreed to my plan . . .

She wanted to know which piece was the most fun to write, and which piece I thought was my best. It turned out that my mom didn't like [my best piece] too much, and the piece I thought was middle class writing, she thought was excellent because I got right down to the point and didn't have repetitions. She also asked me if I liked to write. I was stumped for about a minute, then I finally answered, that it was a pleasure for me to write down my thoughts on paper and to be complemented on them.

I think writing is very important, and the better the writer you become, the better you are as a person because your vocabulary expands, and when people read your writing they get shocked that it is so good. I'm very happy I got stuck with a teacher like Mr. Burkhardt because he is a writer himself and I think of his pieces as masterpieces, especially the booklette for his mom, and also the writing activities are extremely fun and humerous (sometimes).

—Magda Jedlinski, age 13

How well do the parents of your students understand what you are teaching? How often does a student get the opportunity to look good in front of Mom or Dad? These two questions prompted the idea of the Parent Writing Conference (PWC).

The PWC was simple in concept. The student was asked to:

- review the ten assertions about writing;
- select several compositions and place them in a portfolio;
- explain the PWC assignment to a parent;
- after setting a conference date, give the writing portfolio to the parent to be reviewed prior to the PWC;
- conduct the half-hour writing conference at home with the parent, with no teacher present;
- reflect on the experience in a journal entry (the parent was also invited to offer feedback).

The Parent Writing Conference was a celebration of writing during which students presented themselves to their parents as accomplished learners in the field of writing. Since the teacher was not present, the PWC truly addressed the child-parent relationship, making the two partners in the learning process. Student and parent could examine writing at home in a structured, yet unhurried, setting; the instructions insisted that the half-hour discussion be "uninterrupted by any other concerns." That was cru- cial. In today's hurry-up world, it is not always easy to find half an hour where parent and child can focus on academics. If you do this activity, give your students at least a week to schedule and then conduct their PWCs.

We did Parent Writing Conferences in late March. At that point in the year the students had accumulated numerous pieces of writing from which to select a representative sample for their portfolios: different forms, different audiences, and different tasks. On regular occasions earlier in the year, students had filed their papers in the classroom filing cabinet, preparing unknowingly for the PWC. Echoes of "Save all drafts!" rang in their ears, and suddenly they knew why I had been so persistent with that instruction all year long.

In theory, the portfolio would represent the best writing the student had created during the year to date. Since each student by then had more than sixty pieces of writing from which to select, the odds were good that the writing conference would be a positive experience for both parent and child.

The idea for the Parent Writing Conference stemmed from a conversation I had in 1993 with Dr. Joyce Epstein, now Director of the Center on School, Family, and Community Partnerships at Johns Hopkins University. The two of us were engaged in committee work for the National Board for Professional Teaching Standards at the time. On a flight to Baltimore, she asked me about the ways in which I was involving the parents of my students in their learning. As I thought about her question, I realized that there were some deliberate steps I could take to help parents both understand the curriculum and see their child as a learner. The PWC was one of several activities that stemmed from that conversation.

Reviewing the Assertions

As preparation for the PWC, my students and I began by reviewing the assertions about writing. I gave a copy to each student. As we discussed each one briefly, I noticed students nodding to themselves as they saw in print the philosophy that had guided their writing since September. For homework that evening I asked students to select any three assertions and write about each of them in their English journals.

Nicole waxed eloquently about topic selection:

I find that I (a) have more fun, (b) do better on, (c) finish faster and (d) learn more when I pick my own topic to write about. For example: Let's consider the Bill of Rights [American Legion] essay [contest entry] with the Gift of Writing. If you read both of these pieces you will see a significant [difference] in presentation as well as content. The B.O.R. essay was an assigned topic. Added to that, it was boring, on top of that there was a limit on words! . . . It is stupid to have to cut down on words. This limits what you have to say. And it makes for a fruitless and dull essay to read . . . On my GOW, although we were given a vague outline of what was expected to be written, we were mainly left to use our imagination. With an endless source of ink and paper, I was able to pull through with a strong piece of writing.

—Nicole Guippone, age 13

Dan expounded on "Volume + Variety = Fluency":

Quite a true equasion. I'm completely convinced that this is true in all cases! Of course, not just writing but, practice always makes perfect. Since the beginning of the year, we've had to do many pieces of writing. When I first started I saw too many corrections for my own good! I was really frustrated and got sick of writing quickly. Since then my writing has matured in not only grammatical terms, but word usage has improved as well as my content and for this I am so grateful that we did so much writing and continue to do so.

—Dan Brickley, age 14

By asking students to reflect on the ten assertions, I not only prepared them for the PWC and strengthened their understanding of the philosophy of our writing program, but I also learned the degree to which they comprehended the assertions.

Explaining the Assignment

Sometimes when explaining assignments to the class, I pretended to be speaking to only one student in order to get the others to listen. I turned to Magda, a very responsible student, tennis player, and member of the chorus, and said, "These instructions are for Magda, and I invite the rest of you to listen in, or else ask her when I'm done, or even call her up tonight."

"Magda," I explained, "you're going to do an activity called the Parent Writing Conference. I want you to go to your writing folder and select at least seven pieces, all created since school began last fall, that you want to have represent you. Then, using the form I just distributed—the Writing Portfolio Checklist [these and other PWC forms are in the appendix]—tell me why you want to share those particular pieces of writing with your parents. If you want to use one or two entries from your English journal, that's fine also.

"Next," I continued, "I've got some other forms and instructions for all of you. This first one—the Parent Writing Conference Appointment Form— may be the most important piece of paper of all. Use it to set up an appointment with one of your parents. You and your mom or dad need to agree on the time, the place, and the date. It's kind of like the game of *Clue*—Colonel Mustard, in the study, with the hammer. I need to know all that."

I paused while Magda and her classmates examined the PWC Appointment Form, then continued. "Notice that it has two parts, Magda.

After you and your parent agree upon a time and place, fill it out and cut it into two parts. Put the top part on the kitchen fridge, or wherever you keep important papers in your house, and return the bottom half to me, signed. I need both your signature and your parent's signature."

Then I turned to the whole class and said, "When you prepare for your PWC, you get to go through all of your writing this year and select your best work, so you are totally in charge of what pieces you show to your parents and the sequence in which you present them. But remember, you can't have the conference until you tell me *why* you selected the pieces you did."

This last admonishment ensured that students would understand both the *what* and the *why* of the PWC—which pieces were going into the portfolio, and why those pieces had been selected to be shared with their mom or dad. I wanted students to be clear about their choices.

"Now, Magda, and everyone else," I added, "you've probably forgotten what I just said, so here is a general instruction sheet. If you follow these step by step, I promise you that it will work." I then pointed to a familiar sign ("Follow the instructions.").

As a class, we went over the instructions and reviewed the two objectives of the Parent Writing Conference:

> to increase parent-child communication regarding learning.
> to promote a better understanding of the task of writing.

I said that I expected every student to review the ten assertions about writing with their parents.

"Magda," I continued, "here is a letter from me to your mom or dad. On the back are some guidelines for them. And here is my letter to you, with your own guidelines" (see Figures 17.1 and 17.2). By this time the class was awash in a sea of letters, forms, writing assertions, instructions, and guidelines.

"Show your letter to your folks so they know that the PWC is something I am asking you to do for English class," I said. "And when you have completed the writing conference, Magda and everyone else, please invite your parents to give me some feedback. I will not be there at the PWC with you, and I am very interested in what your folks have to say.

"Also," I emphasized, "understand that you are not done with your PWC until you have completed the journal entry—all six questions. Today is Tuesday; by Wednesday of next week, the assignment must be complete. You will have the next two days in class to prepare your writing portfolio. But first and foremost, set a date with your parents! Do not wait until next Tuesday night to do this, because if something happens, you won't complete your PWC on time."

By the time they left class, each student had a clear idea of how to prepare and conduct a Parent Writing Conference. I also made sure they had Magda's phone number, just in case.

Figure 17.1 Letter to the Parents

Dear Team 8-1 Parent:

Since September your child has done writing in several different modes and for several different purposes. I know that you are interested in what your child is learning in school. Your child's current assignment is to have a writing conference with you based on at least *seven* of the following pieces of writing:

(a) free-verse poem, interior monologue, personal essay (September/October)
(b) PEEC pieces (October)
(c) newspaper article (November)
(d) Holiday Memory Piece (December)
(e) Lessons Learned (January)
(f) Gift of Writing (February)
(g) American Legion essay (March)
(h) *Miracle Worker* pieces
(i) one other piece of writing done this year in English/social studies (selected by your child)
(j) an English journal entry of your child's choice
(k) a social studies journal entry of your child's choice

This Parent Writing Conference (PWC) should take from thirty to sixty minutes. My request is that you schedule a time with your child when the two of you can sit down and discuss writing *uninterrupted by any other concerns.* It is appropriate for your child to share both unpolished drafts and final versions of these pieces. On the back of this letter you will find "Guidelines for the Parent." These guidelines should be helpful when you do the Parent Writing Conference.

Upon completing the Parent Writing Conference, your child will write an English journal entry in which he or she will respond to *all* of the following questions:

- What did you learn by examining your writing with one of your parents?
- What questions did your parent have about your writing?
- How has your writing improved since last September?
- What are your current writing strengths?
- What areas of your writing need improvement?
- What else do you have to say about your writing this school year?

The journal entry is due on Thursday, March 28. Please schedule this Parent Writing Conference between now and next Wednesday, March 27, so that your child can complete the English journal entry assignment on time. I also invite you to complete the Parent Writing Conference Reaction Form.

Let me know if you have any questions about this activity. My intention is that you learn more about your child by looking at some of the writing she or he has produced so far this year. Thank you, and enjoy this experience with your child.

Sincerely,
Ross M. Burkhardt

Note: *"Guidelines for the Parent" and the PWC Reaction Form are in the appendix.*

Figure 17.2 Letter to the Student

Dear Team 8-1 Student:

Since September you have done writing in several different modes and for several different purposes. Your parents are interested in what you are learning and how you are progressing. Your next assignment is to have a writing conference with one of your parents based on at least *seven* of the following pieces of writing:

(a) free-verse poem, interior monologue, personal essay (September/October)
(b) PEEC pieces (October)
(c) newspaper article (November)
(d) Holiday Memory Piece (December)
(e) Lessons Learned (January)
(f) Gift of Writing (February)
(g) American Legion essay (March)
(h) *Miracle Worker* pieces
(i) one other piece of writing done this year in English/social studies (selected by you for reasons of your own)
(j) an English journal entry of your choice
(k) a social studies journal entry of your choice

Your Parent Writing Conference (PWC) should take from thirty to sixty minutes. Schedule a time with one of your parents when the two of you can sit down and discuss your writing *uninterrupted by any other concerns*. It is appropriate to share both unpolished drafts and final versions of these pieces. On the other side of this letter are instructions for conducting the Parent Writing Conference. Follow them.

Upon completing your Parent Writing Conference, write an EJ entry and respond to *all* of the following questions:

- What did you learn by examining your writing with one of your parents?
- What questions did your parent have about your writing?
- How has your writing improved since last September?
- What are your current writing strengths?
- What areas of your writing need improvement?
- What else do you have to say about your writing this school year?

The EJ entry is due on Thursday, March 28. Be sure to schedule your Parent Writing Conference between now and then.

Let me know if you have any questions. Enjoy this activity.

Sincerely,

Ross M. Burkhardt

The Writing Portfolio

That evening Magda made the obligatory appointment with her mother. The next day in class she looked through her writing folder, eventually selecting eight pieces, one more than required (Magda often went beyond the minimum), that she felt presented a range of her best writing.

We spent three class periods completing PWC preparations: one to explain it, and two for students to sift through their writing folders, decide which pieces they wanted in their portfolios, then fill out the form explaining their reasons for selecting the pieces that they chose.

Magda justified each of her choices on the Writing Portfolio Checklist as part of the process of creating her portfolio:

Title: The Distinctions
I included this writing because: I want her to read my first piece of 8th grade.

Title: Flowers—Free verse poem
I included this writing because: My mom loves flowers and the poem is about flowers.

Title: Some Say—Anthony, Dan, Chad
I included this writing because: so she could see what was happening around us in school.

Title: Holiday memory piece
I included this writing because: it's about Poland and I want my mom to see that I still remember my heritage.

Title: Lesson's Learned
I included this writing because: its a different type of writing, I want her to see a veriety.

Title: American Legion Essay = Good citizens equal a strong democracy
I included this writing because: I want my mom to know that we [care] about our democracy and how we can help it.

Title: Olga—Gift of writing
I included this writing because: my mom will now know that I do care about her and I write about my family.

Title: Miracle Worker piece
I included this writing because: because I put a lot of hard work in to it, revising and editing over and over again till I had every word right.

By completing this form, Magda gained clarity on which pieces of writing she had selected and why she wanted them to represent her, and I gained valuable insight into Magda's understanding of the PWC.

Conducting the Conference

Students conducted Parent Writing Conferences at home, in the evening or on a weekend, without a teacher present. I always included a weekend with this assignment, introducing it on a Tuesday and having it due the following Wednesday (eight calendar days later).

The student met with the parent for at least half an hour and talked about writing. If a parent was not available, the student could conduct the PWC with a trusted teacher, an advisor, a coach, the principal or assistant principal, an older brother or sister, an aunt, uncle, or grandparent—someone who cared about that student and would provide the requisite feedback on his or her writing.

In my community I could count on parents being available. If they aren't readily available in yours, work out an alternative.

Journal Entries

After students completed their PWCs, they responded to six questions in their journals:

- What did you learn by examining your writing with one of your parents?
- What questions did your parent have about your writing?
- How has your writing improved since last September?
- What are your current writing strengths?
- What areas of your writing need improvement?
- What else do you have to say about your writing this school year?

Reading through their journal entries, I learned a great deal about my students and their perceptions of the writing program. In almost all cases, they saw improvement in their own writing over time and expressed positive sentiments about the many writing tasks they had performed earlier in the year.

Magda, a tiger when it came to tackling assignments, wrote a five-and-a-half-page entry detailing her experiences during the PWC:

> For my mom, she was very interested to see from my point of view which I thought was my best piece of writing or the most fun to write. I never thought of my writing as most fun. I know I am repetitive in some of my sentences but my mom pointed it out constantly and made sure it was clear. I also did not know my mother enjoyed reading my writing, I thought she was bored by it, that why I only read to her about one or two of my stories to her a month. Now I will try to read my pieces of writing to her when she has any free time, also so I can get some advise from her, because she will tell me what she really thinks.

Reflecting on seven months of writing several times a week in English class, Magda asserted that she had made progress in her ability to write:

> Right now, as I am writing this, I know for a fact that my writing has improved from September. The reason I know this is because I now catch myself when I use the same word to many times. Just a couple of nights ago when I was writing my fast moving poem I couldn't find the right word so I threw the whole poem out. Also, now I always read my stories out to myself one or two times before I hand them in. My first piece of the year "Distinctions" actually wasn't that bad, I thought I wrote pretty well in it considering that I wrote it and had no idea what writing was all about. Now, the pieces I write are much longer, have better and bigger vocabulary, and the sentences are phrased more the way I want them to be. What I mean by this is that I make them what I want and not what they turn out to be.

Magda also saw areas where she could improve her writing skills:

> My main weakness that is seen by many people and myself is repetition, I usually go to a thesurus, but for names I often tend to repete the same name over again. My mom points that out often to me, and I will correct myself in that piece, but then when I write again I sometimes forget. Now I have that in the back of my mind always and correct myself most of the time, but still I repeat names to often. Another weakness I find myself having is coming up with good titals for my writing. I can never find a perfect one. They are always middle class titals. So I have to work on these two weakness, and keep catching my mistakes.

Parent Feedback

Students gave parents a three-question "Reaction Form" and, on my instructions, invited them to provide feedback regarding the PWC. The questions were:

1. What did you learn about your child's writing through the Parent Writing Conference?
2. What suggestions do you have regarding your child's writing?
3. What comments do you have about the Parent Writing Conference?

Many parents accepted the invitation and responded thoughtfully, helping me to see how they perceived the overall writing program as well as providing me with specific suggestions for improving their children's writing. Most appreciated the time they spent with their child.

Andrea's father noted that the demands placed on his daughter increased appropriately as the months passed:

Andrea's writing matches the feelings she shares with us about fairness and justice. She is very sensitive to the conditions faced by people in turmoil. Please continue the methods you are using. I observe that the demands for concise thought, careful spelling, and sentence construction seem to become more demanding as the year progressed. This is good because it keeps kids writing but does not excessively burden them with too many corrections too early.

—John Campbell

Tara's father used the feedback form to acknowledge a positive interaction with his daughter:

I think the PWC was a good idea. It gave Tara and I an opportunity to review her writings together and discuss them. Usually I review her work as an assignment, with a critical eye, which I'm sure you know can lead to a more confrontational attitude. With this conference I attempted to just discuss with Tara her writing and how she feels about it. Of course Tara let me know that we were over the suggested time [limit] and we should finish up. As I write this I just realized that we left the table not grumbling and annoyed with one another but civil; there must be something to this. Thank you.

—Mike Bowden

Another parent commented: "You learn about your child's thoughts, ideas, and dreams." Still another wrote that the PWC was "a panacea to the universal response to 'What did you do in school today?'"

Follow-Up

In a class discussion afterwards, most students described the PWC as a positive learning experience. Some complained that their parents had not read through the portfolio ahead of time. In a few instances, both parents were present for the conference, but this was the exception. One or two students said it was "scary" to conduct the conference; most, however, enjoyed parading their knowledge of writing in front of their parents. A third of the conferences lasted under thirty minutes; a fifth lasted more than fifty minutes. One student said that her parent focused too much on spelling and not enough on content and growth. Another student, referring to a piece written in the fall, asserted that he could not have improved it when he first wrote it, but seven months later he felt that he could. Most parents were impressed by the amount of drafting and revising their children had done; several asked if this activity could be repeated later in the year.

I did not grade the PWCs. How do you evaluate such a personal exchange between parent and child, particularly when you are not present?

The journal entry and the student portfolio can be assessed, but since the teacher is not there for the actual conference, that experience stands alone.

As with the other activities in this book, the PWC format should be adapted to your students and your particular school setting.

Some do's and don'ts:

- *Do* give students at least a week to complete this activity. Scheduling PWC time with busy parents is not always easily done.
- *Do not* schedule this activity too early in the school year. Students need to have a sufficient number of writing pieces from which to select a representative sample for the portfolio.
- *Do not* allow the absence of a parent to result in the student's not completing the PWC. Enroll a colleague to serve *in loco parentis*.
- *Do* let students decide what pieces to include in their PWC portfolios. Have them explain their reasons, and let them have the final authority for representing themselves as writers. I recall occasions when I felt that a student had selected the "wrong" piece. Then I reminded myself that it was their writing, not mine.

Why have each student conduct a Parent Writing Conference? Essentially, to give them the opportunity to have a positive discussion about academics with their parents.

Assertions Addressed

As they put together their writing portfolios and discussed writing with their parents, the students addressed several of the ten assertions:

- Each parent saw samples of the child's writing, both early drafts and polished pieces; in this way parents came to know their children as writers.
- During the PWC the student read at least two pieces aloud to the parent.
- Students reflected in journals on their abilities as writers; they saw areas of strength, areas for improvement, and how far they had come since September.
- The experience was real for students; they "published" their writing by sharing it with an important audience—Mom or Dad.
- The questions parents asked helped students to understand their writing process; also, the discussion that a parent and child had about the ten assertions led to greater understanding on the part of the student regarding the philosophy of the writing program.

Closing Thoughts

Often when we give assignments to our students, we cannot anticipate where they will lead nor the impact they will have on others. Krystle's unvarnished PWC journal entry spoke eloquently to these very points:

> I was always so imbaresed to show my wrighting to my parents. I don't know why but I was. When I heared that we had to do the PWC I flipped out. That night when I got home I gave my mom all the sheets and explained to her what it was. I did not know what work to show her. I had to pick seven pieces and I only wanted to show her 5 I wrote. I picked 2 more pieces out and showed her. I also showed her my A.A.H. [All-American Hero essay] as an extra piece. The essay was about my grandpa. She very much enjoyed my stories, so she said. When I showed her my A.A.H she got halfway through it, and then I looked at her and she started to cry. My writing has never had as big of an impact as that essay. It was about her father. I guess she found it very emotional. She asked me to wright up another coppy and bring it to my grandpa. So that was the first thing I did. I never asked her why she was crying but I think I know why. When I brought [the A.A.H. essay] to my grandpa he wasn't home. I felt kind of stupid giving it to him so I hung it on the refrigerator. When he came home he noticed it and grabbed it off the refrigerator. I ran out the door. When I came back he gave me a kiss and said he loved the story. That was all that mattered to me.
>
> I am really glad that we got to have a PWC. I think it has changed part of my life. I now have a better relationship with my family, and I feel comfortable shareing my wrighting.
>
> —Krystle Gavin, age 13

18

The Individual Magazine

The Individual Magazine

Basic idea:	As a culminating activity, each student produces an individual magazine containing several pieces of writing in several modes, all related to an overarching theme.
Assertions addressed:	All ten *(see p. 17)*.
Skills addressed:	Sentence structure, paragraphing, sequencing ideas, listening, reading aloud, drafting and revising, preparing writing for publication, proofreading.
Class time needed:	Four to five weeks.
Advance preparation:	Earlier in the year, introduce forms of expression that can be revisited during the magazine project.
Time of year:	The last two months of the school year.
Neat feature:	Students become engaged in writing.
Assessment:	Journal entries can be graded; students can be assessed on their drafting and revising process; final drafts can be assessed; the magazine as a whole can also be assessed.
Follow-up:	Students distribute copies of their magazine to family and friends.
Journal entry:	One per week during the project; students respond to seven questions:

a. What successes are you enjoying with your magazine?
b. What problems are you having with your magazine?
c. How is your writing group functioning?
d. What ideas are you considering now?
e. What resources are you consulting to learn about your topic?
f. What specific questions do you have for Mr. Burkhardt?
g. What else do you have to say about your magazine or anything else?

Caution:	Allow sufficient time for students to meet in writing groups, type in the computer lab, and confer with you.
Forms:	An overview of the individual magazine requirements and deadlines.
Why do this?	To bring the year's writing program to a successful conclusion by having students employ everything they learned previously by producing a magazine.

The school year builds inexorably toward June. Writing assignments and activities done in October or January might have appeared to students to be episodic and unrelated, but for me they were part of a slow crescendo leading to the individual magazine project. In the spring, all skills came into play.

Whenever I walked through an art class, I was struck by the collaborative nature of the environment. Students who had been sitting passively in my classroom the previous period were now animated and purposefully engaged in creative activities. Part of the attraction of the arts is the hands-on quality of the work: students are producers, not just consumers, of information. I wanted to generate that same sense of engagement in English class. A colleague who had taken the National Writing Project Summer Institute suggested having each student create a magazine of his or her best writing. Touting the magazine project, she described her students as "authors." I wanted to see my students, too, as authors, and I asked them to create magazines. They did so, gloriously.

Format

The individual magazine had certain elements: a foreword; an "About the Author" segment; a unifying theme of the student's choosing (friendship, field hockey, courage, cats, whatever); eight or more pieces of writing exploring that theme, composed in at least three different forms of expression; and a required length—a minimum of three typewritten pages, single spaced, in 12-point type.

Once students determined their theme and had drafts to share, they met in writing groups, read handwritten pieces aloud to one another, and sought ideas for revision. They used word processors both at school and at home. Liberated from the drudgery of recopying text by hand, one diligent girl went through fourteen drafts of a twenty-five-line poem before she was satisfied. She changed line order, added and deleted words and phrases, and experimented with layout in each new draft. Most students settled for four or five drafts.

I created a weekly schedule for the five-week project. On Monday we met as a class; I announced deadlines, shared one or two exemplary items that students had just submitted, reviewed expectations, and answered questions. On Tuesday and Thursday, half the class met in their writing groups while the other half went to the computer lab to type. On Wednesday and Friday, the students switched activities.

The magazine project grew over the years; I raised the requirements, and students responded positively. Kids enjoyed assembling magazines for many reasons: they could choose their own theme; they could write in many forms; they met in writing groups and received feedback on their writing; and they had fewer class lectures to sit through as we shifted to a workshop mode.

My original magazine assignment, distributed over twenty years ago and limited in scope in those pre–word processor days, contained the following instructions:

Assignment: Each student will publish his/her own magazine containing original pieces of writing which have been drafted, revised, edited, and prepared in manuscript form for typing.

Requirements: Your magazine must be at least three (3) typewritten pages and not more than five (5) typewritten pages.

All writing must be your original work.

Your magazine must contain pieces written in at least three different forms of expression. These include:

> poem
> essay (personal or impersonal)
> letter
> diary/journal entry
> report
> 1st person narrative (fact or fiction)
> 3rd person narrative (fact or fiction)
> play
> interview

Your magazine must have a cover designed by you with the following information on it:

Title; your name; the date

Inside the front cover, two short pieces must appear. One is a piece entitled "About the Author," a paragraph or two of 150–200 words giving biographical information about you, your interests, etc. The other is a "foreword" to the magazine telling the who, what, where, when, why, and how it came into being. This foreword might also contain a dedication, thanks to the typist, thanks to anyone who was helpful to you in preparing the magazine, etc.

Optional Activities: You may wish to include illustrations, drawings, etc. for your pieces of writing. You may wish to choose a theme or central focus for your magazine and have all pieces relate to that theme.

Deadline: All pieces should be written, revised, edited, and prepared in manuscript form for typing no later than May 22.

Some pieces will be done sooner than this. As pieces get revised and put in final draft form, let me know and I will schedule editing groups to do the final editing and proofing. This way the typist can work on pieces as they are completed.

Looking back on this assignment, I note the tentative modesty of its instructions ("you may wish to choose a theme," "not more than five (5) typewritten pages," "at least three different forms of expression").

Ten years later, the magazine project required an interdisciplinary theme, called for at least twelve pieces of writing, was completely typed and revised by the student on a school Macintosh or home computer, and generally placed much heavier demands on the author. My tweaking of the assignment continued every year.

About the Author

We began at the end.

"For homework tonight," I announced one day in early April, "I want you to write an 'About the Author' piece on a separate sheet of paper and bring it in tomorrow. Do it in the third person."

I deliberately did not mention the individual magazine project. As far as my students knew, this "About the Author" homework assignment was a stand-alone writing exercise. Again, when introducing complex writing tasks, I liked to begin with something both small in scope and accessible to students.

The next day I asked students to take out their "About the Author" pieces. A rustling of papers ensued. "I'd like each of you to read your opening sentence, please. Chad, we'll start with you and go right around the room."

Chad read, "Chad Chinalai was born on December 15 in Bahrain . . ."

"Thanks, Chad. Tori?"

"Tori Schappert was born in Hicksville, New York, on September 21 . . ."

And it continued.

"Holly Galla, an eighth grader, was born February 9 . . ."

"Kevin Morgenstern was born in Mineola, New York, on March 13 . . ."

"Eighth grader Dan Brickley was born on January 16 in Manhattan . . ."

After the tenth student read his opening line, I asked, "Does anybody notice anything?"

"Boring," cried Jake. Everybody laughed.

"They're all the same," said Perri. "They all just say when people were born."

"Right you are, Perri," I confirmed. "Now, listen to these first lines of some 'About the Authors' from past students. 'When he was one, Joshua Silverstein was sent to his room for a no-no he didn't commit.' 'Magic, movies and money are what motivate Théo Burkhardt.'"

I could tell by the subdued silence that the kids were catching on.

"Check out this one: 'Life being unfair, Magda Jedlinski has to suffer six times a week because she can only go horseback riding on Thursday.' And one more: 'Shopping, talking on the phone, and being with friends is what Susanne Campo likes doing best on her own time.'"

"What do you think of those?" I asked after I'd read a few more.

A hand went up.

"Yes, Chad?"

"Can I have mine back? I want to revise it."

"Twist my arm, Chad. Anyone else?"

Twenty-two other hands shot up. The peer examples had worked their magic once again. That evening, students revised their "About the Author" pieces, adding zest to their introductory sentences.

Peer Models

"I'd like you to read something," I said the following day, randomly distributing some of the better magazines from years past. As was my practice, I used exemplary examples but passed them off as average.

"Take a few minutes and look through the magazine that you were given, then switch with a neighbor. Make sure you look at three or four different magazines. You've got five minutes to do this, so don't get bogged down."

The students began leafing through the magazines. Intense silence told me they were into it.

After a few minutes I asked, "What do you notice about these magazines?"

"These are cool, Mr. B.," said Jake.

"It looks like a lot of work," Chad offered.

"I like this cover," Bean exclaimed, holding up Alison Montgomery's *Competition* with its telescoped effect. Alison had glued a small yellow rectangle, actually a xerox-reduced copy of her cover, onto a slightly larger pink copy of her cover, which in turn was affixed to a still larger green copy. The word "Competition" ran from the upper left to the lower right in a diagonal line through all three pieces of colored paper.

"Now I think I know what that 'About the Author' homework was all about," Susanne observed. "Are we going to do something like this?"

"Indeed you are, Susanne and everyone else. In fact, you only have one English assignment for the next five weeks: create an individual magazine. What you have been looking at are magazines created by last year's students. The good news is," I continued, "you already have completed your first piece of writing. That 'About the Author' piece you revised last night will go on the last page of your magazine."

On that positive note, I handed out the magazine assignment sheet. We discussed it, I answered questions, and before the period ended the students had a good sense of what was expected of them. The combination of their examining models, revising their "About the Author" pieces, and studying the magazine requirements grounded students in the task ahead.

"Do we get to pick our theme, Mr. B.?" Tori wanted to know.

"Absolutely," I replied.

"I know what my theme is gonna be," Bean announced. And she did.

Theme Statement

A few days later I gave each student a form titled "Individual Magazine Theme Statement." Eileen "Bean" Wind had decided upon her theme the day I announced the magazine project. A Disney fan from way back, she completed her form:

Name: Bean Wind   Theme: Disney World

A. When I say (my theme), what I mean is . . .
B. This theme is important to me. I want to write about it because . . .
C. What I plan to say about this theme—my message—is . . .
(Respond completely to these THREE questions in the space below)

To me, Disney World is a fun place for learning, exploring, imagining, and see-ing that dreams really do come true. Even though I've been to Disney World 5 or 6 times, I still discover new things. I plan to let people know how educa-tional but fun Disney World can be. Some people think of it as crowds and long lines but I see it as a place for fun and imagination. That is the point I want to get across.

I informed students that they had to list at least five ideas for their mag-azine on the back of their theme statement; this was to let me know that, in fact, they had some notion about how and where to begin. An industrious student, Bean listed seven:

1. 1st trip to Disney World
2. Space Mountain
3. Poem of the rides—Magic Kingdom
4. My favorite rides
5. Imagination
6. Walt Disney
7. Disney World: A Place for all ages

She was off and running; my insistence on students' preplanning their magazine served her well. If, a week or two into the magazine project, a stu-dent faltered, I would ask him or her to reread the theme statement; in most cases, that put the student back on track ("Oh, yeah, that's what I'm writing about").

The theme statement for most students also served as draft one of their foreword. Three and a half weeks into the project, when I announced that the first draft of the foreword was due, I suggested that students look at their theme statements. The vast majority used that text as a starting place for their foreword.

Brainstorming

Once students had determined their themes, we did a brainstorming activ-ity. When they walked into the room they saw an instruction on the chalk-board: "Form a co-ed group of four or five people."

Once they were in their groups, I said, "You each have identified a mag-azine theme. Today we are going to do some brainstorming. Here are the ground rules. First, decide the order in which you do this; everyone will have a turn." They buzzed for thirty seconds and sorted it out.

"Who will go first in each group?" I asked. Five hands shot up, one from each group.

"Great. You will be known as the 'suggestee,' the rest of you are 'suggesters,' and everybody needs one of these," I continued, quickly distributing the Brainstorming forms, which were nothing more than two sheets of white paper stapled together, with the following heading at the top of the first page:

Name: _____   Magazine Theme: _____

Instructions: Write down everything suggested to you by the members of your group. Don't censor. If you do, you may miss some great ideas.

"Now, when I give the signal," I continued, "the suggestee, the person who goes first, has thirty seconds to explain his or her magazine topic to your group. Then, for the next four and a half minutes, the rest of you will suggest to the suggestee as many ideas as you can about what he or she can do with that theme. Be as specific as you can. Suggestee, get ready to write!"

I clapped once, and they began. The room was instantly noisy as students fired a constant stream of ideas at one another.

After two minutes I said, "If any of you hears an idea that you can use, even if it isn't your turn, write it down on your brainstorming sheet."

I suspect that both of the following occurred: a student who was suggesting something to the suggestee realized that he or she could use the same idea in his or her own magazine; and another group member who heard a suggestion made to the suggestee realized he or she could also use it.

After five minutes, another student in each group became the suggestee, and we repeated the process. After twenty-five minutes, each student in the five-person groups had taken a turn as the suggestee. By the end of the class period, all students were able to walk out of class with a list of new possibilities for their magazines.

The Five-Point Scale

A few years into the project, I developed a five-point scale to rate items submitted for magazines (we used the term "item" because it easily encompassed everything, from graphs to glossaries, maps to monologues, poems to persuasive essays, lists to letters, and diary entries to diagrams). When a student brought in an item, I rated it instantly, on a scale of one to five, using several criteria: creativity, length, complexity, originality, breadth, appropriateness, and informational content. A two-line couplet rarely earned more than a one; most three-page essays were rated three or better.

Occasionally, breakthroughs occurred. One Monday I held up Christine's board game; her theme was witches. She had researched the 1692 witch trials in Salem, Massachusetts, and invented a game called "Crossing Salem Village." Fate cards resulted in all kinds of disasters, including sick cows and failed crops. Christine's ingenuity prompted me to invent a rating of six on the spot, which I promptly announced to the rest of the class. Christine glowed, as did lightbulbs over the heads of several other students. The next day three more board games appeared, none of which earned higher than a three.

"But," Merri complained, "you gave Christine a six. Why did I only get a three?"

"Merri, my dear, first of all, life is unfair," I reminded her, pointing to the sign and smiling.

"Second, Christine broke the mold, and you merely imitated her. Third, the quality of her board game is better than yours, at present. Now, if you revise your game and add some interesting features, you might convince me to raise your score." She did, and I did; Merri was very sharp, as I was to learn later, during the Death Chair process.

Writing Groups

By springtime, students had participated in numerous writing groups; they knew the drill. But because the magazine writing groups were going to stay together for five weeks, I sought student input.

"Let me know who you would like in your writing group," I told my students. "I can't make any promises, but by now you know with whom you work well or not. If there is a classmate who you think would be a good writing group partner, put his or her name on an index card and return it to me by the end of the period."

In most cases, students made responsible suggestions. Factoring in what I knew about them as learners, I used their requests and my own intuition to construct writing groups of three or four students. Most groups included members with similar writing abilities. In many cases, when two good friends asked to work together, I honored that request. I had previously told them, "This is the most important project of the year—it will determine your grade in English. Do your absolute best work." Students understood the stakes, and they wanted to succeed.

Once I decided on the composition of the writing groups, I posted the lists. Much backslapping and congratulations followed: "We're in the same group!" Just before students went off to meet in their groups for the first time, and in support of the frequently referred-to poster in the classroom regarding instructions, I distributed a handout:

Follow these instructions for your Writing Group, also:

- Always meet in the same location.
- Writing group time is only for writing group—no library, computer room, etc. Be on task; stay on task.
- Have your drafts and a writing implement with you.
- You have at least four pieces to begin with—your "About the Author" and three first drafts (as of 5/5). Remember, the final draft of your "About the Author" is due Friday, May 6.
- Begin by explaining your magazine topic to the rest of the group.
- Do some additional brainstorming (as we did in class Tuesday) to add to your list of ideas for your magazine.

Deadlines

Each week I handed out a set of updated magazine deadlines to let students know what was due, and when. They appreciated these updates; there were many details of which to keep track. The list of deadlines also helped me manage the flow of paperwork and plan my time accordingly.

On the deadline sheet, I indicated both what was due and how many pieces in that category had to be completed by that date. For example, "two pieces revised in Draft 2 (total of four)" meant that by the specified date, a student had to turn in at least two new pieces of writing in second draft and have already submitted two others in second-draft form, for a total of four pieces in second draft by that date.

A typical handout read:

Individual Magazine Deadlines

Monday, May 14—2 pieces revised in Draft 2 (total of four).
Tuesday, May 15—3 pieces typed (total of nine, including AA)
Thursday, May 17—2 pieces revised in Draft 2 (total of six)
Friday, May 18—Cover, Draft 1; three pieces in final edit
Monday, May 21—Draft 1 of foreword; 2 pieces revised in Draft 2 (total of eight)
Wednesday, May 23—2 pieces in final edit (total of five)
Thursday, May 24—2 pieces in final edit (total of seven)
    Note: No new pieces for magazine after this date!
Tuesday, May 29—Cover in final draft
Wednesday, May 30—2 pieces in final edit (total of nine)
Thursday, May 31—Foreword in final edit
Friday, June 1—All other magazine pieces due in final edit

Some students had written pieces earlier in the year that fit the theme of their magazine. Students could use them in their magazine; but, since these pieces had already been graded and published, they did not count in any way toward the final magazine grade.

Students also found short pieces by other authors, mostly poems, that added something extra to their magazine. Joanna Kalb's *Baseball* began, appropriately enough, with the lyrics to "Take Me Out to the Ball Game." I set a limit of two such "outside author" pieces per magazine; on the rating scale, they earned a one.

Magazine journal entries were due each week; students responded to a set of seven questions for each entry:

a. What successes are you enjoying with your magazine?
b. What problems are you having with your magazine?
c. How is your writing group functioning?
d. What ideas are you considering now?
e. What resources are you consulting to learn about your topic?
f. What specific questions do you have for Mr. Burkhardt?
g. What else do you have to say about your magazine or anything else?

Two Student Magazines

Susanne selected friendship as her theme, a not uncommon concern of young adolescents. She decorated her gray cover with a two-piece "Best Friends" locket; her title, *Friendship,* ran diagonally from upper left to lower right in block letters; and four carefully chosen words—communication, respect, risk, and trust (Distinctions all)—were placed here and there on the cover.

Along with her foreword and "About the Author" segments, Susanne typed eleven pieces of writing in seven different modes: four poems, a dialogue, a letter, a list, an interior monologue, an editorial, and two personal essays.

In the foreword, Susanne explained her theme:

This magazine is based on what friendship is and what it means to me. One of the poems I wrote was about what friendship should be like. This poem shows all the qualities in a friend, and it shows what I expect of my friends. This poem is called "Friendship Is."

One of the reasons why I chose "friendship" as my theme is because I really dedicate my life toward all of my friends. Most of the time I'm doing something with my friends, whether it be hanging out at each other's houses, shopping together, or just talking on the phone with them. They are really important to me, and I feel that after you read my magazine you will have a better understanding on what friendship is, and you will get a better idea on how I feel about friendship in the world.

I give special thanks to my writing group who has helped me create and organize my theme. I also want to give special thanks to my two best friends, Danielle Marx and Jen Brander because if it weren't for them I wouldn't have had any of the feelings that I wrote about in my magazine, and I wouldn't have been able to use friendship as the theme. The last and most important person

person that I would like to acknowledge is my English teacher, Mr. Burkhardt. I want to give special thanks for helping me create this magazine, and for making it turn out a success.

    —Susanne Campo, age 13

Throughout her eighth-grade year, Susanne could always be found with either Danielle (Dani) or Jen, or both. Her magazine became a tribute to her two closest friends; they were the intended audience. In fact, three pieces in Susanne's magazine specifically celebrated Dani and Jen. One described a field trip they took to Albany to do a slide show presentation at Niskayuna Middle School, an event for which I specifically invited the trio because of their strong friendship. Another piece was titled "Letter to a Special Friend." In it, Susanne lamented the fact that she would be moving to Florida in a year and a half; she wanted Dani to know that "I will always consider you someone that was special in my life." The third piece, "Dani," was a memoir of their first encounter:

> I can still picture it now. Me, walking into a full room of kids, and all of them staring at me.
>
>   It was the month of October, around the 15th. It was when I first moved to Wading River.
>
>   As I walked into the room and sat at a desk, I could feel my heart beating. It was probably beating as fast as it could go. My hands were shaking, and I felt my stomach aching from all of my nervousness.
>
>   The first person that came over to talk to me was Amy Sill. I became friends with her for the first week until Danielle Marx moved to S.W.R. a week after me.
>
>   As soon as she walked into the classroom, I knew that I would probably be best friends with her immediately, and I was right. When we started to talk to each other for the first time, we both had a lot in common, so we decided to become friends. Danielle was really nice to me, and I started to like her.
>
>   As the months of that year went along, we were still good friends, and I had a weird feeling that we always would be.
>
>   Now, three years later (in 8th grade), we are still the best of friends, and we probably always will be. I appreciate her for being my friend and for always being there when I need her. I hope we will stay friends forever.

To this day, Susanne and Dani continue to be close friends.

After three days and several false starts, Josh still had no theme. I pressed him: "Decide now!"

    He immediately responded, "Chocolate."

    Somewhat dubious, I asked, "What's your first step?"

    "I want to borrow that poster," he said, pointing to an aerial view of the World Trade Center in Manhattan, its two towers distorted outward and upward as they rose 110 stories above the Big Apple.

I didn't see any connection between the poster and chocolate, but I handed it to him. Josh immediately disappeared out the classroom door. He was back five minutes later, clutching the twin towers poster in one hand and several sheets of writing paper in the other.

Ten minutes later Josh showed me a mock-up of his magazine cover. The word "CHOCOLATE" appeared in brown, arched over Manhattan's twin towers. The towers themselves had been transformed into candy bars. Using a brown marker, Josh had printed the word 'Hershey' on one tower and 'Hershey with Almonds' on the other.

Josh saw something that I hadn't in a poster that had been on display in the room since September. At that point I realized that Josh's theme—chocolate—would work for him. All I needed to do was get out of his way.

Ultimately Josh created six pieces of writing, including a list poem, "The Choice," which contained the names of 45 different chocolate bars, and his masterpiece, an homage to Robert Frost:

Stopping by Greg and Its Chocolate I'm Eating

Whose Mounds this is I think I know
His locker's in the third wing, though;
He will not see me stopping here
So I can eat it really slow.

I tremble and I shake with fear.
If he finds out he'll kick my rear.
Between the wrapper and coconut flake
The darkest chocolate I have right here.

The fourth verse began:

The chocolate's lovely, dark and deep . . .

The Death Chair

Assembling the final copy of the magazine was a challenge. Consistent formatting is not a task at which many young adolescents excel. Pagination, sequencing of items, titles exactly the same in the table of contents as on the numbered pages—all became opportunities for minor flaws. To heighten student consciousness about formatting magazines properly, I invented the "Death Chair."

"Now that you are almost done with your magazines," I said, "I invite you to sit in the Death Chair." I pointed to an unoccupied chair in the corner.

"Starting tomorrow, I want you to take all of your final drafts, put them in order, number them exactly as they are in your table of contents, and then meet me at the Death Chair."

"The Death Chair gets its name," I explained, "because no student has ever survived it the first time through. Everyone makes a minor error in pagination, in a title, or what have you. So here's the kicker. If you make it through the Death Chair on your very first attempt, with absolutely no error of any kind—spelling, punctuation, page numbers, title agreement, everything—I will add five points to your magazine grade."

A quick buzz filled the room. Since the magazine represented their entire English grade for the fourth quarter, the Death Chair caught their attention.

The following day, we began. Josh was first. He numbered his Frost parody incorrectly. *Goodbye!*

Tori forgot to put the date on her front cover. *Gone!*

The foreword to Bobby's Lacrosse magazine was not signed. *Scram!*

In her table of contents, Susanne misnumbered her tribute to Dani. *Outta here!*

Brooke's baseball magazine had a misspelling: she had typed "Forward" instead of "Foreword," in spite of my repeated warnings to the class. *Later!*

Lauren placed her "About the Author" on page 23 in her table of contents, but the "About the Author" page itself had no number. *Next!*

Perri's magazine on fashion began with page 1 on the left side of the staples. *Zap!*

Seth misspelled "Metallica" in one of his item titles. *Ding!*

Watching from the edge of the crowd as peers bravely took their turns, Merri carefully studied each student, going through her own magazine page by page in a dry run as the student in the Death Chair presented each final draft page for me to inspect. Three times in a row I heard Merri mutter, "I think I've got it." But she waited, checking and rechecking her work.

Magda spelled my name wrong in her foreword. *Blam!*

Chad had an item not listed in his contents. *Boom!*

Jake opened his folder of finished drafts, took one look at them and said, "Excuse me," and left. He saw something I hadn't seen. *Bang!*

Heidi got to page 3 before we found an error. *Badda-bing!*

Jessica made it to page 8 without a mistake. *Ka-boom!*

Greg survived until page 11 of his magazine. *So long!*

Then Merri stepped up with a smile. The rest of the class watched in hushed anticipation.

Cover . . . page 1 . . . page 6, no mistakes yet . . . page 12 . . page 16. On page 17 I stopped, then pointed to the bottom. The students edged closer.

"Oops, my error," I said. "There's no mistake there." An audible sigh of relief from Merri and her classmates.

Page 19 . . . only six more to go. Page 22. Finally, her "About the Author" on page 25. It was perfect.

I stood up.

"Ladies and gentlemen," I announced in stentorian tones, "I give you Merri Montenare, the only student in the history of the magazine project to survive the Death Chair. Five points! Congratulations, Merri."

Merri beamed, her classmates cheered her success, and I teared up—for joy, for Merri's well-deserved victory, and for the fun of it all.

Assessment

Magazines were assessed using several criteria. First, each piece in the magazine was rated on a scale of one to five, with five being the highest score. Second, I kept track of the degree to which students met deadlines. Items were due every day in first, second, or third draft, or typed. A student who turned in an item early received an E, and a late item received an L; an E canceled out an L. I was of the opinion that a student who amassed 57 E's during the magazine project demonstrated more diligence and industry than a student who complied 64 L's; effort was rewarded accordingly.

I kept track of the numbers of drafts of each item. A student who took each item to a fifth draft probably invested more of herself than the student who did just two drafts. Magazine journal entries were graded, and kids were given an overall journal grade.

Students were also graded on their participation in writing groups. Much of my time was spent walking from group to group, monitoring their activities and answering questions. Each member of the writing group received a group proofreading grade. The quality of each foreword and "About the Author" were noted, as was each cover. At the end of the project, students completed evaluation forms, which provided more information about the making of their magazines. Finally, I looked at the finished product and gave it an overall grade.

Assertions Addressed

During the five weeks that students worked on their individual magazines, they addressed each of the ten assertions several times:

- Each student communicated numerous ideas about a self-selected theme.
- Each magazine was an accurate representation of the current writing ability of its author.
- Students became invested in their magazines because they selected their topics.
- A kind of "family learning" was in effect: one student would "invent" a piece of writing, and others would follow suit the next day.
- In writing groups, students read pieces aloud to one another again and again, seeking the right wording, the right tone, the right pace.

- Every student completed and published a magazine. In sixteen years, only one individual, a school-phobic student who had been hospitalized for much of sixth and seventh grade, did not complete a magazine.
- The writing process reached flood tide as students invented, drafted, revised, edited, then drafted and revised some more, and eventually published twenty copies of their magazines for distribution to family and friends.
- Students considered audience, purpose, and topic throughout the project. Some switched topics early on, but most made a decision and stuck with it.
- Including weekly journal entries, the required eight pieces, plus the foreword, "About the Author," and extra items they created, students did more writing during the five-week magazine project than during any other five-week period of the year. The typical student composed six journal entries, an evaluation, and multiple drafts of ten to twelve items for the magazine. Volume and variety were hallmarks of this project.

Closing Thoughts

The individual magazine project was the most rigorous and demanding activity I did with students. It represented the culmination of the year's writing, one in which students drew on all they had learned previously to create something of which they were quite proud. I asked a lot of my students, and they responded accordingly because it met one of their needs: to be engaged in worthwhile, demanding work.

Starting in September, students learned to express themselves in a variety of modes: free-verse poems, interior monologues, personal essays, letters, narratives, journal entries, newspaper articles, editorials. They reflected on their learning (Lessons Learned) and themselves (Letter to Self), always through writing. They considered audience when they wrote (Gift of Writing). They created booklets of poetry, composing, then selecting, pieces and preparing them for publication. They reflected on their writing (Parent Writing Conference).

Thus, when it came time for them to create individual magazines, they were prepared. The process had been incrementally ratcheted up during the course of the year, culminating in this project. Students said in retrospect that assembling their magazine required the kind of work they expected to encounter in high school. I believe that it prepared them for life.

19

Writing for Closure

The year ended as it began, with music and poetry.
Walking down the hall toward their last English class, students heard music: "Hello, Goodbye" by the Beatles. They entered an unadorned classroom and took their seats. All the posters had been removed the day before, in storage for next year.

As the last notes of music faded away, I began reading a poem:

The Last Day

It's the last day.
In they come—
Some pausing hesitantly
At the door,
Reflecting and reminiscing,
Others familiarly announcing
Their presence
As they stride to seats.

Heads turn,
Eyes contact the now-barren classroom:
Posters and pictures
(Relics of yesterday)
Gone . . .
Saving seats for friends,
Listening to the music,
Awaiting the lesson,
They sit, comfortably,
Facing the finale.

For some,
The boredom of school
All but over.
For some,
The restraints of structure
Almost undone.
For most,
An explored world
Now transformed to memory.

The student asks:
"What did I gain from this experience?"
"What did I give to it?"
"What happens next year?"
The teacher asks:
"What did I gain from this experience?"
"What did I give to it?"
"What happens next year?"

A simultaneously shared journey
Through days and months past
Has ended. And now,
All is quiet and still
Because
It's the last day.

"Nobody Even Said Goodbye"

In 1984, my colleague Tony Messina served as master of ceremonies for the "moving up" ceremony we held the evening before the last day of school. Tony lived in another school district; his daughter Micheline, an eighth grader, attended another middle school. He invited her to our Eighth-Grade Night.

Along with almost two hundred students and over four hundred teachers and parents, Micheline watched as her father, a music teacher, performed "Wrap-Up Song," an original composition for synthesizers and percussion. She then saw a forty-five-minute, three-screen slide show celebrating the eighth grade via music and pictures from the past three years.

The following day, Tony asked his daughter what she thought of Eighth-Grade Night. Micheline replied, "Dad, it was great. At my school, nobody even said goodbye."

Earlier in this book I raised the question, "How well do we say 'Hello'?" A corollary question at the end of the year asks, "How well do we say 'Farewell'?" Young adolescents need closure, particularly if they have been members of a close-knit team. "After spending three years together sharing teachers, classes, field trips, sports, clubs, assemblies, community service, music groups, plays and more, kids have stored up a host of memories. When they walk out the doors for the last time in June, they should have no regrets about leaving" (Burkhardt 1985, p. 9).

Four closure activities brought our school year to completion: letters to teachers, striking the set, the last class, and Memory Minutes.

Letters to Teachers

Five days before school ended, I said to my students, "Put your name on the sheet of paper you were given as you walked into class." They did.

"Now, draw two vertical lines from top to bottom so that you have three vertical columns." They did.

"Put the numeral 8 at the top of the left-hand column." They did.

"Where is this headed, Mr. B.?" Érica asked.

"Just follow . . . ," I said, pointing to the sign to my right.

"I'm now going to ask you to do some remembering. No talking with neighbors, please. You will all have a chance to share in a moment. In the column marked 8, make a list of your best memories from eighth grade," I instructed. "Put down activities that you enjoyed, that taught you something, and that were important to you. The only requirement is that they be school-related. If you fill the first column, go on to the second one."

"Tori," I said, "I know you are a volunteer Candy Striper at the hospital, and Justin, I know you play trumpet in the community band, but those are not what I'm asking for here. Your list should be school experiences only. You have five minutes. Get started."

Kids began scribbling furiously, occasionally laughing to themselves. I watched, enjoying it all. Five minutes flew by.

"Finish your thought," I said.

"Now we're going to share our lists," I explained. "As each of you read one item from your list, I will make a master list on the chalkboard. If a classmate says something that you forgot, feel free to add it to your list."

Students recalled field trips, the Letter to Self, the undefeated soccer team, individual magazines, the school play, writing for the school newspaper, jazz band, playing lacrosse, building a CO^2 race car in technology class. As each student volunteered a "best memory," others added it to their lists.

"Okay," I said, "now things get a little more difficult. Just below where your list ends, draw a line and write the numeral 7.

"That's right," I said as the kids smiled, "we're going to do seventh grade."

They began listing memories from the previous year. I watched and waited as they wrote. Kids shared, and I continued the master list on the chalkboard. Frog dissection drew groans and laughter.

"Okay, now reach way back," I said, "and list your best school experiences from sixth grade." Again they wrote, then shared items. Lists grew even longer; puberty education sparked numerous giggles. Twenty minutes of class had elapsed.

"Kids," I said, "look at your entire list and circle the three best experiences you had. They might be all from this year, or one from each grade, or two from seventh and one from sixth, whatever. It's your call."

"Oh, Mr. B.," Tori pleaded. "I need to pick four." Several other students nodded in agreement.

"This is an 'intentional' school," I asserted. "Everything that you wrote on your list happened on purpose. One or more staff members decided that you should have those activities. So," I continued, "for the three 'best' items you selected—or, in Tori's case, four—put down the name of the staff member who enabled you to have that experience." They did, naming the play director, the band leader, coaches, the art teacher, their math/science teacher, and the assistant principal.

"Each of you now has a sheet of paper on which you have identified the best things you did in middle school," I said. "You also know the names of the persons responsible for your having had these experiences. And you have only five days left in your middle school career."

I paused dramatically, a technique by now quite familiar to the students. A few had already figured out where this was going.

"What can we possibly do with this information?" I asked. "Your best school experiences, the teacher responsible, only five days left? Can anyone think of anything that we could do with that information?" I repeated, hamming it up a bit and pausing again.

Chad raised his hand. "I guess we could write them letters of thanks," he suggested.

I slapped my forehead in mock surprise.

"Wow, why didn't I think of that! Chad, that's such a great idea, I think you should write *two* letters. So here's your assignment," I announced, "and it is the absolute last English assignment you will ever have in eighth grade." This wasn't exactly true, since they were also about to be assigned Memory Minutes, but it was a useful white lie at the time.

"Your task is to write letters to two staff members, thanking them for whatever it was they did for you," I explained. "Think of your letters as thank-yous to the entire staff for these last three years. Since this is your very last assignment, do your best work. I do not want you to sit bolt upright in bed in mid-July and say, 'I left without thanking anyone.'"

"Mr. B.," Tori blurted out, "now that I know what this assignment is about, can I write to someone not on my list, because I really want to thank—"

"Of course you can, Tori," I said.

"One other thing," I added. "We have had a great year, I have enjoyed having you as students, and some of you may be thinking of writing to me. I appreciate that, but if you do, it will cost you a third letter."

The assignment was not about generating mail for me but rather thanking the rest of the staff. Nevertheless, in the end I received several letters.

I'm not sure what it is like for you during the last week of school, but I remember how it was for me. Have you ever seen a World War II movie where the B-17s are coming back from a bombing run over Germany? The left engine is gone, black smoke billows from the right propeller, the fuel tanks read empty, bullet holes perforate the tail assembly, the wing tips catch the choppy waves of the English Channel, the bombardier slumps over the controls, and the White Cliffs of Dover are visible in the distance. *Will I make it?* the pilot wonders. *Can I hang on long enough to land?*

I identify with the pilot, because that was how I felt at end of the year: out of gas. Final exams, report cards, closure activities, the last field trip, textbook collection, and budget requests for next year demanded precious time as the grains of sand slipped through the hourglass.

During the last week of school I was able to pour fuel in the empty tanks of colleagues. The letters of appreciation that I put in their empty mailboxes brought tears to teachers' eyes. A colleague came to me and said, "Did you see what Billy wrote? He remembered fractions. He thanked me for teaching him!"

Few of us entered this profession for the money. Our dividends are more intangible; being acknowledged by a student at the end of the year is one reward. Letters to teachers are a wonderful closure activity and such a real writing assignment that my students didn't even ask about grades.

Striking the Set

Three days before school ended, I asked students to help me "strike the set"—that is, take down all the posters. During the preceding 180 days, they composed and questioned and listened and learned in a room covered with visual stimuli. In two short periods the decorations abruptly came down.

I gave away the handmade signs as souvenirs; kids walked out of class proudly bearing "Life is unfair" or "Do or do not; there is no try." The day after we took down the signs, kids still sensed where many of them had been; invisible posters were imprinted on their minds. I would raise my hand and point back and to the left in the now-naked classroom, and as in a Greek chorus they would shout, "Follow the instructions!"

By dismantling the "set," students moved one step closer to completion.

The Last Class

Every year, the day comes when you teach your final lesson to your students. I saw this as an opportunity for a closure ceremony.

After reading my poem "The Last Class" (which echoed "The First Day"), I presented humorous awards to each student, did group acknowledgments ("Stand up if you were in the band—chorus—orchestra . . ."), offered parting advice, spoke about my own summer plans, and thanked the students for all the writing they had done.

Then I read one last poem from my well-worn copy of *Poems for All Occasions*.

The Last Poem of the Year

How do I write
the last poem of the year
when what I want
is to still hold you near?

How do I find
the words that conclude
and punctuate our parting,
something I've rued?

How do I say
what is really inside
when I want to look back
without having cried?

How do I speak
of the love that I feel
when my pain at your parting
is vivid and real?

How do I tell
each one of you
how much you have meant
this whole year through?

And when you are gone,
how shall I recall
the tears and the happiness
of knowing you all?

Thank you, good friends,
for laughter and fun.
I'm better for knowing you.
Now we are done.

As a token of appreciation, I presented a copy of *Poems for All Occasions* to every student. All the weekly poems I had composed that year were included.

Memory Minutes

The Memory Minute activity was unique: how often in life before age thirteen do you have an opportunity to say farewell, formally (albeit eighth-grade style), to peers with whom you have worked closely for three years?

At the beginning of the last week of school, I passed out a Memory Minutes assignment sheet. The instructions read:

> Think back over the past school year—all the people, places, and events that were part of the tapestry of the year. Think about what is really important for you to say in your Memory Minute, your "last words," in a sense, to your classmates and teachers on Team 8-I. When you have decided on your topic, prepare a presentation that lasts about a minute. Your Memory Minute may take the form of an anecdote, a poem, a story, a letter, a song, etc. You will present this Memory Minute by yourself—a one-person task. Since this is your last assignment of the year, make it a good one. Get the job done.
>
> Write it out in advance! Keep it a surprise! No regrets!

"Kids, don't miss this chance to say what you need to say. Step up and do it. You'll never have this opportunity again," I told them. And they rose to the occasion, magnificently.

No student ever asked for a grade on Memory Minutes; it was so beyond an academic assignment that it never occurred to them that it "counted." The kids saw Memory Minutes as something they had to do in order to complete their middle school experience.

For many years we did Memory Minutes during our end-of-the-year field trip to Boston, in a rented function room in the restaurant next to our motel. Following a talent show, which gave students one last opportunity to show off in front of their friends, we gathered in a circle and spent three hours saying goodbye.

Jen's Memory Minute paid homage to my "first day" poem:

It's the last day.
Out we go—
Most rushing energetically
Out the door.
Others pausing hesitantly,
Not wanting to leave eighth grade.

Heads swivel,
Eyes look for their buses.
Hoping to get a ride with someone next year,
Getting on your bus,
Saving seats for friends,
Holding your report card carefully,
Filled with good grades and bad,
We sit, expectantly,
Wondering what the summer will bring.

For some, the boredom of summer returns.
For others, the boredom of school ends
Finally . . .
For most, wondering who they'll be friends with.
New perspectives, possibilities, people.

The next year
You return to school
Only it's a new school.
New faces, teachers, classrooms.
You sit waiting.
The student asks:
What does he expect of me?
What is this room all about?
Who is this teacher?
The teacher asks:

Who are these people?
What are they all about?
What do they expect of me?

What was once a simultaneously shared journey
Is now only a journey alone.
As you think back to the great Team 8-1 memories
And realize it will never be the same again,
All is new and trembling
Because
It's the first day.

—*Jen Campisi, age 13*

In front of the entire team, Rio Longacre apologized to me for his disrespectful behavior during the year; he wanted to clean it up before the year ended. He then turned to a girl and, again in front of his peers, apologized to her for having teased her.

Maggie Brazelton, a popular girl, used the occasion to announce that she was moving to North Carolina the week after school ended. Her unexpected bombshell disrupted Memory Minutes for almost half an hour as her close friends rushed to her and sobbed. Maggie deliberately had kept the information quiet in order to spare her friends premature anguish; at the appropriate time she told them all at once, they all cried together, and then they could all move on.

Luke Trusnovec gave a skateboarding demonstration. Jenn Hill sang "Somewhere" from *West Side Story*. Jay Urgese played a tape of special song cuts he had recorded as his Memory Minutes. It was quite a night.

Twelve years later, Eileen "Bean" Wind recalled the impact of her Memory Minute:

I vividly remember sitting in a conference room at the hotel in Boston sharing our "Memory Minutes." We all sat in a circle, facing one another. I remember feeling that I never wanted 8th grade to end. But, after going through the Memory Minute experience, I felt much more comfortable with the changes that would take place: leaving 8th grade, going to HS, being separated from some friends, friends moving away, etc. What I really liked about the Memory Minute is that it was an open-ended writing activity. We had the freedom to say what we wanted in any way that we wanted to say it. People wrote stories, shared a memory, wrote a poem, played a song, sang a song, said things in general to the whole class, said things to specific people—it was an anything goes activity, which allowed people who may have felt uncomfortable with sharing their feelings to feel more comfortable, knowing that they could share them in any way and to whatever extent they chose.

The memory lingers because it was such a powerful experience, the first real opportunity that I had to share my feelings and a piece of myself in that type of forum. Part of the assignment was to produce a written copy of what we planned to say. I spent a great deal of time writing out what I wanted to say, revising and editing it to make it clear and to make sure that my word choice was exactly what I wanted. After coming up with a final draft, I spent a great deal of time rehearsing. The experience took me through the stages of the writing process in a much more meaningful way—I really cared about what I was going to say because it was personal. My Memory Minute was probably one of the most meaningful pieces I've ever written.

Assertions Addressed

As they completed the last two writing assignments of the year, students continued to address the assertions about writing:

- Each student was a writer all year long, engaged in communication.
- Each student gradually improved in written expression.
- Each student selected topics for the letters to teachers and the Memory Minute.
- All students "published" both assignments: the letters went to important audiences beyond the classroom; Memory Minutes were shared with peers at a final class gathering.
- Right up to the last day of school, all students added to the volume and variety of writing assignments that characterized their year.

Closing Thoughts

Not only do we need to help students create positive memories during the year; we also need to help them achieve closure. Recently Larissa Figari recalled the end of her middle school experience eight years earlier:

> It was cyclic . . . we began with a poem and ended with a poem. (I don't remember if it was the same one!) The year was ending, and it felt like we were losing everything . . . Moving on to high school . . . releasing from our tight niche, we had one more thing to look forward to: BOSTON. Absolutely amazing! The talent show was hysterical. We all laughed and showed off amongst the people that we had grown so close to. Memory Minutes was even more amazing and more touching than anything we had experienced as a team. We ended the year with a bang and slowly untangled from our tight mesh.

20

Reflections on Writing

A fter attending the National Writing Project Summer Institute in 1980, I reflected in my journal:

> I see my role much differently now. My job is to observe, encourage, and extend the writing of my students. I should lead by following one step behind, encouraging the child to go ahead, risk, say what he wants to say in the way he wants to say it. Rather than react immediately by saying, "What a great piece of writing!" I can better help a student by asking questions: "What do you intend to do with this piece? Does it say what you want it to say? How do you feel about it?"
>
> Becoming intellectually aware of the writing process was exciting. The challenge of translating the ideas into practical, sensible, manageable operations in a classroom is a task that will require more than a year of work. Now that I have the ideas (rehearsal), I'm ready to move on. Next year will include a good bit of trial and error as I find what works for me (drafting). The following years should bring consolidation of ideas and less experimentation (revising). I look forward to nurturing the seeds of ideas planted (editing). I do confess to tinges of trepidation at the enormity of the task before me (publishing), but I certainly will not miss correcting those commas.

We grow, and we learn by growing. Twenty-two years ago I was filled with hope and promise. Looking back, I have a sense of mission accomplished, promise fulfilled. The wonderful ideas about teaching writing that I encountered in the National Writing Project Summer Institute came to fruition; they served a generation of students well.

In one of my favorite movies, *Groundhog Day,* Bill Murray is forced to relive the same day over and over as he attempts to learn from and correct his mistakes. Teaching was like that; I would redo the school year, but each time with new students and new ideas, informed by the successes and failures of previous years. And I learned—sometimes joyfully, sometimes painfully, often unexpectedly, usually haphazardly. Yet the learning seems, in retrospect, to have emerged logically, building as the years passed.

Learning to Teach

Ultimately, I learned how to teach writing by writing, by thinking about writing, by reflecting on what I did in the classroom, by listening to students speak about assignments and noticing their enthusiasm (or lack thereof) for particular activities, and by acting on what I observed, sensed, and heard.

Many of the strategies described in this book I put into place during my first year of teaching after the Summer Institute: the Letter to Self, the Gift of Writing, the individual magazine, letters, journals, writing groups, poetry. But each activity went through yearly tweaks and transformations as

I learned via the sobering gauntlet of experience how to introduce, model, explain, assess, and celebrate it. The first year my students did the magazine project, I required five pieces of writing; a unifying theme was optional. A decade later, students were creating interdisciplinary magazines with a minimum of twelve pieces of writing.

How did my ideas about teaching writing change over time?

- I gave up an approach based on teaching skills that might—eventually, with luck—lead to results. Instead, I began coaching my students in the writing process and trusted them to come up with the product.
- At first I used my own writing as models because I did not have many peer examples to share with students. Later, when I began using student models, I discovered their power. More than anything else I did, sharing peer models when introducing assignments played a crucial role in allowing students to see new possibilities for their own writing.
- When reviewing student writing, I learned to look for what was right, not what was wrong. I passed over spelling errors in early drafts and focused on what the student was aiming for, rather than the near miss he or she had. Mina Shaughnessy, in her book *Errors and Expectations,* taught me that lesson.
- I no longer taught by telling. Students learned by constructing their knowledge.
- Writing improved as students came through classes in the elementary grades where teachers used National Writing Project approaches.

Clearly, the "successful teacher who had a bad year" in 1981–82 moved past that episode and enjoyed fifteen more years in the classroom, not as a corrector of commas but as a teacher of writing.

Keywords

Computer searches call for keywords. What keywords would access my teaching? Choice, engagement, response, drafting, revising, and publishing.

Choice. It's simple—when students choose, they assume responsibility for their choices, and they are more invested in the task.

Engagement. Students come to school overstimulated by media and technology. I combated that reality by designing activities that captured their interest. Some succeeded year after year; others worked once, then flopped the second time.

Response. A key element in improving writing was providing useful response. We did that through journal comments, notations on drafts, writing conferences, writing groups, and class discussions.

Drafting. Once students learned that they didn't have to get the piece correct the first time and that their writing would become stronger through successive drafts, they relaxed and improved as writers. Writing is a craft; elegant prose requires many drafts, a handy thesaurus, and a good dictionary.

Revising. I asked students to revise their writing regularly. I also found myself revising my pedagogy as I tried new approaches, added new wrinkles, introduced new techniques, and invented new activities.

Publishing. When you take your writing public, you care more about it because you know that it will represent who you are. By asking kids to publish regularly, I made them become more invested in their work. And by publishing my own ideas through journal articles, workshop presentations, and books, I modeled appropriate behavior for my students as I tested my ideas about writing in the marketplace.

Why I Taught

Teaching writing as I did took considerable time, both to learn how to do it effectively and to actually get it done on a day-to-day basis during the school year. The responses of the students constantly renewed me; after reading a set of journal entries I would be invigorated. I spent less classroom time on reading and more on writing, counting on the fact that the seventh- and ninth-grade English teachers were emphasizing literature.

All of the strategies presented in this book were, at one time, brand-new ideas for me. I did not know how to do them properly. But as I taught them again and again, they became new and improved models of the original exercise.

The numerous writing activities had a cumulative effect. Jessica Cepelak, for example, made a Gift of Writing, composed a Letter to Self, created both a poetry booklet and an individual magazine, wrote thirty-five journal entries, entered an essay contest, crafted a newspaper article, contributed to ten class anthologies, sent scores of letters, and more. All of these tasks, along with her writing-group experiences and my models, enabled Jessica to grow as a writer.

But the learning writer is always in process; the writing is never done. Another student, Beth Ann McEnany, put it this way: "Your writing is never in final form even if you think it is . . . [T]he only way you get good at writing is by writing." Her words still resonate with the wisdom of experience.

Who do we want emerging from our language arts classrooms? Reflective students like Tori, Adam, and Rebecca? Imaginative students like Josh, Nicole, and Jessica? Industrious students like Lauren, Mike, and Carolyn? Responsive students like Jake, Heidi, and Bobby? Or all of them?

What activities can we provide that draw out the talents of our students so that they have opportunities to be reflective, imaginative, industrious, and responsive? Who are we seeking to nurture if not Dan, whose positive attitude toward writing was all but contagious:

I used to think of [writing] as a drag, but now I love it! Not so much the idea of writing but what happens when I start writing. It comes very easily to me! I guess I just have so many thoughts going through my mind that getting some of them on paper is not very hard. I think writing as well as any other type of art is a great way to productively release energy. Especially when you just need to do something, writing is just so easy.

—Dan Brickley, age 13

My objective each year was to turn students on to writing; I knew they had ideas they wanted to share, and my job was to enable them to do this as well as they could. I taught writing to help kids communicate, not to get grades.

Words of Advice

Reflecting on my seventeen years of teaching writing using ideas acquired in the National Writing Project Summer Institute, I offer the following advice:

Write. As the educational leader of the community of writers in your classroom, you should write with your students. Be the model.

Share. Let your students see both early and late drafts of your work. Share your struggles and your successes.

Expect. Expect your students to be writers with ideas to share. Interact with them on the basis of that assumption.

Invite. Invite your students to participate in writing. Make them feel welcome. Don't force them. Lead by example. Be the first to volunteer to read aloud.

Encourage. Support, encourage, praise, and reinforce your students' writing. They do listen; a kind word goes a long way.

Ask. Ask your students to attempt new challenges. Ask them to reflect. Ask them what worked and what didn't. Ask them what they learned. Ask them to go beyond wherever they are as writers.

Listen. When you ask your students about writing, consider their responses and learn from them. Incorporate the best of their thinking into your writing program.

Provide choice. As much as possible, on any given writing assignment let students choose the topic, or the form, or the audience, or all three.

Respond. Give your students both written and verbal feedback on their writing. Ask them about audience, purpose, intent, word choice, specific details, beginnings, endings, titles, form, and sequence.

Invent. Try something new every year. This year's students should not get only retreads from last year.

Be flexible. Each student is an individual; no one assignment works equally well for all. Consequently, individualize instruction as much as possible.

Be low key. Don't oversell an assignment. Young adolescents become skeptical when you tell them, "This is a great assignment, you'll love it." Maybe they will, and maybe they won't. Let them discover the assignment, and then let them tell you what they like and dislike about it.

Reflect. Think about what worked for you when you were a student. Think about the writing activities you used last year. Discard what didn't work, and strengthen what did.

Evolve. The writing activities you are using may, and probably should, change; in three years you will be teaching somewhat differently, your practice informed by reflection, experimentation, and experience.

Have fun. Life is short. Laugh with your students. Celebrate them and their writing. Give them lasting positive memories.

Use peer models. Give your students models of assignments created by their peers. Save the best examples from this year; ask student authors for permission to use them, then make them a part of next year's curriculum.

Carpe diem. Seize the moment every day. Expect the unexpected, and be ready to shift in order to capitalize on an unanticipated event.

Honor youth culture. Kids appreciate it when you demonstrate specific knowledge of their world. You don't have to like the music, but it is helpful to be familiar with the latest incarnation of Alfred E. Newman or Elvis, James Dean or Doris Day.

Make reading a priority. Ask students, "What are you reading?" Be ready with your own answer; let them know your literary tastes. Show them the books you read. Be a model reader.

Make writing a priority. Spend time on it. Honor it. Publish it. Do it.

Life Lessons

My students often said that I was teaching them life lessons. And I was, every day. Beyond forms of expression, placement of commas, and the inviting intricacies of a Frost couplet, I always felt that I was teaching students to be mature; I went beyond the English language arts curriculum and raised questions about life.

Now that I have retired, what are my life lessons? What would I teach my students today, if I could?

Write poetry regularly.

Communicate with those dear to you; tell them how and why they are important. Do it in writing.

Celebrate both special and everyday occasions with poems, stories, proclamations, menus, scrapbooks, captions on photos—insinuate the written word into all you do.

Reread and revise, as needed, whatever you have written.

Read books, go to the movies, create art, participate in your community, travel, take up a hobby and make it a passion, reflect on life, enjoy the beauty of nature, meet new people, visit old friends, respect your elders, love your kids, and be yourself.

Yearlong Writing Summary Review

At the end of one school year I asked students to compose a Yearlong Writing Summary Review (YWSR). I wanted them to reflect on their experiences and help me understand what they found worthwhile, what didn't work for them, and what suggestions they had for me.

Clayton remembered the "many assignments and lessons concerning the quality of our writing" during the year. He recalled that when "students first came into Mr. Burkhardt's room, the first thing Mr. Burkhardt told us was that this class was a course in communication." He's right: I did; it was.

Clayton continued:

One way I grew as a writer is in my creativity. When I came into Mr. Burkhardt's classroom I didn't know much about how to pick things out of thin air and make a poem out of whatever I found. After several months of reading other [students'] poetry I have found that it has helped my poems grow into a very powerful ball inside of my head just filled with ideas that are ready to go.

I'd have to say that when the whole class got together and read poetry from all different [student] poets it helped my mind more than any other kind of writing activity. It gave me more of a sense as to how far you can go with poetry. The only criticism that I had for that writing activity was that we had to write in all different forms of poetry. I thought that was bad because we had to write poems around the kind of outline that we were practicing. I had written a good poem and then I noticed that I hadn't followed the correct way of writing it. I was not happy that I was limited as to what I could write in my poetry. It just took all the fun out of it.

I thought that the writing activity that was the most fun for me was the Letter to Self. I can't wait until my senior breakfast to open it. I will be so much more mature and I will have changed so much. It's so exciting. The thing that made it so fun was that we had so much freedom and no matter what we wrote, we still got an "A."

I thought that the writing activities that didn't work for me were the ones that involved writing groups. I don't like writing groups because all of the students who are in your writing group are always correcting your papers while enforcing their ideas on you. It just didn't work for me.

The coaching Mr. Burkhardt mostly gave to me was to relate what I enjoy in life into my work. He would always be helping me, and then he'd start talking about doing it the way I played guitar, or to do it like the Beatles would have done it. So I'd have to say that the coaching that Mr. Burkhardt always gave me was just to be myself while writing.

I really don't think that I can write down what I learned about writing this year. It's all too much that I would forget things here and there about what I learned and it would take me years to finish. But what sticks out so much about the teaching Mr. Burkhardt gave us about writing was that you always must have fun. He also said that life is unfair, but that's besides the point. When Mr. Burkhardt was teaching us how important it is to communicate, in my mind he was saying, what good is writing if you don't want to do it? . . .

I've noticed a change in my writing when I look back at what I did in the beginning of the year, and what I'm doing now. I have noticed the writing in the beginning of the year was absolutely terrible. I have become a much better writer from doing it Mr. Burkhardt's way instead of writing the ways that other teachers have taught me to write.

—Clayton Bowman, age 13

Clayton's analysis of his writing experience helped me see ways in which my writing program was helpful to him, and some ways in which it wasn't. His thoughts were echoed by Beth Ann, who began: "This year I sure have written a lot . . . This had to be the year of writing."

Beth Ann offered this self-assessment: "When I first started eighth grade I wasn't a strong writer, and as the year comes to an end I think that I really have improved a lot."

When a student asserts that he or she has improved as a writer, I am both pleased with that assertion and curious as to what motivated it. Beth Ann, who had a more positive writing group experience than Clayton, noted:

[T]he most helpful thing this year was writing groups. You are able to read people you[r] piece and get feed back and see what can be changed. The first writing group was the hardest because everyone in my group was scared to read their piece of writing, but the more we had writing groups, the better we got. We were able to put more input into each other's pieces.

The things that didn't work for me were the ones that had a limit on what you could write. There should not be a limit because that doesn't make the piece better; it makes it worse because you are too worried about the amount, and then the quality doesn't come out as good as you would have thought it would have.

The coaching that was most worthwhile for me from Mr. Burkhardt had to have been that your writing is never in final form even if you think it is. That helped me because I was able to always go back and fix something if I needed to. I learned the only way you get good at writing is by writing. You can't stop writing because if you do, then you won't be able to learn as many new things you could. The reason why is you are too busy relearning the old stuff to learn the new stuff. Mr. Burkhardt, just keep making your future students write - it works.

—Beth Ann McEnany, age 13

Full Circle: Reflections

This book began with reflections by three students, written in March of their eighth-grade year. Seven years later, I asked these same students what they recalled and retained, what value the writing activities had for them, and what difference, if any, all the writing made in their lives.

The life of a thirteen year old is one of conflicting emotions, confusing experiences, and inspiration. When I was thirteen it felt as if with every piece of writing that poured on to the computer screen I was taking another step into adulthood. Boy, did it feel terrific.

Spending a year immersed in a curriculum that placed such emphasis on writing, and letting go of inhibitions, was exactly what I needed to begin to understand the value of quality literature. Although I have always been an avid reader, 8th grade was the first time in my experience with the written word that I was struck by the idea of an author's "voice." The concept that the way a story or poem was written could affect its theme was thrilling to my young mind; it changed everything about the way I wrote and read. I began reading books in the second person, like Tom Robbin's "Half Asleep in Frog Pajamas," just to see what that was like, and then tried to mimic them to see how far I could bring that "voice."

By consistently writing for class assignments and on my own, I also began understanding the difficulty of writing, but more importantly the thrill. I really meant it in 1995 when I said, "Once the year ends I'm not going to want to stop writing," because I didn't. I honestly wrote just about every day the summer before entering ninth grade, and while I now often look back and laugh at the innocence and simplicity of that early writing, those first steps into literature were fundamental for any future steps I would take. Now a college junior, I am so grateful for my 8th grade writing experiences, because I honestly believe my writing is what has brought me such success through the years. Every student has to write college essays before they are admitted to the college of their choice, and my college essays not only helped me get in, but I was granted writing scholarships as well.

Of course, I never wrote an autobiography after I finished 8th grade, but the love for writing that I expressed in that journal seven years ago still runs just as fiercely through these fingertips. While I am now studying courses that will eventually lead to a medical career, I also will graduate with an English major and as an editor of my college newspaper. It is a love that no matter how hard I try I just cannot let go of, and I honestly have Mr. Burkhardt and his own love and understanding of writing to thank for the skills that have brought me where I am today.

—Jessica Cepelak

Looking back on what I wrote, I realize that my opinions and preferences about my writing have changed a lot over time. My writing has improved since eighth grade, and being a Sociology major in college, I get a great deal of practice. Most of my school work consists of essays and research papers. The years of English classes I took from middle school, through high school, and the few I took in college made me realize that creative writing is, and probably never will be my strong point. I said in my journal entry [in 1995] that I enjoyed the challenge of writing poetry. I can say now that poetry is the one writing style that I dislike the most. None of the poetry I wrote in eighth grade actually meant anything—as long as it rhymed, I thought it was good. I gave up on creative writing after completing my general education English requirements in college, and have not really written "for fun" since then.

One benefit of all of the English courses I've taken over the years is that they gave me the ability to elaborate. Having the skills to expand and add details to research papers make them much easier to read and, in my experience, pleases most professors. The writing we did in eighth grade helps me more now than it did then. I kept most of the writing I did, and I look at it every once in a while and laugh. It shows me exactly what I shouldn't be doing when I write now.

I still think that sharing your writing is a good thing. It allows you to have an outside opinion other than your own, and usually other people catch small mistakes that you may overlook. When I write a paper for school, I have someone look over it, and I read it aloud to myself before handing in the final draft. This enables me to correct passages if they sound awkward.

The writing we did in eighth grade was fun, and it made us use our imaginations. Although creative writing isn't something I'd like to do for the rest of my life, it was a good experience.

—Heidi Lipinsky

As I'm sure everyone thinks or feels when they look back on their writing from about 10 years ago, "My how I've changed!" And yet, after you sit back and think about it for a day, and then a week, and then a few weeks more, you come to the realization . . . maybe I'm not as different as I thought.

I don't know how much I see of the boy that I was in that writing piece, but I'm sure bits and pieces are recognizable. The beginnings of arrogance, surely (even then I was impressed with myself, which is never a good sign), and the strong leanings toward fantasy as my genre of choice are both obvious. So how does that fit into my life now?

Well first, seeing as how I'm having trouble even writing this short piece, I don't do much creative writing anymore. What was once a free-flowing style has become an ability to crank out university level "papers," you know, those things that you never need to write again once you leave academia. I guess in a way I feel disappointed, reading my own thoughts from back then. I remember feeling so much hope, so full of pride in myself and my ability to become anything, and I lived out that dream in many of my writings. Whether I was a wizard, a warrior, a rogue, or a king, I could imagine that the world of my dreams truly did exist somewhere, and that when I was an adult, I could give up on this world and journey there instead.

Now, the grip of reality surrounds me. Self-deprecating science fiction has replaced the naïve utopia of fantasy. Tolkien's Middle Earth no longer seems to be the peaceful, tranquil, happy world that I at first envisioned, and I can see within his Earth the sadness and despair at the loss of beauty as the Age of Man began. My mind and the minds of others are my battlegrounds now, as Freud would say, but I think, looking back on it, I always knew I would end up a psychologist. My plan, as of now at least, is to go to NYU and get a doctorate in psychology. But for each decision made, a thousand doors are closed behind you, and I wonder sometimes. I think back to a poem a certain 8th grade teacher made me memorize, and I wonder how many people live their lives feeling like that old king, and if they they will all be forgotten, just as Ozymandius was.

—Mike Clair

Ultimately, students such as Mike, Heidi, and Jessica saw me as another writer in the classroom, albeit a leader in our community of writers. They were influenced by my style and ideas, as I was influenced by theirs. I was a role model for almost all writing activities, and my students knew that I was dead serious about the task of writing. I am convinced that one of the reasons for the general improvement in the quality of writing in my classroom over the years was that I modeled appropriate writing behavior by sharing early drafts and finished pieces as well as the frustrations and successes that came with them.

Through it all, poetry was the connecting link. Consider the interrelationships of poetry memorizations, my *Poems for All Occasions,* free-verse poetry as the first form of expression taught, class anthologies of poetry, individual poetry booklets students created later in the year, the weekly poems, and the celebration of writing from day one to day 180. Something positive happened to students on our "simultaneously shared journey": they enjoyed writing, and not just occasionally.

Looking through my threadbare copy of *Poems for All Occasions* recently, seeking a verse to end this book, I recalled a day in late January just before one of my students moved away. Ever the teacher as writer, I composed a poem for his farewell celebration. May its words resonate for you and your students.

Have you ever had the feeling
of time flowing by
and you aren't really sure
if hello means goodbye?

Have you ever known the pain
of losing a friend
and you find difficulty
in accepting the end?

Have you ever sensed the rush
of haste all around
and you barely feel your feet
skimming over the ground?

Have you ever been confused
by demands on your time
and you modify your pace
to the angle of the climb?

Have you ever asked yourself
what the melody means
and you dream rainbow thoughts
filled with monochrome scenes?

Have you ever read a poem
where the meaning isn't clear
and you push it away
in a gesture of fear?

And if I can question
and touch who you are
can the distance between us
be very far.

Epilogue

I never wanted to be a teacher. I remember sitting restlessly in an oak seat hinged to a desk bolted to the floor, listening to the endless drone of my third-grade teacher. She gave me a C- because I could not recreate a cursive lowercase *e* between the solid and dotted lines on a sheet of exercise paper. I cried and felt inadequate, yet at the same time I knew that life was not just about lowercase *e*'s. Those hours wasted in elementary school taught me a powerful lesson: do not become a thief of youth. Brautigan's allusion to Jesse James comes to mind.

And yet, for thirty-five years I taught English and social studies. The daily task of interacting with young adolescents nourished me more and more each passing year. I loved what I did and strove constantly to avoid riding with Jesse. Teaching called to me, beckoned and enticed me. Each September the year stretched ahead as a marvelous journey. Opportunities seemed boundless, and Frost's untraveled roads awaited—all was possibility, all exciting.

We create our own circumstances. In my classroom I invented a realm in which students made real decisions, took real risks and assumed real responsibilities, interacted with others in meaningful ways, acquired useful life skills, drafted and revised and published their writing, and enjoyed the process. I composed poetry, traveled with students, developed lasting relationships with young people, discovered new approaches to teaching and learning, and experienced the stimulation of beginning anew each fall.

Why did I teach? Because it fulfilled me more than anything I could imagine. Because it spoke to my sense of service. Because it drew on everything I knew or could do. And because my students kept me young and laughing.

Appendix

Sample Forms and Typical Assignments

Letter of Appreciation and Acknowledgment

Prepare an appropriate Letter of Appreciation and Acknowledgment for an important individual in your life. You will send your completed letter to that person. Your letter should make it clear to the recipient both why you are acknowledging and why you appreciate her or him. Your letter will contain several paragraphs, since there undoubtedly are several reasons why you appreciate and can acknowledge this important individual in your life.

Writing for Real: Strategies for Engaging Adolescent Writers by Ross M. Burkhardt. Copyright © 2003. Stenhouse Publishers

Holiday Memory Piece

By [date], prepare a Holiday Memory piece of writing that you will share in class. In class your teacher shared an example of a Holiday Memory. Consider all the holidays that your family celebrates. Select on activity, memory, or tradition, and celebrate it through a piece of writing intended to be shared with others. Practice reading your piece aloud. A prop may be useful when you share your Holiday Memory. Remember, accurate details create interesting writing.

Letter to Self

As your first writing assignment of the New Year, write a letter to yourself.

This Letter to Self (LTS) has five parts. You can do any part in any order. You will have time in class to work on your Letter, and you are expected to complete one part of it as homework each evening. You may want to view your LTS as a personal time capsule.

The purposes of doing this Letter to Self are:

- to provide a record of your life and who you are now;
- to anchor in time your current views, attitudes, philosophy, and outlook;
- to explore your feelings and opinions about a variety of issues;
- to create a document that years from now will have significant value to you.

The five parts of the Letter to Self are:

Me, Now: my hopes, fears, dreams, intentions, goals, problems, concerns, likes, dislikes, joys, frustrations; what I like about myself; what I don't like about myself; what I'm proud of; what I think about; what bothers me; who I am; etc.

My World: a description of my home, bedroom, school, neighborhood, town; favorite places to go, chores, allowance, pet(s), possessions, clothes, religion, current events; favorite books, music groups, movies, TV, etc. Include a map of your room, street, etc.

What I Do: my hobbies, pastimes, sports, school activities; what I do when I'm alone; what I do with friends; favorite snacks and foods; chores; how I spend my weekends and vacations; special activities I do, organizations I belong to; etc.

People in My Life: my family, siblings, aunts and uncles, grandparents, friends, best friend(s), teachers, the opposite sex, people I like, people I'd like to know better, people I admire and respect, important people in my life, people who annoy me, etc.

My Future: predictions, what I want to do, my long-range intentions, what I'm looking forward to, what I'm dreading; my goals, my hopes and fears for the world, the second half of eighth grade, summer vacation, high school, college, marriage, employment, etc.

In doing this Letter to Self, you do not have to write about each subtopic mentioned above; just write about what is important to *you*. You should write *at least* two (2) pages for each part (total: 10 pages minimum). You may also want to write about something important to you that isn't mentioned above. Create your own categories. This Letter to Self is for *you*, and it should deal with the things that are important and real in your life—the good, the bad, and the ugly. The more honest you are with yourself, the more you will appreciate and value your LTS in years to come.

I will collect each LTS part as you complete it (one part per day), and your completed Letter to Self will be returned to you in June. No one will read your LTS except you and those you choose to share it with. Have fun! Write extensively!! And create something memorable that captures your life today and who you are!

Writing for Real: Strategies for Engaging Adolescent Writers by Ross M. Burkhardt. Copyright © 2003. Stenhouse Publishers

Letter to Self: Planning Sheet

Me, Now:

My World:

What I Do:

People in My Life:

My Future:

Letter to Self: Memory Quiz

Create a list of all the important people, nicknames, code phrases, inside jokes, slang terms, special events, memories, etc., that are currently part of your life. You don't need to explain them (since you'll never forget them); just list them. Four years from now, how many of these will you actually remember?

I'll never forget . . .

Writing for Real: Strategies for Engaging Adolescent Writers by Ross M. Burkhardt. Copyright © 2003. Stenhouse Publishers

Letter to Self: Ideas and Activities for Enhancement

As you work on your LTS, consider the following suggestions. They could improve and enhance your project:

- Include photographs of you, your family, and your friends.

- Draw a map of your community and mark special locations.

- Create a personal montage/collage with quotes, souvenirs, pictures, clothing labels, candy wrappers, etc.

- Record an audiotape or videotape of you, your family, and your friends.

- Cut out articles from newspapers or magazines about significant current events and issues important to you and your world.

- Be on task during class time.

- Use the coming weekend to reread what you have written, to add new information, and to improve and lengthen your LTS.

- Create a new section of your LTS called "Favorite Memories."

- Write a secret letter to another student on the team; surprise him or her four years from now (I have envelopes if you need some).

- Make a list of your favorite activities, TV shows, foods, movies, songs, rock groups, books, sports teams, music videos, video games, etc.

- Are you typing your LTS? Read through your current drafts, make notes where you have forgotten people, places, events, ideas, and circumstances, and then revise and lengthen your LTS.

- Ask your friends to sign the outside of your LTS packet.

- Decorate the outside of your LTS packet.

- Include some sample e-mail messages.

- Put in some homework assignments and tests from other subjects.

- Think of something not on this list to include in your LTS.

- Number the pages of each separate LTS section (People: P1, P2, P3, etc.; Future: F1, F2, F3, etc.).

Letter to Self: The Appendix

Follow these instructions:

1. Reread all five(+) parts of your LTS.
2. As you reread it, ask yourself, "What's missing? Who did I leave out? What did I forget? What topic(s) can be explained more fully? What do I want to add? What else do I have to say?"
3. As you reread your LTS, take notes in the appropriate spaces below.
4. For homework, complete "Letter to Self: The Appendix." In this section include the things you left out earlier. Write at least two pages.

Me, Now:

My World:

What I Do:

People in My Life:

My Future:

Letter to Self: Evaluation

This English journal entry is due on: [date].

Think about all the writing you did for your LTS and the many thoughts that went through your mind as you created it. Then respond to the following questions:

- How do you feel about your completed LTS and the overall LTS project?

- How many pages did you write for your LTS? (If you both typed and wrote longhand, give totals for each.)

- Which part of the LTS was most difficult for you to do? Why? Be specific in your explanation.

- Which part of the LTS was easiest for you to do? Why? Be specific in your explanation.

- What did you learn about yourself while doing your LTS? Be specific in your response.

- What special things did you do to enhance your LTS (secret letter, collage, videotape, etc.)? Be specific in your response.

- What suggestions do you have so the LTS can be a better project next year?

- What else can you tell me about the process of creating your LTS?

Letter to Self: End of Year Update

Create a two-page update to your Letter to Self. Here are just a few possible memories and events about which you can write:

final exams

spring sports season at the middle school

Eighth Grade Night

going to the high school—ninth grade!!

summer movies

the last concert

summer plans and family trips

middle school teachers

what I've now realized

what I still don't like

four years from now

current events

TV shows

what's changed

friends

"Life is unfair"

"Things change"

the Super Bowl, the NCAA "Final Four," the baseball season

topics of your choice

The more you write, the more honestly you write, the more you will appreciate your LTS four years hence.

Writing for Real: Strategies for Engaging Adolescent Writers by Ross M. Burkhardt. Copyright © 2003. Stenhouse Publishers

Gift of Writing Preparation

Using the space below, fill in the names of three important people in your life, people you actually know. For each person, mention two or three events or aspects of your relationship—experiences you shared, attributes you value, memories you have in common, etc.—so that it is clear why each person is important to you.

Name of person: _____

Relationship info/event:

Name of person: _____

Relationship info/event:

Name of person: _____

Relationship info/event:

Writing Portfolio Checklist

Title: _____
I include this writing because:

Title: _____
I include this writing because:

Title: _____
I include this writing because:

Title: _____
I include this writing because:

Title: _____
I include this writing because:

Title: _____
I include this writing because:

Title: _____
I include this writing because:

Title: _____
I include this writing because:

Use additional sheet(s) if necessary.

Writing for Real: Strategies for Engaging Adolescent Writers by Ross M. Burkhardt. Copyright © 2003. Stenhouse Publishers

Parent Writing Conference: Appointment Form

We have scheduled our Parent Writing Conference for:

Day:

Time:

Place:

_____   _____
Parent Signature   Student Signature

(Sign and post this half on the refrigerator or some other prominent location in your home as a reminder of the PWC.)

- -

We have scheduled our Parent Writing Conference for:

Day:

Time:

Place:

_____   _____
Parent Signature   Student Signature

Sign and return this half.

Parent Writing Conference: Instructions to the Student

1. Make sure your writing portfolio is neat, complete, and in chronological order. Mark the specific pages in your journals if you intend to use journal entries.

2. Find an appropriate time to first mention the Parent Writing Conference (PWC)—i.e., just before, during, or after dinner, or at a time when your parent can read my letter to them explaining the assignment. ("Dad, Mom, do you have a couple of minutes? I have a request regarding my schoolwork.")

3. Give my letter of explanation [see Figure 17.1] to your parent. Wait until he or she has completed reading the letter. Then point out the guidelines printed on the back.

4. Have your writing portfolio with you, ready and available.

5. Make sure your parent understands the request (having a conference with you to discuss your writing) and your follow-up assignment. You will need from thirty to sixty minutes *uninterrupted by any other concerns* to conduct the writing conference properly. Plan ahead!

6. Agree on the *day, hour,* and *place* for the Parent Writing Conference using the appointment form (the sooner you schedule it, the better).

7. Give your writing portfolio to your parent so he or she can read your writing *in advance.* Also, review your writing and prepare some questions and comments to share at the conference.

8. Remind your parent about the PWC on several occasions prior to the date and time you both agreed on.

9. Arrive on time for the PWC with your English journal, notes, and a writing implement.

10. Conduct the Parent Writing Conference. Share your feelings about writing with your parent. What have you learned about writing so far this year? What was the most difficult piece for you to compose? Why? Which piece was easiest? Why? Respond to your parent's questions about your writing.

11. Read two or three of your pieces aloud to your parent.

12. Share and explain the ten Assertions About Writing with your parent.

13. You may do the Parent Writing Conference with both parents if you choose. This is more difficult to schedule, however.

14. Your Parent Writing Conference must be completed no later than [date].

15. Thank your parent when the conference is over. Invite him or her to complete the Parent Writing Conference Reaction Form and return it.

16. Complete the PWC journal assignment after you have your conference with your parent.

Objectives for the Parent Writing Conference
To increase parent-child communication regarding learning.
To promote a better understanding of the task of writing.

The Purpose of Writing
To communicate with a particular audience about a specific topic for a particular reason.

Writing for Real: Strategies for Engaging Adolescent Writers by Ross M. Burkhardt. Copyright © 2003. Stenhouse Publishers

Parent Writing Conference: Guidelines for the Parent

1. Agree on a *time and place* for the Parent Writing Conference with your child. You will need from thirty to sixty minutes *uninterrupted by any other concerns* to conduct the Writing Conference properly.

2. Prepare for the Parent Writing Conference by reading the several pieces of writing in the portfolio *beforehand* so that you can spend the conference time discussing them with your child.

3. At the Parent Writing Conference, ask your child about his or her writing: which piece does he or she like best? Which piece was most difficult to create, and why? What has he or she learned about writing so far this year? How does he or she feel about writing? What does your child see as his or her strengths and weaknesses when it comes to writing?

4. Ask your child to read two or three pieces aloud to you.

5. Ask your child to explain the ten Assertions About Writing to you.

6. What do you notice about your child's attitude toward and understanding of the writing process and writing in general?

7. Both parents may choose to do the Parent Writing Conference. This is more difficult to schedule, however.

8. You are invited to complete the Parent Writing Conference Reaction Form following the conference.

Objectives for the Parent Writing Conference
To increase parent-child communication regarding learning.
To promote a better understanding of the task of writing.

The Purpose of Writing
To communicate with a particular audience about a specific topic for a particular reason.

Parent Writing Conference: Reaction Form

Parent:_____ Student: _____ Date: _____

1. What did you learn about your child's writing through the Parent Writing Conference?

2. What suggestions do you have regarding your child's writing?

3. What comments do you have about the Parent Writing Conference?

Use the other side for additional comments.

Bibliography

Atwell, Nancie. 1987. *In the Middle: Writing, Reading, and Learning with Adolescents.* Portsmouth, NH: Boynton/Cook–Heinemann.

Beane, James A. 1993. *A Middle School Curriculum: From Rhetoric to Reality.* 2d ed. Columbus, OH: National Middle School Association.

Belair, Jerome R., and Paul Freeman. 2001. "Communication Skills Are the Key to Content." *Middle School Journal* 32 (5): 5–6.

Brautigan, Richard. 1970. *Rommel Drives on Deep into Egypt.* New York: Dell.

Burkhardt, Ross M. 1985. "How Well Do We Say Farewell?" In *Transition: Journal of the New York State Middle School Association* 2 (2): 9–12.

———. 1987. "How Well Do We Say 'Hello'?" *T•E•A•M—The Early Adolescence Magazine* 2 (1): 2–3.

———. 1988. "Peer Pressure and Peer Perspectives." *T•E•A•M—The Early Adolescence Magazine* 2 (5): 10–15.

———. 1995–96. "Appropriate Instructional Strategies for Early Adolescents." New York State Middle School Association Professional Pamphlet. Series 2 (2). Niskayuna, NY: New York State Middle School Association.

Casals, Pablo. 1998. "You Are a Marvel." In *Joys and Sorrows: Reflections by Pablo Casals, as Told to Albert E. Kahn.* New York: Simon & Schuster.

Easton, Lois Brown. 2002. *The Other Side of Curriculum: Lessons from Learners.* Portsmouth, NH: Heinemann.

Ehrmann, Bertha K., ed. 1948. *The Poems of Max Ehrmann.* Boston: B. Humphries.

Frost, Robert. 1949. *Complete Poems of Robert Frost.* New York: Holt, Rinehart & Winston.

Frovik, Nicole Clendening. 2001. "Writer's Workshop Creates Community of Learners." *Middle Ground* 5 (1): 38–39.

Fulwiller, Toby, ed. 1987. *The Journal Book.* Portsmouth, NH: Boynton/Cook–Heinemann.

Gibson, William. 1960. *The Miracle Worker, a Play in Three Acts.* New York: S. French.

Hunter, Alyce, and Peter Blat. 1994. "Middle-Level Content Teachers Can Do Whole Language Too." In *Transition: Journal of the New York State Middle School Association* 11 (1): 16–18.

Jackson, Anthony W., and Gayle A. Davis. 2000. *Turning Points 2000: Educating Adolescents in the 21st Century.* A Report of Carnegie Corporation of New York. New York: Teachers College Press.

Johnson, Holly, and Lauren Freedman. 2001. "Using Adolescents' Oral and Written Narratives to Create Classroom Communities." *Middle School Journal* 32 (5): 35–44.

Lawrence, Jerome, and Robert E. Lee. 1964. *Inherit the Wind.* New York: Bantam.

National Middle School Association. 1995. *This We Believe: Developmentally Responsive Middle Level Schools*. Columbus, OH: National Middle School Association.

Parsons, Les. 1990. *Response Journals*. Portsmouth, NH: Heinemann.

Perl, Sondra, and Nancy Wilson. 1986. *Through Teachers' Eyes: Portraits of Writing Teachers at Work*. Portsmouth, NH: Heinemann.

Rubinstein, Robert E. 1994. *Hints for Teaching Success in Middle School*. Englewood, CO: Teacher Ideas Press/Libraries Unlimited.

Shaughnessy, Mina P. 1977. *Errors and Expectations: A Guide for the Teacher of Basic Writing*. New York: Oxford University Press.

Weasmer, Jerie, and Amelia Mays Woods. 2000. "Shifting Classroom Ownership to Students." *Middle School Journal* 32 (2): 15–20.

Weber, Alan. 1992. "Evaluating the Writing of Middle School Students." *Middle School Journal* 24 (1): 24–27.

Index

Also of Interest

Why Workshop?
Changing Course in 7–12 English

Edited by Richard Bullock

Why Workshop? offers English and language arts teachers in grades 7 through 12 sound advice on using writing and reading workshops as the primary organization of their classrooms. The book's nine essays are written by experienced teachers who are making their teaching work day by day. In the process they give a good mix of testimonials (Here's how I did . . .), specific methods (Here are the steps . . .), and real-life results (This worked well; this flopped . . .). Their stories aren't too seamless, their successes too easy, their students and their work unbelievably good—rather, these teachers, their courses, and their students represent the range of possibilities in middle and high schools from college preparatory to vocational, from the compliant to the difficult.

A real strength of these essays is the contributors' willingness to articulate the development of their methods, to show how adopting a new teaching philosophy and the methods that it implies takes time and a willingness to persevere in the face of results that weren't intended or that weren't as good as they desired. These teachers show that to make change, they couldn't say, "I tried it and it didn't work" and abandon new ways; they learned from their initial attempts and tried again. Good teaching takes time to develop because methods can't be adopted wholesale from a book (even this one!) or a curriculum.

Why Workshop? offers both overviews of workshop teaching and focused essays on specific elements of workshop. In addition to chapters that offer philosophy and methods in the context of teachers and students working through the school year, the appendix provides an outline of a sample classroom structure based on workshop teaching, with specifics on organizing the year, the semester, the quarter, the week, and the period. It includes forms for students, letters for parents, assessment tools, and all the basic information one teacher used in creating a workshop teaching environment.

paperback • 160pp • 1-57110-084-9